The Alderley Sandhills Project

ENGLISH HERITAGE

MANCHESTER 1824

Manchester University Press

The Alderley Sandhills Project

An archaeology of community life in
(post)-industrial England

Eleanor Conlin Casella and Sarah K. Croucher

Manchester University Press

Manchester and New York

distributed in the United States exclusively by Palgrave Macmillan

Published by Manchester University Press
Oxford Road, Manchester M13 9NR, UK
and Room 400, 175 Fifth Avenue, New York, NY 10010, USA
www.manchesteruniversitypress.co.uk

Distributed in the United States exclusively by
Palgrave Macmillan, 175 Fifth Avenue, New York,
NY 10010, USA

Distributed in Canada exclusively by
UBC Press, University of British Columbia, 2029 West Mall,
Vancouver, BC, Canada V6T 1Z2

British Library Cataloguing-in-Publication Data
A catalogue record for this book is available from the British Library

Library of Congress Cataloging-in-Publication Data applied for

ISBN 978 0 7190 8198 9   paperback

First published 2010

Typeset in 10.5/12.5 Sabon
by Servis Filmsetting Ltd, Stockport, Cheshire
Printed in Great Britain
by CPI Antony Rowe, Chippenham, Wiltshire

ENGLISH HERITAGE

To Mr Roy Barber, Mrs Molly Pitcher and Mrs Edna Younger
for generously sharing their memories of life at the Hagg

edith wharton's lovely figurines
still speak to me today
from their mantelpiece in time
where they wrestle and they play

with passions and with prudences
finances and fears
her face and what it's worth to her
in the passing of the years

(Suzanne Vega, 2007, EMI Records)

Contents

Illustrations

Foreword

The Alderley Sandhills Project represents a set of unique collaborative relationships between the Manchester Museum and School of Art History and Archaeology in the University of Manchester, English Heritage, and the National Trust. Previous work in the region included the Alderley Edge Landscape Project (AELP), begun in December 1996 as a multidisciplinary programme to survey the wider landscape for traces of human activity above and below ground. This site combined such mineralogical variety that it has been classified as both a Site of Special Scientific Interest (SSSI) and a Regionally Important Geological and Geomorphological Site (RIGS) with archaeological importance – apparently the earliest metal mine in England – and a fascinating social history, all this set in a 'honeypot' that regularly attracted large numbers of visitors from the Manchester conurbation and beyond. Indeed, this very popularity was causing great concern to the National Trust as the principal landowner. In 2001 parts of the site were scheduled as ancient monuments. Funded by the Leverhulme Trust with support from Cheshire County Council and others, the Landscape Project set out to learn the Edge's story with the aim of compiling a management plan for the site, raising public awareness through exhibitions, teaching and publication, and identifying avenues of further research.

Over two years the Project surveyed and mapped the wide-ranging topography of the Edge as well as the mines beneath (this in collaboration with the Derbyshire Caving Club), thereby providing a jumping-off point for further archaeological research. Two small test excavations threw light on the industrial mining processes of the eighteenth and nineteenth centuries, as well as confirming the Early Middle Bronze Age date for the earliest mines and revealing the first Roman mine-shaft in England, apparently dug late in the first century AD, as the Romans were penetrating into northern Britain. Where the Bronze Age miners were looking for copper, the Romans probably came for the lead, while the later miners added a quest for cobalt. The study of the 'villas', built after the coming of the railway in 1842, was supported by research into the place names, the routes up to and over the Edge, the history and the vernacular architecture and above all by an ever-growing series of interviews recorded with members of the local community; all these greatly extended our knowledge of 'them and us' in a village that combined an artisan and mining community with one of this country's earliest wealthy commuter dormitories. The mines finally closed by 1920, but the rest of the picture remains true, and the way in which the community came together in support of our researches was moving and exciting, as they gave us information and provided photographs and documents for a hugely valuable archive.

At the same time a thorough study of the underlying geology and the geomorphology helped to put the anthropogenic part of the story into its proper place. Despite such a rich mineral history, the flora and fauna of the Edge itself are surprisingly 'ordinary' – although research has identified two hitherto unknown bramble hybrids and the presence of a Copperwort otherwise virtually unknown outside Cornwall, which must have come here on a miner's boot. With 4,000 years of lead, copper and cobalt mining history the site has great potential as an open-air laboratory for the study of soil pollution. Behind or, more likely, underneath all this lies the legend of the king and his knights sleeping beneath the Edge and watched over by a wizard, all waiting to save England in the last battle of the world. The Edge is still a special place, and study of the way the legend lives on takes one to the edge of fantasy, and sometimes beyond. That the Project's most recent research has found good evidence to take the legend back into prehistory merely adds a further dimension to the expansive history of this area.

This first stage of the Alderley Edge Landscape Project created a momentum which carried it well beyond the two years originally envisaged, and sparked numerous ideas for research, site management and teaching, quite apart from a series of lectures, an exhibition, research papers and books. The most important of these publications are the specialist volume on *The Archaeology of Alderley Edge* edited by Simon Timberlake and A.J.N.W. Prag (British Archaeological Reports, British Series No. 396, also published by J. & E. Hedges for the Manchester Museum, 2005) and a book intended for the general reader which covers all the facets of the project's research, entitled *Living with the Edge: Alderley's Story*, edited by A.J.N.W. Prag and to be published by Manchester University Press.

However, the original project has produced other offspring too. In combining the resources which we had built up with *The Stone Book Quartet*, written by the internationally renowned local author Alan Garner, our landscape research created a context for educational projects that could guide children into an understanding of the history and geography of their own village or town – to give them a sense of place and of their own role within that place. Pioneering in its approach, the 'Edge Landscape Project:

Educational and Heritage Resources' (AELPHER), created jointly with
the Cheshire Education Authority and funded principally by the Heritage
Lottery Fund, but with further support from numerous other bodies, provided a model for other similar schemes elsewhere in the country, perhaps
most notably the Cheshire Young People's Learning Journey. One of the
innovative features of AELPHER was that, at a time when the mind set of
such projects was still largely paper-based, this one was planned from the
outset as a two-part website: one section is the Learning Resource, for teach-
ers and their pupils, and the other gives public access to the Project's results
and archive through a series of 'themes'.

The terms of the Leverhulme Trust's funding permitted only small
research excavations, that also conformed to the policy of the National
Trust. Yet Alderley Edge still lacked a detailed study of a domestic site that
could bring together these several different approaches and techniques and
use them to answer a group of linked and focused questions. Just outside
the Trust's boundaries in the part of the Edge known as the Hagg lay the
'Sandhills', an area where huge quantities of highly polluted sand, derived
from the acid-leaching process used to process the copper ores during the
nineteenth century, had been dumped. The sand had been largely removed
and reused as aggregate, particularly between the 1930s and 1960s, but the
area had remained all but sterile – what little plant regeneration had taken
place had not yet progressed beyond the stage of an algal crust. As such it
had naturally attracted the interest of the Landscape Project's botanists and
entomologists, as previously this area had been surveyed but no detailed
research had been carried out.

The Alderley Sandhills Project gave an opportunity – probably for the
first time – for a research excavation of a small English domestic site of the
historical period as it moved from the agricultural into the industrial era.
Not a rescue project, but a proper research excavation. Although funds for
a parallel investigation of the flora and fauna of the Sandhills themselves
did not become available, the skills of the Museum's botanists could still
be deployed in studying the environment of the cottages before and during
excavation, and used as a further control of the memories of the three 'children' about their cottage gardens and vegetable patches, even their privies
and middens. Thus the Alderley Sandhills Project could combine the archaeological perspectives with a detailed environmental survey of the site, while
also drawing the local community fully into the project, both as providers of
information and as participants in the excavation.

In the lee of the Sandhills stood two pairs of cottages known variously as
the Miners' Cottages or the Hagg Cottages. Records suggested that they had
been built in the 1740s, and they had been demolished by the Nield family
of White Barn Farm in the 1950s. Aside from census records and other
documentary evidence, photographs of the cottages survived, and perhaps

more important (and exciting) so did three people who had lived in them as young children. Two, who still lived in Alderley, had already contributed to the oral archive their memories of life in the Hagg before the Second World War. Roy Barber was the third person. He moved away from the village to Scotland, but came back while the project was running and also contributed to the oral history record.

With the availability of funds from the Aggregates Levy Sustainability Fund came a special and possibly unique opportunity for collaboration between English Heritage, the Manchester Museum and the School of Art History and Archaeology to compare the 'myth' of remembered history with the photographic evidence combined with the results of a research excavation, carried out according to methods developed in the New World, where investigation of such domestic sites of the historical period is much more common than in Britain.

The two-way involvement of the public was a very important element in the project. Naturally the local communities were a prime consideration, as a source of information, but also as an enthusiastic and receptive audience for tours of the site and for descriptive pamphlets, lectures and a small travelling exhibition. It was also part of our commitment to provide permanent signage to interpret the site for visitors, whether hailing from the local area or from further afield. It was clear to us from experience gained on the original Landscape Project that interest in Alderley Edge extended well beyond the confines of the local area. The Sandhills Project addressed this outreach element both through its own website within the Manchester Museum's web pages and by arranging visits and participation for urban schools as part of the government's Excellence in Cities scheme.

Even this is not the end of research at Alderley Edge by the university and the National Trust. The study area is suffering from the growing pressure of increased visitor numbers as well as damage to the surface by weather erosion; the Edge's fragile make-up is under substantial threat. The Trust is working in collaboration with the University's archaeologists, building on the management plan created from the Landscape Project's work, to conserve its delicate ecology but with due respect for the archaeology and the history that lie underneath. Thus the story goes on.

A.J.N.W. Prag
Hon. Professor in the Manchester Museum and
Professor Emeritus of Classics

Acknowledgements

Special acknowledgements are naturally due to Mr Roy Barber, Mrs Molly Pitcher, Mrs Edna Younger and Miss Pamela and Miss Mary Parkinson. As former residents and neighbours of the Hagg Cottages, their childhood memories transformed the excavated site into a living place.

The authors also wish to thank the following individuals and organisations for their valuable contributions to the Alderley Sandhills Project: Paul Sorensen, the Hagg site landowner; William Harris, of neighbouring White Barn Farm; Tristram Besterman, John Prag, Irit Narkiss and Clare Pye, of the Manchester Museum; Steve Mills, Doug Kidd, Nigel Dibben and Phil and Elaine Taylor, of the Derbyshire Caving Club; Wendy Scott and Meg Barnett, of the Wizard Tea Room; Jeremy Milne, Paul Rutter and David Standen, from the National Trust; Tony Wilmott, Jennie Stopford, Kath Buxton and Andrew Davison, of English Heritage; and Adrian Tindall, formerly of Cheshire County Council.

Various participants assisted during the field and laboratory stages of archaeological research. We would particularly like to thank the following for their special contributions: Darren Griffin, Russell Palmer, Sam Bolton, Devin Hahn, Sophie Pullar, Laura Brenton, Sarah Whitehead, Steven Price, Osamu Maeda, Jo Wright, Matthew Watkins, Alice Hall, Zoe Sutherland, Jonathan Pickup, Jo Laycock, Martin Burgess, Katherine Baxter and Shari and Leigh O'Regan. Non-invasive surveys were undertaken by Malcolm Bailey of UMIST and Graham Mottershead of UMAU, University of Manchester. Sean Edwards, Galina Gussarova and Ed Bellinger of the Manchester Museum completed the botanical survey of the site before excavations. Finally, post-excavation analysis was undertaken by the ARCUS team at the University of Sheffield, with particular thanks due to Jim Symonds, Joan Unwin, Chris Cumberpatch and Hugh Willmott.

Thanks are due to Sarah Whitehead for special dedication to her duties as Laboratory Manager after August 2004. Derek Trillo of G10 Photography and Design Unit, University of Manchester, undertook the specialist photography of artefacts drawn from the ASP Collection, and Leigh O'Regan completed line drawings of selected items.

A number of generous colleagues directed us towards comparative materials from unpublished field reports: Noel Boothroyd and David Barker, Stoke on Trent Archaeological Service; Ian Miller, Oxford Archaeology North; Mike Nevell (University of Manchester Archaeological Unit), Robina McNeil and Norman Redhead (Greater Manchester Archaeological Unit); Jim Symonds and Anna Badcock, ARCUS, University of Sheffield; Richard Buckley, Audrey Horning and Marilyn Palmer, University of Leicester; Paul Belford, Ironbridge Gorge Museum Trust; David Cranstone, Cranstone Consultants; Roy Stephenson, Jacky Keily and Nigel Jeffries, Museum of London Archaeology Services (MOLAS); and David Gwyn of Govannon Consultancy.

Finally, we would like to thank our patient and supportive editors at Manchester University Press, Matthew Frost and Ange Brennan. Their friendly enthusiasm helped sustain us throughout the final writing stages of the Alderley Sandhills Project.

1

An archaeology of community life

You felt part of a very big family. That's gone now, hasn't it? I mean, if you live in a town you don't belong to anyone but your own few people, do you? Whereas you felt belonging to everybody in the parish. You felt safe with everybody.

(Mrs Edna Younger, ASP Interviews, August 2003)

Material studies have greatly enhanced our appreciation of the dramatic transformations of domestic life forged over the industrial era. Traditionally, this research has focused on the changing nature of workers' housing from the early eighteenth century, emphasising the socio-economic impact of industrialisation on both accommodation patterns and architectural forms. This study builds upon such scholarship by exploring the internal intricacies of material life within a rural working settlement from the late seventeenth through to the mid-twentieth centuries.

Households, settlements and community life

How have scholars identified the material existence of a 'community'? Previous studies have tended to adopt a spatial approach, linking specific households into wider settlement groups, typically defined by a bounded environmental landscape (Clarke, 1977; Flannery, 1976; Tringham, 1973). Recent work has questioned the underlying political economy of communities, identifying three basic functions for this scale of settlement: social reproduction, subsistence production, and self-identification/social recognition (Kolb and Snead, 1997). By characterising the community as a unique 'socio-spatial' phenomena (Kolb and Snead, 1997: 611), this approach has correlated traditional archaeological indicators – such as labour investment, distance patterns and exchange relations – to aspects of identity formation and economic status *within* community groups.

Particularly when applied to sites of the recent historical past, this scholarship has illuminated the varied nature of community life – with exca-vated artefact assemblages from specific households given social meaning through comparison with broader material patterns on neighbourhood, regional and even global dimensions (Praetzellis and Praetzellis, 1990; Karskens, 1999; Nevell and Walker, 1999; Cantwell and Wall, 2001). While the micro-scale perspective delivered through archaeological excavation has offered an intimate understanding of the daily internal dynamics within working households (Casella, 2005; Clark, 2005; Groover, 2003; Lawrence, 2000; Matthews, 1999), regional surveys of historic industrial landscapes have revealed highly significant patterns in the position, design and multiple functions of workers' housing (Hughes, 2000; Mrozowski, 2005; Palmer and Neaverson, 2004; Timmins, 2000, 2005). The increasing sophistica-tion of such detailed case studies has in turn fostered a global comparative approach – with local instances of colonial settlement, land tenure patterns, commodification, capitalism and community migration critically juxtaposed to reveal the complexities and contingencies of these key historical phenom-ena (Orser, 1996; Johnson, 1999; Hall, 2000; Gosden, 2004). Shifting our analytical focus to the interplay between these varied scales, these settlement studies reveal how specific material patterns of production, distribution and consumption shaped the underlying nature of everyday society from the eighteenth century (Palmer, 2005). They demonstrate, in other words, how the archaeologist must 'think globally, dig locally' (Orser, 1999: 281) to appreciate the internal material world of community life.

Drawing from sociological theories of agency (Bourdieu, 1977; Giddens, 1984), an increasing number of archaeologists have adopted ideas of prac-tice and interaction to explore how past individuals were able to manipu-late, protect, sustain and negotiate their specific 'place' within a community (Saitta, 1994; Johnson, 1993; Horning, 2000; Beaudry and Mrozowski, 2001; Tarlow, 2005). Defining a 'community' as a socially constituted human phenomenon, these studies have explored patterns of internal hier-archy, class distinction, social mobility, embodied and habitual practices and extended kinship networks to illuminate the underlying social fabric of human settlements. For these scholars a community exists 'not [as] a spatial cluster of material remains to be observed, but rather a social process to be inferred' (Yaeger and Canuto, 2000: 9).

Adoption of such an interpretive approach immediately generates ques-tions on the comparative nature of the evidence itself. Particularly for periods of the recent past, available research sources are characterised by their rich, sometimes overwhelming, diversity. However, the subtle nuances of affilia-tion, kinship, competition and identity can be grasped only as points of both harmony *and* dissonance emerge through this miscellany. Indeed, contradic-tory stories frequently appear when we try to cross-check evidence gleaned from historical documents, memories and excavated objects – a process of epistemological exchange that has been characterised as a 'conversation' or triangulation between different forms of 'knowledge' about the recent past (Schrager, 1983; Lummis, 1987; Purser, 1992; Beck and Somerville, 2005). Nonetheless, it is those very contradictions that illuminate the complicated, negotiated and interactive nature of social life within human communities.

Since the 1990s, oral historians have begun to move away from questions of authenticity and verification to instead explore how social memories and inter-personal narratives are themselves created. Drawing from the work of Graham Dawson (1994), Penny Summerfield (1998: 17) adopted the term 'composure' to describe the production of memory. Playing on the double meaning of the verb 'to compose', her study examined the dual process of crafting accounts of past experiences and achieving personal composure (or equilibrium). Crucially, the production of oral histories is not indiscriminate – the story told is always 'the one preferred among other possible variations' (Dawson, 1994: 22–23). Composition, in other words, necessarily requires the inclusion *and* omission of specific memories to produce both a coherent narrative and a comfortable version of one's self. Further, individual narratives are composed as 'social memory' through their association with broader collective contexts – ranging from kin affiliations to regional or national identity groups (Halbwachs, 1992 [1950]; Misztal, 2003). These personal stories draw upon, and thereby reinforce, broader social themes of gender, age, nationality, locale, class and culture to create, shape, challenge and sustain their underlying social meanings (Cattell and Climo, 2002).

The metaphor can be extended to material culture on both personal and collective scales of analysis. Through their dwellings and possessions, each community resident actively cultivates a constellation of social meanings that in turn establish an 'acceptable self' (Summerfield, 1998: 17). However, these acts of material 'composition' serve as a communal process, with individual residents habitually linking their personal memories and memorabilia with their deeper understandings of local norms and shared narratives. Thus the community group belongs to a 'memoryscape' (Nuttall and Coetzee, 1998: xii), a patterned collective of stories and recollections materially anchored together through the architecture and artefacts of the local settlement.

'It were a beautiful place': understanding the Hagg

Building upon such an explicitly social perspective, the Alderley Sandhills Project explored the transformative roles of industrialisation and deindustrialisation on a small rural hamlet in north-west England. Known as the 'Hagg', the study site contained the subsurface remains of two post-medieval brick-and-sandstone cottages, in addition to their associated outbuildings, privies, middens, gardens and a well. To address the multi-layered nature of this historic period community, archaeological investigations were originally designed to examine two central and interrelated themes:

- Transformations of domestic life and consumer culture over the industrial era.
- Changes in the broader cultural landscape of Alderley Edge brought about by local intensification of mineral extraction industries from 1750.

The research results eventually demonstrated a far greater range of historic, economic and social influences present within the material evolution of this study site. Nonetheless, these initial topics provided a starting point – a place to begin to untangle the complicated networks of kinship, affiliation, employment, support, competition and obligation that forged community life at the Hagg Cottages of Alderley Edge.

History of the Edge

Located approximately 25 km south of Manchester, Alderley Edge is a natural rocky outcrop with views across both Greater Manchester and the Cheshire plain. A distinctive natural landscape, the Edge supported a variety of economic activities from early prehistory through the twentieth century. Over both the Bronze and Romano-British periods the local region was extensively mined for copper deposits. From the late Middle Ages the region was predominantly supported by agricultural production, although industrial extraction of copper, lead and cobalt was re-established by the Alderley Edge Mining Company during the nineteenth century.

By the 1840s an early rail line linked central Manchester with the growing service town, thereby making Alderley Edge the first commuter suburb of Great Britain. Over the early 1850s a series of Italianate 'villas' were constructed at Alderley Edge, and sold to the *noveau riche* mill barons desperate to escape the urban grime and crowding of industrial era Manchester. These wealthy urban migrants provided a new source of employment for the working classes of Alderley Edge. Thus from the eighteenth century the region supported a complex mix of agricultural, industrial and service-based economic activities.

The Alderley Sandhills Project

Funded by English Heritage through the Aggregate Levy Sustainability Fund, the Alderley Sandhills Project was undertaken as a research partnership between the Manchester Museum and the Archaeology Programme at the University of Manchester. Following initial geophysical and topographical surveys of the Hagg site, four excavation trenches were opened during the summer 2003 field season (see Figure 2.6). Areas A and B consisted of two open area trenches positioned to reveal structural remains of the eastern and southern Hagg Cottages.

Area C was a small 1 m × 1 m test pit opened to investigate a geophysical anomaly recorded during the early non-invasive surveys. Unfortunately, no significant material deposits or features were recovered in this third research area. Finally, a 2 m × 2 m trench was opened on adjoining National Trust land to investigate the nature and date range of an artefact scatter eroding from a walking track at the northern end of Hagg Lane. Post-excavation analysis results of assemblages collected from this Area D trench indicated a strong correlation with the last major occupation period of the Hagg Cottages. Thus Area D artefacts were directly associated with late nineteenth through mid-twentieth-century deposits from both Areas A and B.

In addition to archaeological excavation and historical archival research, the Alderley Sandhills Project benefited greatly from enthusiastic involvement by the local community of Alderley Edge village. Over the summer 2003 field season, former residents Mrs Edna Younger (*née* Barrow), Mr Roy Barber and Mrs Molly Pitcher (*née* Barber) visited the site to watch their childhood homes emerge from the soil. Their memories, narratives and family photographs of life at the Hagg offered an intimate personal perspective on everyday life within this rural working hamlet. These stories not only demonstrated how residents composed their sense of community at the Hagg but also located our excavated features and assemblages within a living (yet past) social landscape.

A research framework

At the close of the summer 2003 field season the site archive was re-evaluated to identify constructive avenues for post-excavation research and analysis. After consultation with material specialists from English Heritage project officers, the National Trust's regional archaeologist and the Archaeological Research and Consultancy at the University of Sheffield (ARCUS), a new set of research objectives were established. To address the diverse nature of this historic site, three categories of analysis were undertaken: material, methodological and interpretive.

Material

This first category of research examined archaeological questions specific to the site itself. Work was undertaken to characterise the nature, distribution, deposition and demolition of the archaeological resources collected and recorded during excavations. To properly understand the material residues of local events a stratigraphic sequence for the Hagg site needed to be developed. How early was the initial occupation of the Area B cottage? Were local or imported materials used for construction of the Area A cottage? How and when were these structures modified over their use-life? How did the various occupants adapt these structures to deal with local environmental problems, such as rising damp, land erosion or foundation subsidence? When were they demolished? Had their building materials been substantially cleared or recycled after demolition?

The post-excavation work also sought to locate and identify intact sub-surface remains that could be directly linked with the Hagg Cottages. While a large quantity of early twentieth-century artefacts had been recovered from the Area D midden, its exact relationship to the Hagg Cottages needed to be established by comparing material assemblages across the various trenches. Similarly, the Area B cottage demonstrated an ambiguous structural layout. Did it relate to landscaping efforts by cottage residents? Or would could its remaining features be associated with a particular chronological period? To answer these site-specific research objectives, a combination of photographs, historical documents and stratigraphic recordings were utilised to interpret the excavated archaeological remains.

Methodology

In addition to researching the specific material history of this site, the project questioned elements of how archaeological fieldwork is itself undertaken. A second strand of research objectives examined methodological techniques used for the recovery of data about the recent past. While standard field recovery methods, in both Australasia and the Americas, include coarse-sieving of all stratified soils, this technique is not typically practised in Europe. This project adopted full coarse sieving, with the excavated soil matrix processed through a combination of 4 mm and 2 mm mesh screens. Thus post-excavation research questioned whether this time-consuming field practice actually improved recovery rates for small finds. Did the technique impact either the number or diversity of artefacts recovered?

Through the enthusiastic participation of former residents the project also examined the research potential of oral history as a new source of data on the recent past. Like historical and material sources, these narratives introduced their own 'difficulties, constraints and grammars' (Purser, 1992: 28). This second methodological research objective addressed the relation-ship between ethnographic and archaeological sources of evidence on the recent past. Do oral histories merely offer idiosyncratic, nostalgic or even inaccurate representations of past lives? How would these narratives reveal the subtle 'intermingling of neighbourhood, friendship and kin links' (Rule, 1986: 157) that defined life at the Hagg? When do memories support and/or contradict artefactual evidence? Did material evidence of household activities correlate with recorded oral histories? To what degree is this source altered by the social identity of the interview subject? These research objectives enabled a reflection on how the archaeology was carried out as well as presenting an archaeology of the site itself.

Interpretation

A final category of research objectives was developed to explore the significance of the Hagg site within its wider temporal and social context. While British archaeology has maintained a proud tradition of industrial era scholarship since the mid-1950s (Symonds and Casella, 2006), only a few detailed studies have been completed on domestic settlements associated with the nation's leading industries (Palmer and Neaverson, 2004; Timmins, 1998; Hughes, 2000; Gwyn, 2006). Post-excavation research and analysis were undertaken, therefore, to illuminate the transformative roles of industrialisation and deindustrialisation on everyday life in these rural working households. What forms of domestic labour were required for home maintenance? What other income-generating activities were undertaken to supplement formal modes of employment? How did the structures themselves negotiate the overlap between domestic and work-related space? Did the four households respond in unison as the region evolved from an agrarian, through industrial, and into a service-based economic framework? Or could we interpret different employment patterns through the material goods of these separate households?

To understand the growing influence of mass-produced commodities and ever broader distribution networks on the English working household, final research questions were developed to explore the material nature of consumer behaviour over the industrial era. How did the introduction of a waged economy change what foods were purchased and prepared by the Hagg residents? Did different types of mass-produced commodities appear within household assemblages at different periods of industrialisation? Why did certain goods appear first? Why were certain types of home or locally based production retained? Did the availability of consumer goods change how residents maintained both themselves and their houses? Did the material assemblages hold evidence of specialised artefacts, such as tablewares, cutlery, food storage vessels, personal grooming tools or interior ornaments, that could be associated with a yearning for social mobility? Could aspects of social identity (gender, class, age, etc.) be interpreted through the material world of the Hagg Cottages? Ultimately, such explicitly social research questions supported a contextual perspective, by demonstrating how the archaeological remains at the Hagg simultaneously reflected material patterns specific to the settlement itself and illuminated broader changes to English rural life over the later historic period.

Outline of chapters

Offering a synthesis of preliminary results from the Alderley Sandhills Project, this volume seeks to demonstrate how the men, women and children of one rural working settlement experienced a community through their internal material world. Chapter 2 will introduce the local site history and environmental landscape of the Hagg Cottages. Drawing from a multidisciplinary range of sources such as archives, cartography and oral history, this chapter illustrates the origins, architectural development and eventual demolition of the study area. Additionally, results of various non-invasive surveys will be combined to characterise how three centuries of residential and industrial activities influenced the topography, botany and soils of the surrounding natural landscape.

Forming the primary focus of the volume, Chapters 3 through 6 explore four themes central to the daily experience of life within a post-medieval working rural community. Chapter 3 considers foodways at the Hagg Cottages and demonstrates how social ties both within and between the households were created through practices of food preparation and consumption. Integrating results from artefact collections with oral histories of former residents, the chapter continues by examing the impact of mass-produced commodities on working households by illuminating the different roles of home-produced and store-purchased provisions. Changing concepts of nutrition and the 'English' diet are explored through evidence from ceramic, glass and metal assemblages. Finally, the nineteenth-century introduction of increasingly exotic foods and affordable tablewares is considered in relation to changing scales of product distribution and availability within the globalised world of the industrial North West.

The maintenance of a working household will be examined within Chapter 4. Summarising the architectural history of the Hagg Cottages, this chapter tracks the evolution of these houses from their seventeenth-century origins as estate farmhouses for a stronghold tenant family to nineteenth-century sub-leased accommodation for itinerant employees of the local mineworks, and eventually to twentieth-century rental cottages for local service workers at the commuter suburb village of Alderley Edge. Archaeological evidence for the expansion and abandonment of particular spaces across the site will be mapped against changes to living and working patterns over the industrial era. Concepts of health and hygiene are examined on both personal and household scales, with artefacts related to grooming, cleanliness, sanitation, drainage and pest control discussed. Finally, evidence of various ornaments and decorative techniques is considered, as residents of the Hagg Cottages transformed these rented dwellings into their personal homes.

Building upon these practices of domesticity, Chapter 5 explores how Hagg residents enhanced their daily lives, and sustained their local community through shared moments of recreation and relaxation. Comparing assemblages related to alcohol and tobacco consumption between the households, this chapter examines how leisure activities became materially inscribed. Aspects of gender, age and social status, evidence from artefact assemblages, photographs and oral histories will be combined to show how these families nurtured kinship and camaraderie through their material world. Stories and photographs shared by former residents illuminate their play activities at the Hagg Cottages. By juxtaposing these nostalgic memories against excavated artefacts, this chapter will explore the nature of childhood over the inter-war decades of the early twentieth century. Finally, the continuing theme of consumption will be explored through relative concentrations in specific brands of leisure-related food and beverage containers. Changes in the commercial distribution of beer and ale will demonstrate the increasing participation of Hagg residents in the consumer society of north-west England.

Chapter 6 will explore how site residents materially sustained their neighbourhood life. The influence of status, inter-generational relationships and inter-household relationships will be examined through analysis of artefact patterns and oral histories. To demonstrate how internal class relations were actively composed within the Hagg community, this chapter also considers the simultaneous networks that structured everyday rural life – those hierarchical identities created through employment, kinship, neighbourly and landlord–tenant relations. By exploring the social meanings of assemblages related to tools of trade and personal dress, specific material practices will be linked with broader spatial patterns of gender, work, residence and status. Ultimately, this chapter will demonstrate the impact of wider community affiliations on the material record of the Hagg Cottages.

Finally, Chapter 7 will summarise the major outcomes of the Alderley Sandhills Project by considering what material perspectives have contributed to our understanding of community life from the pre-industrial to the post-industrial era. By situating results of the project's material, methodological and interpretive research questions within an international comparative perspective, this chapter will demonstrate the ways people use material culture to express and experience social belonging. By exploring the community as an essential aspect of social affiliation in the working households of rural England, this chapter summarises the creative ways in which the Hagg residents gradually modified their daily lives, their family organisation and their physical dwellings to maintain themselves over three centuries of dramatic social and economic upheaval. This chapter provides an archaeological narrative of the Hagg site, a rural working community of north-west England.

2

The Hagg of Alderley Edge

This chapter presents an archaeological overview of the Hagg Cottages. Through its broader geology and prehistory, the site is first located within the northern Cheshire region of north-west England. A cultural history is also constructed, drawing from archival sources on four centuries of occupation at the Hagg Cottages. The final section of this chapter offers a detailed overview of fieldwork results, summarising material evidence for the archaeological stratigraphy and features recorded within each excavation trench. Finally, the post-excavation treatment and sampling of recovered artefacts are introduced to demonstrate how excavated objects were used to interpret broader patterns of everyday life within this rural working community.

The Alderley region: a long-term history of human habitation

The study area is located immediately east of Alderley Edge (Figure 2.1), a modern commuter village located approximately fifteen miles (25 km) to the south of the city of Manchester, one of the main urban centres of north-west England. The area in question is dominated by a spectacular natural sandstone escarpment know as the Edge. Rising 179 m above sea level, this dramatic landscape feature has defined the local region since prehistory. Although now overgrown, the site of the Hagg Cottages lies approximately 500 m south of the Edge.

The Edge escarpment forms part of a larger tongue of high land extending in a north-westerly direction above the Cheshire plain (Prag, 2005: 1; Timberlake, 2005: 11). Spatially, this dramatic feature appears on the edge of two distinct geological regions. From the Edge itself, on a clear day, the local vista reaches both across the Cheshire plain to the south and across to the Pennine hills to the north and east. Described as the 'backbone of England' (Hebbert, 2000), the Pennine Chain consists of an upland hill region that effectively divides the island from the Midland counties of Derbyshire, Staffordshire and Cheshire at its southern extent to the northern

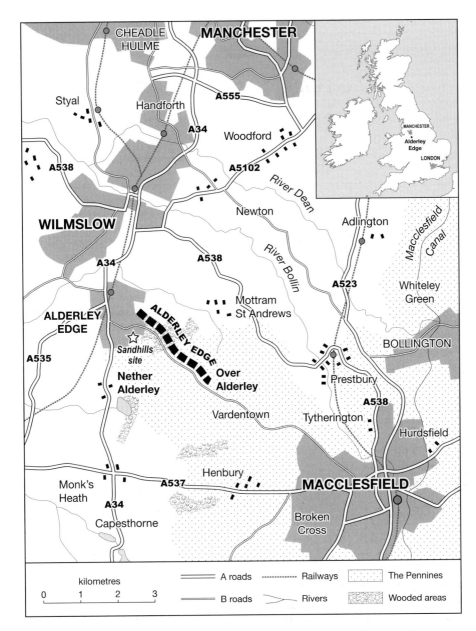

Figure 2.1 Location map of study region, with inset of England

counties of Lancashire and Yorkshire. While the Pennine Chain formally rises from Macclesfield, only 5 km away from Alderley Edge village, research has linked the Alderley uplift and formation of the Edge escarpment to this dominant geological feature (Prag, 2005).

A natural rocky outcrop, the Edge provided an excellent vantage point, in addition to shelter and water. As a result, the Edge served as a centre of human habitation throughout prehistory. Mesolithic remains, primarily flint flakes dated from *c.* 8700–4000 BC, have been recorded in the immediate Alderley area (Timberlake, 2005: 7). Excavations and landscape surveys have also demonstrated that the Edge was mined for copper ore from the early Bronze Age (*c.* 1900–1700 BC) (Timberlake and King, 2005: 50).

Pollen records demonstrate that, approximately 2,000 years ago, regional Iron Age societies engaged in extensive farming practices, cutting back local woodland and developing pastoral agriculture (Timberlake, 2005: 16). Over this transitional period, Romano-British garrisons also actively occupied the north-west of England, with settlements established in nearby Manchester and Northwich. Despite this regional presence, no evidence suggested Roman military use of the area between Macclesfield and Alderley Edge, or any significant routes passing through the upland area (Timberlake, 2005: 17). However, industrial work at Engine Vein – one of the historic mines on the Edge – has been dated to the first century AD. Additionally, an early fourth-century Roman coin hoard was famously recovered from the top of Pot Shaft, one of the underground sections of the Alderley mines (Timberlake, 2005: 18). Thus the mineral wealth of Alderley Edge was likely exploited over the Romano-British era. Nonetheless, no existing archaeological evidence has linked this industiral activity with any contemporary regional settlements.

From the medieval period, the dual character of this geological region shaped the local economy. Until the advent of rail transport, trans-Pennine access was slow and arduous, with few roads crossing the high moorlands (Hebbert, 2000: 379). Hill farming of sheep provided the main agricultural activity on these Pennine uplands, in addition to small-scale mining of stone and lead along the rocky hillsides. In contrast with these uplands, the lush pasture land of the Cheshire plain supported a dairy pastoral economy (Simpson, 1957: 143). As a result, the local Alderley region has been dominated by agricultural activity since the late medieval period (McClure, 1939: 514), most famously including the production of 'Cheshire cheese' (Lawton and Pooley, 1992: 49). While Alderley is located on the northern edge of this famous dairy region, farms in the north Cheshire area typically cultivated potatoes, wheat, oats and hay, as well as rearing dairy cattle (Simpson, 1957: 148). Specifically at the nearby village of Styal – located 5 km to the north of Alderley Edge – eighteenth-century tenant farmers were recorded as growing wheat, oats, and potatoes, tending gardens and orchards attached to their homes, and producing cheese for local sale (McClure, 1939: 515). Historically, the closest and most important economic centre in the area was Macclesfield. Located approximately 5 km south-east of the Hagg Cottages site, it functioned as the market town for local residents (Wallis, 1917: 33), who came to socialise and trade their produce.

Regional land tenure was traditionally ascribed to two landlord families. The original medieval Alderley landscape consisted of two settlements – Over Alderley and Nether Alderley, named for their spatial location relative to the Edge escarpment. The Hagg site was located approximately 2 km from each of these medieval settlements. The feudal landlords responsible for these historic settlements consisted of the Stanleys, a gentry family established in north-east Cheshire since the fifteenth century. Until the Second World War the Stanleys occupied the grand stately home of Alderley Park, located in the medieval village of Nether Alderley. Additionally, this family owned the majority of land within both Over Alderley and Nether Alderley, including the Hagg site itself.

The Hagg Cottages were situated very near the parish boundary between Chorley and Nether Alderley. Chorley also supported its own medieval village, approximately 2 km west of the Hagg site. The Trafford family were the main landholders in Chorley, and lived further out towards the north-west of the parish. Far more welcoming of commercial development, the Traffords sold their land throughout the later industrial period, thereby hastening the absorption of Chorley into the Victorian-era town of Alderley Edge. Thus, while the specific history of the Hagg Cottages reflected the socio-economic concerns of the Stanleys (who owned the site), the wider historical landscape also reflected crucial differences in the commercial interests of these two gentry families over time.

Post-medieval history of the Hagg cottages

The study of the Hagg Cottage site can, therefore, be seen as a microcosm of the social, political and economic developments of the area spanning from the post-medieval period to the present day. To provide a background context for archaeological research on the Hagg Cottages, the major characteristics and historical shape of this distinctive region must first be considered.

The eighteenth-century history of the Hagg

The first archival mention of buildings at the Hagg appeared in 1735. A notebook belonging to the Stanley family included a transcription of the 1735 Poor Law assessment, in which 'Widow Dean' was recorded as living at the Hagg (CRO [Cheshire Records Office] DSA 3752/1). The family name of Dean was not an uncommon one – for example, nearby Brynlow Farm

was simultaneously occupied by members of the Dean family. It has therefore proved difficult to trace the earliest residents of the cottages through
their wider family connections. Another mention of this same 'Widow Dean'
appeared in 1745, when the parish registers record the burial of Frances
Dean of the Hagg (CRO P/143/1/1). A later written account from the
early 1840s recorded that a farmhouse had been erected at the site in 1747
(AELP [Alderley Edge Landscape Project] archive), a date corroborated by
a datestone above the door of the eastern cottage inscribed 1747 (Alderley
Park Estate, 1939: 82). In a memoir written in the early 1840s the first Lord
Stanley (John Stanley, born 1765) observed that around this time a second
Hagg dwelling was 'rebuilt as a small farmhouse' for Daniel Dean (most
probably the son of Frances) (AELP archive).

Land enclosure and the Hagg

By the mid-eighteenth century, historical records suggest, two farm buildings occupied the Hagg site. The 1775 enclosure map of the Alderley area
roughly indicated the location of these two structures. The purpose behind
this map revealed a crucial element in the history of the Hagg Cottage residents over the late eighteenth century. As an enclosure map, it represented
the transfer of land use, specifically the removal of common land, throughout the Alderley region. Since the Stanley family already owned the majority
of this land, the 1775 enclosure was by agreement, rather than as a result of
a formal Act of Parliament. Nonetheless, enclosure meant that the villages
of Nether and Over Alderley no longer held communal land rights or admin-
istrative responsibilities over such land. This process was part of ongoing
changes in land ownership and subdivision undertaken by Cheshire landowners into the nineteenth century (Barnwell and Giles, 1997). As a further
development of his Alderley estate land, Sir John Stanley established a plantation of various tree species across the Edge. Over the following years, he
continued buying out small leaseholders who still held common rights over
the Edge, completing the legal process of enclosure by 1778, thus securing
his dominance and management of the area.

   In addition to these alterations to the traditional agricultural landscape of
the Alderley region, mining activity began around the Edge during the later
eighteenth century. Charles Roe, a Macclesfield businessman, was involved in
copper mining in the area from 1758 to 1871, with forty to fifty people in the
Alderley area involved as waged labourers. The road system around Alderley
was also largely defined by enclosure, with precise details recorded within the
enclosure maps. These documents clearly show that Hagg Lane was intended
to be eight yards wide, in keeping with other local lanes. The main turnpike
road system was also created in the mid-eighteenth century, with the local
Knutsford to Macclesfield Road, over Monksheath, significantly improving

transport links in the area. The development of the road infrastructure also created a market for alehouses and inns, and many of these establishments soon appeared for the use of local miners along these roads. By 1780 the present Wizard Inn had been built to accommodate the needs of the local Alderley miners on their journeys between their workplace and homes.

Rental records showed that the Dean family continued their occupation of the Hagg site throughout the late eighteenth century. Archives held at the Alderley Park estate also indicated that a man named Frank Timperley married the daughter of Daniel Dean, and took over the farm upon the death of his father-in-law in the late eighteenth century (AELP archive). During this time the Stanley family continued their patronage of the area: a school for girls was established by Maria Stanley in 1799, and smallpox vaccinations were extended to Alderley children in 1802, but despite these paternalistic improvements, life for the working families of the Hagg could be difficult. Even though male wages had increased over the 1790s, agricultural wages in Cheshire were low, and a bad harvest in 1799 was followed by a particularly harsh winter, causing hunger among the poorer residents of Alderley parish.

By 1800 the Hagg farm was most like those on the uplands of the Alderley estate. Although holdings on the lower Cheshire plain tended to be large dairy farms, the Hagg site lies within the transitional boundary between the two dominant geographic zones, as mentioned earlier. Records from the period 1800–1808 depicted the Hagg tenement as a small farm, about half the average size for leases within the Stanley estate. Such a small concern would not have generated much income for Hagg tenant farmers over the early nineteenth century.

Mining the Hagg

The geological character of the Alderley region proved crucial to the development of the Hagg site. Copper mining was already part of the Alderley landscape in the eighteenth century. Nonetheless, in 1806 – at the height of the Napoleonic Wars – cobalt was discovered at the Edge. This event served as a catalyst for the development of extensive mining activity in the immediate surrounds of the Hagg Cottages.

The establishment of this extractive industry in the early years of the nineteenth century significantly altered the type of occupation supported by the cottages. The shift from agriculture to mining also affected change in the overall socio-economic status of the Hagg Cottage residents as they transitioned from tenant farmers to waged labourers. By 1808 the Alderley Edge Mining Company had been formed, and was leasing the Hagg site from the Stanleys for £40 a year – double the rent of the previous farm tenancy. Perhaps as a result of this lease transfer and rate increase, the Timperley family – descendants of the original inhabitant Widow Dean – relocated from Alderley to Manchester. The cottages were internally subdivided at this time (CRO DSA 3752/2–4), so that they could accommodate four families within the two structures.

The Stanley family may have viewed the local farming and mining communities as distinct social groups. Certainly, separate celebrations were held in 1810 for the golden jubilee of George III, with the underlying significance of such celebrations discussed in Chapter 5. Unfortunately, the lack of historical sources over this period limited our ability to determine whether the social distinction was established by the landowning familyor whether it was a separation equally felt by the farmers and miners themselves.

The first phase of mining ended at Alderley in 1817, when operations ceased to be profitable. With the end of the Napoleonic Wars, peace with France restored better-quality imports from Continental sources. Although no clear set of records existed for the Hagg Cottage residents over this period, local figures such as the Stanley gamekeeper, Joseph Clarke, were thought to have taken up tenancy during this period. In 1833 Joseph Clarke was recorded as moving to Beachtree Lodge from the Hagg. Since Beachtree was the first purpose-built gamekeeper's lodge on the Stanley estate, Clarke was most likely a member of the estate household rather than employee of the Alderley Mining Company.

Further physical changes to the buildings also occurred during the mid-nineteenth century. Rent books (CRO DSA 3752/2–4) recorded major works on the southern cottage (excavation Area B) in 1839, including reconstruction of the front wall, and a roof replacement with Kerridge stone (local sandstone tiles). The nature of these works suggested that the cottages had fallen in to a state of disrepair by this period.

Railways and the rise of commuter suburbs

From the 1840s, following these repairs to the southern cottage (Area B), our historical knowledge of the Hagg became supplemented by data drawn from national census returns. While this source provided brief snapshots of site residents every ten years, they also permitted speculation on broader settlement patterns and occupational profiles for the male heads of household. In the first census return of 1841, a total of nineteen people were listed as residing at the Hagg, divided among four separate households (with population counts inclusive of the heads): Henry Jackson (family of five), David Toft (family of four), John Ellam (family of two) and George Barton (family of four). All of these men listed their occupation simply as 'agricultural labourer'.

Alongside these labourers, four stone-cutters were listed in residence at the Hagg. These were related to the arrival of the railway to the Alderley region. Railway transport was to have a significant impact on the daily life of this rural community, not least with the arrival of a work force from outside counties and regions of England. In the 1841 national census, all parishes along the track of the new railway line reported a temporary increase of population as labourers and tradesmen relocated in search of construction work.

Previously, the only transport routes within the parish had been by road. Although pivotal in the rapid expansion of neighbouring Manchester, canal transport had come late to this northern region of Cheshire. Indeed, it was only in 1831 that a canal was opened through the nearby market town of Macclesfield. This new water route linked the potteries of the Midlands to the south, with the industrial areas of Stockport and Manchester to the north. However, since the local canal did not run through the parishes of Nether Alderley or Chorley, it was of little consequence to the villages.

As a result, the construction of an innovative rail transport system brought revolutionary changes to the local landscape. The track of the new railway ran directly through the medieval village of Chorley, immediately adjacent to the Hagg Cottages. Around the site of the new rail station, a planned commuter village of 'Alderley Edge' was soon established.

Located 22 km from central Manchester, Alderley Edge offered a convenient rail commute to the thriving industrial city. This encouraged a mixture of both day-trippers and new residents into the area. The Trafford family, landlords of Chorley parish – where the train station was sited – allowed their property to be subdivided for sale to commercial developers. From the 1840s, series of Italianate villas were constructed, in addition to the infrastructure required to support a new rail commuter village (Hyde, 1999). Alderley Edge was a planned settlement, entirely designed to attract wealthy Manchester businessmen seeking an idyllic countryside landscape for their family homes. In contrast, the Stanley family refused to subdivide their property, or develop it for the 'Cottontots' – as this emerging class of *nouveau riche* Manchester commuters became known among the established families of north Cheshire.

Thus the extent of Alderley Edge village grew to roughly mirror the medieval boundary line of Chorley parish. Although located just on the outskirts of this new village (see Figure 2.1), the Hagg Cottages occupied Stanley land and remained firmly within Nether Alderley parish. The Stanley family were a little less dubious of the merits of opening their land for public visitors. They particularly encouraged Sunday and holiday outings to the woods of the Edge, a day trip popular from the second half of the nineteenth century through to today (Hyde, 1999: 26).

Although residents of the Hagg remained tenants of the Stanleys, the 1851 census returns demonstrated that these inhabitants were not isolated from the rapid changes occurring in the new village of Alderley Edge. In

1851 total of fifteen persons lived at the Hagg, with households headed by Benjamin Heywood (family of two), William Ridgeway (family of three), Samuel Oaks (family of five) and John Clark (family of five). Only two of these men were listed as labourers: William Ridgeway and Samuel Oaks. Interestingly, the latter household included Samuel's sister, Sarah Oaks, who had just given birth to a child, but who was not married. John Clark's occupation was listed as gardener, although the identity of his employer was not included. Benjamin Heywood's connection with the expanding Alderley Edge village was clear; his father had been a stonemason involved in the construction of the early villas in Alderley, and Benjamin later assumed management of this family business.

In 1844 one of the first rail venues, the Queen's Hotel, opened in Alderley Edge to cater for urban visitors (Simmons, 1984: 202). One year later, construction of the bourgeois Italianate villas was well under way. Most examples of this type of housing consisted of three reception rooms, three or four bedrooms, offices and service accommodation, all set in approximately an acre of gardens. (See Hyde, 1999, for an architectural gazetteer.) Domestic female staff were drawn from outside of the local area, with live-in accommodation provided as a term of employment. In contrast, male garden and maintenance staff tended to be employed from local working families (Hyde, 1999: 26). Alongside these villas, new terraced housing was also constructed to accommodate the service workers of Alderley Edge village. The built landscape of this planned community was thus designed to cater across the socio-economic spectrum.

Industry at the Hagg

After the mid-century, the mines at the Hagg became operational once again. During the 1860s this industry employed approximately fifty men and boys, working both underground and on the dressing floor. Miners earned little more than agricultural labourers over this period. Nevertheless, when a new workhouse opened in Macclesfield – established to serve the destitute of both Alderley and Chorley – few admissions arrived from either the Over Alderley or Nether Alderley villages. Thus, even though local workers were poorly paid, they were still managed to eke a living, whether down the mines or working the land.

Traditional agriculture-based occupations began to wane from this point onwards, with the national census of 1861 recording an unusual degree of occupational change from the preceding decade. All heads of household were by then listed as working in the mines. The return data included Samuel Oaks – no additions to his family of five – who, although still resident at the Hagg, had changed his employment entry from agricultural labourer to miner. One new household was headed by David Walston (family of five), a copper miner who had moved to the Hagg from Derbyshire, a Pennine county to the south-east which historically supported lead-mining industries. Mineworkers also headed the remaining two households. Thomas Cooper (family of five) was an engine feeder in the copper and lead works of the Alderley Mining Company and William Taylor (family of two) was a mine labourer from Yorkshire – another Pennine county to the north-east of Alderley, traditionally linked with the coal industry. Thus, as industrial mining intensified over the latter half of the nineteenth century, residents of the Hagg Cottages represented a combination of occupational migration and adaptation that reflected broader socio-economic transformations within north-west England.

Throughout the 1860s the Alderley mines continued to operate as a profitable concern, attracting growing attention and a diverse array of visitors. In 1865 a Japanese delegation was recorded taking a tour of the mines. The ongoing prosperity of the area continued to draw a skilled work force, with the 1871 census primarily identifying the adult male Hagg residents as mineworkers, with a total of eighteen persons across the four households. All four heads of household recorded in 1861 had left the Hagg, suggesting a high turnover of tenants over this industrial decade. In the 1871 census return, cottage occupants consisted of John Martin, blacksmith (family of seven); William Davis, copper miner (family of five); George Laeman, mines agent (family of three); and Joseph Pilscombe, copper miner (family of three). William Davis, George Leaman and Joseph Pilscombe had all moved to Cheshire from the south-west of England, probably encouraged by the availability of jobs in that region of the country.

By 1872 the Ordnance Survey map of the area (Figure 2.2) indicated that the Alderley Edge Mining Company had built two main mines close to the Hagg. Named Wood Mine and West Mine, both were connected with the central dressing area by a tramline. Lead, cobalt and copper were all extracted, with the sheer intensity of mining activity forging a new industrial landscape at the Hagg. At the mineworks, hydrochloric acid was used to chemically leach copper from the extracted sandstone. This processing technique produced large amounts of acidic waste sand deposited as the giant 'sandhills' that came to characterise the Hagg until the mid-twentieth century. Despite its environmental impact, this period of profitability was short-lived. In 1878 the Alderley Edge Mining Company lease came to an end, and mining activity in the area permanently ceased. By the end of century, working residents of the Hagg Cottages faced a second period of economic transition.

Service industry workers at the Hagg

Closing of the mines caused a second dramatic shift in the nature of life at the Hagg Cottages. By the 1881 national census, a fifth domestic household

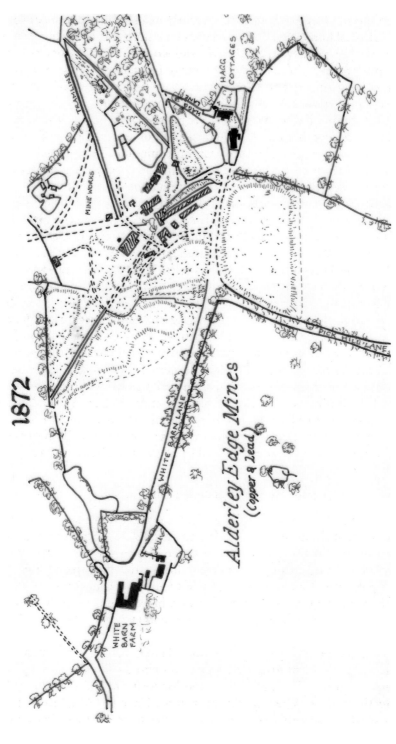

Figure 2.2 Detail of Hagg Cottages with mineworks, sandhills, and White Barn Farm (after the Ordnance Survey map of 1872)

was added to the Hagg site, with the recently disused mine office converted into a residential home. Heads of household included David Ellam, gardener (family of five); Thomas Steele, labourer and woodman (family of five); John Leigh, farm labourer (family of four); George Leaman, commercial brewery agent (family of three); and Joseph Massey, a labourer on highroad construction (family of five). With the closure of the mines, all families recorded in the 1871 census had departed the Hagg, their transience reflecting the domestic flexibility required by the industrial economy. One notable exception was that of George Leaman. A Cornish migrant, he appeared permanently settled into the Cheshire region, having adapted his experience as a mines agent to secure a similar position within a local brewery.

The following ten years witnessed a sharp drop in population at the Hagg Cottages, with only twelve residents listed in 1891 – the lowest total since nineteenth-century census records began. Joseph Massey (by then recorded as living alone), George Leaman (reduced to a family of two) and David Ellam (family of four) retained their tenancies. Further, these men were also all listed with the same occupations as in the 1881 census, suggesting that some degree of job security was available to the people employed in non-industrial work. These families lived alongside George Barber, a general labourer, head of a family of five. One cottage was listed as unoccupied.

From the turn-of-century this pattern of residential stability continued. The 1901 census recorded David Ellam (family of three) and George Barber (family of four), who continued their occupations as gardeners and domestic workers. Joseph Massey was also still residing at the Hagg in 1901, although his household size had increased to two, and his occupation was promoted to township roadman. These residents were joined by another Barber family. Ernest Barber, a stone quarryman, head of a new household of three.

Family lives: oral histories and the Hagg

As the site history entered the twentieth century, information provided by documents such as census returns and rent books becomes powerfully enhanced by oral histories of daily life at the Hagg Cottages. While stories were collected from a range of Alderley locals, the majority of narrative detail reflected the childhood memories of three former residents: Mrs Edna Younger (*née* Barrow), Mr Roy Barber and his younger sister, Mrs Molly Pitcher (*née* Barber). All were born at the cottages over the early 1920s (Figure 2.3).

Mrs Edna Younger's mother, Delphine Massey, had herself grown up at the Hagg as a member of Joseph Massey's household – first listed in the 1901 local census return. Like the Barbers, the Masseys were a long-established local Alderley family. When she was born at the Hagg in 1922, Mrs Younger joined a strong local network of relatives. After their marriage, her parents

Figure 2.3   Roy Barber, Edna Younger (*née* Barrow), Molly Pitcher (*née* Barber), site visit, September 2003. *Inset* Edna Barrow, Roy Barber and Molly Barber at the Hagg, *c.* 1928

had rented the eastern half of the internally divided Area B cottage. Her maternal grandparents and uncle also lived at the Hagg site, occupying the former mines office bungalow near the Hagg Cottages. By the end of decade, her maternal kin left Alderley for the Welsh coast in an attempt to improve her uncle's health with the seaside climate (Mrs Edna Younger, ASP interview, July 2003). Her paternal grandparents (the Barrows) also lived near by, although inside the village of Alderley Edge, rather than the Hagg site itself. A carpenter by trade, her father, Frederick Barrow, set up his own business within Alderley Edge village during the 1930s. By mid-decade, he purchased a family house in the village, and the Barrows left the Hagg (Mrs Edna Younger, ASP interview, August 2003).

The family of David Ellam – recorded in the 1901 census lists – also continued to reside at the Hagg site over the 1920s. By then, the Ellam household consisted of three members: elderly David Ellam and his two adult

Figure 2.4   The Hagg Cottages in the 1920s

unmarried daughters, Gertie and Mary Ellam. Occupying the western half of the internally divided Area B cottage, the Ellams shared strong neighbourly ties with the other Hagg families. When Mr Ellam died during the 1920s, the 'Miss Ellams' continued to occupy their cottage, famously keeping their gardens in 'splendid order'.

The internally divided cottage of Area A was occupied by an extended family of Barbers. Ernest Barber – son of George Barber (elder) from the 1901 census – still occupied the cottages in the 1920s (Figure 2.4). He had a son, also called George, and following the death of his wife in the early years of the century, he and his young son George were joined by relatives when Jack and Lena Perrin moved into the adjoining half of the Area A cottage. Ostensibly, Mrs Lena Perrin had arrived to help her widowed nephew with the cooking, housework and child care, although oral history participants suggested her real talents lay elsewhere, possibly in more commercial pursuits (Mrs Molly Pitcher, ASP interviews, July 2003; Mr Roy Barber, ASP interviews, September 2003).

During the inter-war period, George Barber (younger) brought his new wife to live within this extended household (Mr Roy Barber, ASP interviews, August 2003). The Area A cottage provided a childhood home for Mr Roy

Barber and Mrs Molly Pitcher until 1928, when their parents moved to the nearby town of Wilmslow. This new suburban settlement formed part of a housing boom on the outskirts of many towns over the 1920s, providing accessible and improved housing to working families across England (Hyde, 1999: 56). Ernest Barber and the Perrinses continued their occupation of the Area A cottage following the family's departure.

When faced with high death duties, the Stanley landlords finally sub-divided and sold their Alderley estate in 1938 (Hyde, 1999). Requiring a catalogue of all properties and tenants, the Stanley estate book provided a final archival image of the Hagg Cottages. The divided Area B cottage was identified as lots 497 and 497a (Alderley Park Estate, 1939: 81–82). These were each listed as:

A Semi-detached Cottage
Near the Copper Mines, Nether Alderley.
Accommodation: Living Kitchen, Scullery, Parlour, and Two Bed Rooms,
outside W.C. [toilet].
Company's Water Supply laid on.
(Alderley Park Estate, 1939: 81)

The eastern side was recorded as let to Mr A. Knight, who had assumed tenancy following departure of the Barrow family, for £13 per year in rent (Alderley Park Estate, 1939: 81). The smaller western side continued to be let by the Ellam sisters, although for the lesser sum of £6 12s per year in rent (Alderley Park Estate, 1939: 82).

The internally divided cottage of Area A was listed as a single unit, lot 499, and described in the sale catalogue:

A Substantial Double-fronted
Dwelling House
known as
The Haggs Cottage
at the Copper Mines.
The Property is built of brick, with a tiled roof,
having a panel imposed over the door dated 1747.
Company's Water laid on.
The Accommodation: Sitting Room, Dining Room,
Kitchen, Scullery and Larder,
with Four Bed Rooms.
(Alderley Park Estate, 1939: 82)

Mr Ernest Barber (paying £5 10s per year) and Mrs Perrin (paying £4 10s per year) remained listed as tenants. The former mine bungalow had also apparently been reoccupied by 1938, and was rented by Mr J. Powell for the annual sum of £10.

The 1938 estate sale was a spectacular failure, in that most of the lots failed to sell (Hyde, 1999: 52). Gradually, different parts of the estate were sold off to former tenants and other private investors. Following the death of her great-uncle, Mrs Molly Pitcher frequently returned to the Hagg to visit and bring meals to her grandfather and elderly widowed great-aunt, Mrs Perrin. Mrs Pitcher's recollections portrayed life within the cottages over World War II as ever fewer people inhabited the site.

The Hagg site was eventually bought by Thomas Nield and his son Fred. Over the early 1950s they demolished the cottages and sold off reclaimed building materials from the Area B structure. Additionally, the Nields intermittently removed the majority of the sandhills, by selling the acidic sand to the local council as aggregate for roadworks. The Nields used the abandoned mine shafts and immediate landscape for extensive garbage landfill operations, on contract with the local Macclesfield Council.

Oral history participants remembered Mrs Perrin as the final resident of the Hagg Cottages. She appeared extremely reluctant to leave her home at the site. Indeed, one story told of how the Nields cut off the piped water supply to the cottages in an attempt to force her relocation. Undeterred, she continued to happily occupy her cottage, drawing her water from the original well (Mrs Molly Pitcher, ASP interview, July 2003). Eventually, by the mid-1950s, the Barber family convinced Mrs Perrin to move from the Hagg. With the cottages abandoned, the site's owners soon demolished the buildings (Figure 2.5).

Figure 2.5   Sandhills, *c.* 1955, during aggregate removal

The Alderley Sandhills Project: fieldwork results

This section outlines results from both the preparatory site surveys and the actual excavations. In order to determine the nature of sub-surface material remains, the Hagg site was extensively analysed through a series of non-invasive surveys. A topographical survey was first undertaken to map the immediate excavation areas and to facilitate the laying out of a site grid. A specialist vegetation survey investigated whether it was possible to trace the site's history through remaining plant species. Finally, a set of geophysical surveys were completed to aid the identification of sub-surface features prior to excavation. A metal detector survey was also undertaken during excavations. Its results suggested a general scatter of debris across the intensively occupied area, rather than any locations of specific household or midden features.

When combined with archival and cartographic sources, these non-invasive surveys helped determine the locations of excavation trenches. This chapter will present a site narrative based upon these archaeological excavations. A stratigraphic phasing of the Hagg site is also provided within the following section. These field data will support the more interpretive presentation of results contained in subsequent chapters.

Vegetation

A vegetation survey was undertaken prior to the excavation of the cottages and a map of the findings was created. Since the survey was time-restricted to March through May 2003, some significant plants were still emerging as the survey finished. Nevertheless, interesting results were produced which provide a little more contexual background for interpretation of the Hagg archaeology.

In the fifty years since the cottages were demolished, the vegetation had reverted overall to complex semi-natural woodland, with several garden species still in evidence. Vegetation which would have formed fertile hedges, or crop boundaries, were included in the recorded flora of the site. These consisted of hawthorn (*Crataegus monogyna*), damson (*Prunus domestica*), common elder (*Sambucus nigra*), common nettles (*Urtica dioica*), blackberry-producing brambles (*Rubus fruticosus*), goosegrass (*Galium aparine*), St John's wort (*Hypericum perforatum*) and creeping thistle (*Cirsium arvense*).

In addition, certain species provided evidence of domestic planting within the site, particularly raspberries (*Rubus idaeus*), daffodils (*Narcissus* cv), roses (*Rosa* cv) and primroses (*Primula vulgaris*). The native bluebells (*Hyacinthoides non-scripta*), found in abundance across the site today, may also have been imported or encouraged by the cottages' former inhabitants.

Such plant sources of food, medication and beautification form a constituent part of understanding the lives of the past inhabitants of the Hagg Cottages. Uses of these natural resources are be discussed in greater detail later within Chapter 3.

Topographic, electro-resistivity and magnetometry surveys

A topographical survey was carried out across the Hagg site in order to create a local site grid linked to the national Ordnance Survey grid. Further, land features were mapped in 0.5 m contour intervals to consider the potential presence of below-ground archaeology. Results indicated that the site sloped generally from east to west, and brought to light remains of a well, located slightly to the north of the Area A cottage.

Two non-invasive surveys were carried out, utilising resistivity and magnetometry technologies. Clear anomalies in both surveys picked out structural remains of the Area A 'Stanley' cottage. Further results also suggested middens along the eastern bank that bounded the Hagg site. One particularly visible linear anomaly appeared in both survey results. Since it linked the two cottages together, it was interpreted as the remains of a utility pipeline, although its orientation did not correspond to any of the recorded water or drainage services at the Hagg site. Neither survey was able to pick out any readings to suggest the presence of Hagg Lane or the southern Area B cottage. Following excavations, it became clear that this absence of data was the result of extensive post-demolition recycling of building materials following the destruction of the southern structure. In stark contrast, the demolished remains of the Area A cottage were left relatively *in situ*, yielding a far greater quantity of artefacts and structural features.

Excavation

Four trenches in total were opened at the site (Figure 2.6); the two main trenches, Areas A and B, were initially 10 m × 10 m, which were then subdivided into four equal units of 5 m × 5 m. Drawing upon a combination of physical survey data, historical documents, photographs and oral historical evidence from the last three surviving cottage residents, Area A was situated over what was thought to be the location of the mid-eighteenth century 'Stanley' double-pile cottage. Similar evidence was also used to situate Area B, with trenches sited to examine remains of the southern seventeenth-century 'baffle' entrance cottage. During the excavation season, Area B was extended eastwards to examine the remains of structural features related to an historical privy.

Area C constituted a 1 m × 1 m excavation trench, located to the north-west of the Hagg Cottages (see Figure 2.6), in an area which seemed most

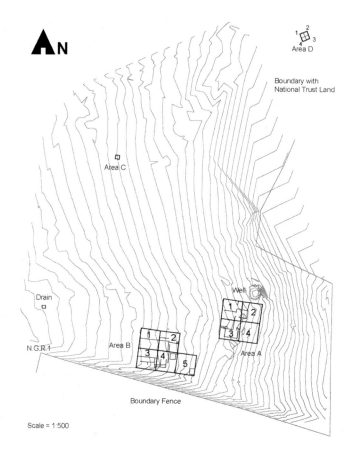

Figure 2.6   Alderley Sandhills Project 2003, site plan. Topographic contours set at
0.5 m intervals

likely to yield the remains of domestic middens. Oral history evidence suggested that cottage residents had been dumping their rubbish in this area,
and the electro-resistivity and magnetometry surveys both indicated the
presence of a large anomaly. Area D was located to the north of the cottages
(see Figure 2.6), on land owned by the National Trust. The area was under
immediate threat of destruction from the construction of a bridle path by
the National Trust, and early twentieth-century artefactual material could
be seen eroding from the path at this location. An initial 1 m × 1 m test
trench here was later extended to a 4 m × 4 m trench, subdivided into four
units.

Excavations in all trenches were carried out by stratigraphic context,
with all removed material then sieved through 4 mm or 2 mm sieves, using
a combination of wet and dry sieving (Figure 2.7). Contexts were numbered

Figure 2.7 Alderley Sandhills Project 2003, sieving station

with four-digit context numbers (sometimes referred to in this site narrative) and Harris matrices were constructed for each trench. Specific details of these stratigraphic contexts and matrices can be found in the project report, lodged with both English Heritage and the National Trust during December 2004 (Casella *et al.*, 2004). An overview of site phasing and a brief narrative for each excavated area is provided below. Over the subsequent four chapters, more detailed interpretations are given to what are considered to be the most important features, including the changing architecture of the buildings, and the structural remains that helped constitute the decoration of the cottage residents' homes. The summaries provided here are simply aimed at imparting an overall introduction to the archaeological phases and findings, and a temporal framework for these later detailed discussions.

Site phasing

Nine distinct phases to the archaeology of the site were identified overall, although not all nine phases were visible in each excavated area. The phases were as follows:

Phase IX. Natural: pre-seventeenth century

Dark red-orangey clay was the characteristic natural soil across the whole of the Hagg area. This phase was visible as the natural basal deposit found in Areas B, C and D. Included in it are interface contexts with low quantities of artefact inclusions within them. No remains in Area A were excavated through to this earliest natural phase.

Phase VIII. Construction period I, c. 1650–1747

The first evidence of house construction at the Hagg comes from Area B only, with no evidence for activity during this early period in any of the other trenches. A small clay-pipe bowl in the base of a wall trench fill in Area B (context [2124]) was specialist dated to c. 1650–1670. The date for this pipe dovetailed neatly with the style of the original structure in Area B, a three-room farmhouse with 'baffle entrance'. Buildings of this style have been provided with a date range of c. 1600–1730 (Brunskill, 1982). The pipe bowl suggested a *terminus post quem* date of 1650, but the easy disposability of pipes during the seventeenth century suggested a date for initial construction of the first Hagg Cottage within this c. 1650–1670 date range.

Phase VII. Construction period II, 1747–1808

A reasonably precise date can be provided for the beginning of this phase at the Hagg site, marking the second period of construction. As outlined earlier within this chapter, archival records included a mention of Lord Stanley arranging the construction of a cottage at the Hagg for Daniel Dean. Further, the Stanley sale catalogue of 1938 recorded a date stone inscribed with 1747 placed above the front door of this double pile cottage (Alderley Park Estate, 1938: 82). Representing an early example of this architectural style – known locally as a 'Stanley cottage' because all Alderley examples were erected by the landlord – similarly designed houses were common in rural regions of England between c. 1760 and 1860 (Brunskill, 1982). There is evidence for extensive construction work during this phase in Areas A and B. Neither Area C nor D contained elements of this eighteenth-century phase of site use. Enclosure of the Alderley land, as recorded by the 1775 enclosure map, took place during this phase.

Phase VI. Construction period III, 1808–1828

Historical records again provide precise dates for Phase VI, the third major construction period at the site. This construction activity was allied to a change in the occupations of the Hagg residents, as this was the phase in which the houses were remodelled to better accommodate families working in the newly established industrial mines. In 1808 the Stanley estate records indicated the internal subdivision of the two houses, yielding a total of four separate households at the Hagg site. Construction work during this phase was in evidence in both Area A and Area B. There was no evidence for any human activity during this phase in Areas C and D.

Phase V. Construction period IV, 1828–1872
The subdivision of the Hagg Cottages was closely followed by further major reconstruction works at the southern Area B cottage. Alterations primarily involved the rebuilding of the front wall and roof. The end of the phase was marked by the 1872 Ordnance Survey map of the area. By the time of that detailed record, an extension had been added to the eastern side of the Area B cottage. A mid-Victorian period extension had also been added to the southern side of the Area A cottage, with its date established by the use of diagnostic red and grey quarry tiles for its decorative flooring. A common architectural material throughout England in the mid-nineteenth century, their distribution from the Midland potteries was enabled by a rapid expansion of the railway network, which provided transport for heavy, yet fragile, building materials. Excavation in Area C recorded an orange and red clay context with large rubble inclusions, probably related to mining activity over this phase. There was no evidence for any activity in this phase within Area D.

Phase IV. Construction period V, 1872–1940s
The start of this phase was dated to the 1872 Ordnance Survey map. As mentioned above, the Hagg Cottages had reached their greatest extent of architectural elaboration. Thus this fifth construction phase was the last in which the archaeological record showed house alterations at the Hagg. By the 1940s, both oral history and artefactual assemblages indicated, the cottages accommodated their final occupants. Over this late phase, construction work in Areas A and B amounted to a series of property improvements and modernisations. These included the creation of new pathways and cement floors around the Area A cottage, and the addition of a boiler room, drains, flower beds and paving to the Area B structure. A new multi-seated privy was added to the site, for shared use by all four households. Area C contained a gradual silt build up above the earlier mining deposits. Forming the bulk of evidence from Area D, the midden dump occurred during this late Victorian through twentieth century phase.

Phase III. Abandonment/demolition, 1940s–1950s
It is not clear exactly when the last residents moved out of the Hagg Cottages, although oral histories suggest it occurred sometime after the Second World

War. All Hagg structures were demolished during the early 1950s. In Area A this post-occupation event was evident through the gradual build-up of silt and debris in and around the cottage remains. Demolition activities in Area A produced a large volume of building rubble and discarded household artefacts. In Area B the evidence for this period was not quite so clear. The privy was filled in with rubble, and the drains were filled with silty soil deposits. In contrast to Area A, no large demolition contexts were excavated from Area B. Area C held no evidence for this post-occupation phase, and in Area D a silty-sand deposit that overlaid the midden appeared to date from this period. In an aerial photograph taken in 1954 the Hagg Cottages were no longer visible as standing buildings.

Phase II. Recycling, c. 1950s

Following demolition of the cottages, the majority of building materials from the Area B structure were removed. Most evidence for this final phase of cultural activity came from Area B, partially through the absence of continuous features, and highlighted by the fact that few structural remains were visible above foundation level. The remnants of a rubble context pushed over a wide area were also visible in Area B, suggesting some ground flattening occurred after demolition. No activity from this phase was visible in Areas A, C or D.

Phase I. Topsoil, post-1950s

Following site demolition, a topsoil of brown humic sandy silt built up across the Hagg site. This phase also included stratigraphic contexts related to the regrowth of vegetation, in addition to cut-and-fill events created by local rabbits. Phase I contexts were recorded in all excavated contexts.

Area A

This was the area in which oral and documentary historical archives suggested the Stanley cottage (built *c.* 1747) had stood. From the excavations a sequence of contexts relating to the original construction of the house, its division into two cottages, their extension and decoration, as well as debris from occupation, were recorded (Figure 2.8).

Contexts relating to the original farmhouse fit within Phase VII (*c.* 1747–1808). During this time the original interior and exterior walls of the farmhouse were built, and the floors were covered with bedding sand and flagstones, symmetrical chimneys were installed as part of the house's design, and the original southern fireplace at the base of one of these chimneys formed part of the archaeology recovered. This architectural design was common, with similar structures recorded in rural England with dates between 1760 and 1860 (Brunskill, 1982).

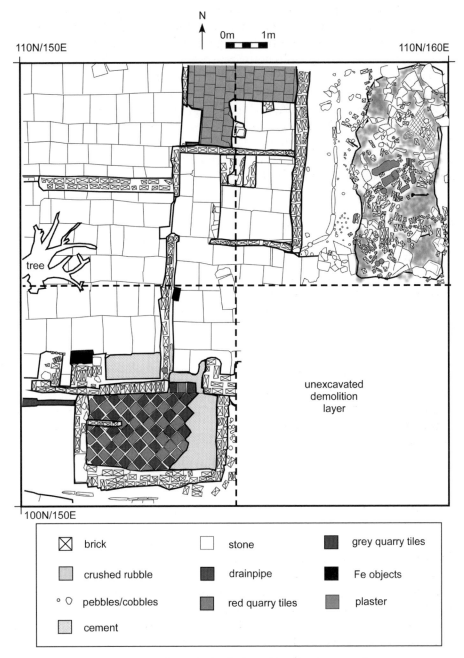

N

0m   1m

110N/150E

110N/160E

tree

unexcavated
demolition
layer

100N/150E

⊠ brick	☐ stone	■ grey quarry tiles
crushed rubble	■ drainpipe	■ Fe objects
° ○ pebbles/cobbles	■ red quarry tiles	■ plaster
cement		

Figure 2.8 Area A, final plan of excavation trench,
Alderley Sandhills Project, 2003

The next major event visible in the archaeology of Area A was the division of the single farmhouse into two smaller cottage units. Occurring in Phase VI, the houses were historically recorded as subdivided by 1808. Contexts related to this internal modification included the extension of walls to block internal doorways, the creation of a doorway between the front and back room in Area A, unit 1, and the construction of an additional kitchen fireplace Area A, unit 2.

Following the subdivision into two cottages, the structures continued to be modified. In Phase V (1828–1872) an extension, including a quarry-tiled floor, was built on the southern wall of Area A, unit 2, and an exterior drain was constructed. Phase IV in Area A involved contexts relating to the decoration and elaboration of the cottage interiors. A blue plaster render was applied to many of the interior walls over this phase. Red-glazed tiles and a wooden mantelpiece were added to the front-room fireplace in Area A, unit 2. Within Area A, unit 1, ferrous metal pegs and a plate set into the original sandstone floor suggested that a kitchen range had been installed. Externally, a flower bed and decorative path edging were added to the northern rear of the divided cottage. Finally, the decorative extension to Area A, unit 2, also appeared to have been converted into a work shed, with Portland cement laid as a floor repair.

Over Phase III (1940s–1950s) contexts related to the abandonment and demolition of the Hagg Cottages. These included the build-up of silts and debris, as well as the collapse of all major structural elements. The context with the largest volume of finds (context [1004]) represented the primary demolition layer of Area A. It included the bulk of household artefacts recovered from the Hagg site, most of which had been discarded when the final residents left their homes. Little recycling of demolished building materials occurred in Area A. The final contexts, recorded archaeologically, related to the build-up of topsoil above the collapsed structure.

Area B

The archaeology of Area B contained the earliest evidence of occupation at the Hagg site (Figure 2.9). Natural clays (Phase IX, pre-seventeenth century) underlay all contexts, although in a few places these deposits held later artefacts, presumably embedded during the extensive recycling activities of the 1950s. Seventeenth-century contexts thought to date to Phase VIII included: wall cuttings, foundation walls, exterior drains, and the brick entrance porch marking the southern entrance of the dwelling. The excavated floor plan suggested a six-room farmhouse, with three rooms on the ground floor and three rooms on the first floor. A common rural house design in seventeenth-century England (Brunskill, 1982), the brick fabric of this house indicated a

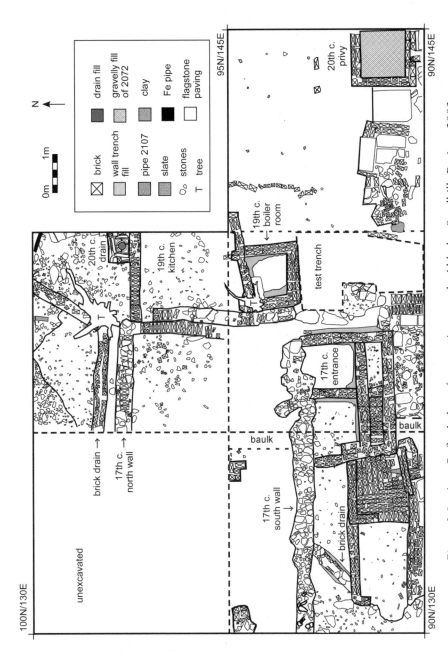

Figure 2.9 Area B, final plan of excavation trench, Alderley Sandhills Project, 2003

relatively high socio-economic status for this property, as this construction material served as an expensive commodity until industrially produced in the subsequent century.

With the construction of the Area A cottage in 1747 the Hagg site was modified to encompass a pair of houses, rather than one single structure. During this phase, the fields of the Alderley estate were enclosed, and the permanent routes of roads and lanes were established. As discussed earlier in this chapter, as a component of these landscape modifications, the orientation of the Area B cottage was flipped by 180°, so that it entered from Hagg Lane on its northern facade. Specific changes included a series of internal walls added to the former entrance porch, which resulted in its division into two small rear utility rooms. Undertaken to adapt to its reorientation, external modifications included a new sandstone path and retaining wall on the eastern side of the property.

No Phase VI (1808–1828) archaeological contexts were recorded within Area B. While the structure had certainly been internally subdivided into a pair of separate households, post-demolition recycling activities had obscured all material evidence of this building phase. Nevertheless, further modifications took place following its subdivision. In Phase V (1828–1872) a new wall was built on the eastern side of the house. A kitchen was constructed on the eastern facade of Area B, with a water pipe installed to service the extension. A front path was added to the dwelling, and further drains were added to the building exterior.

Alterations continued in Phase IV (1872–1940s). Over this later period a separate boiler room was added to the eastern kitchen extension. Sandstone flagging and an area of brick paving were installed to the southern rear of the cottage. In the early twentieth century a privy structure was built on the site, its use shared by all four households of the Hagg. Additional concrete drains were constructed to the rear of the Area B cottage. Because of the extensive post-demolition recycling, no clear archaeological evidence was recovered from Area B for Phase III. Representing the final occupation and abandonment of the cottages in the 1940s and 1950s, the only associated contexts consisted of sandy deposits that built up inside exterior drains after the houses became abandoned.

The recycling phase (Phase II, 1950s) was most clearly visible in Area B, albeit by the remarkable absence of anticipated architectural evidence. Following demolition, the majority of building materials from the Area B cottage had been removed for resale. A thin compact clay with frequent small rubble inclusions suggested that earth-moving machinery swept the demolition site, removing the bulk of cultural materials, and leaving the remnant foundations recorded during excavations.

Area C

Despite its initial promise, the archaeology of Area C proved to be quite simple, containing only seven contexts. Opened to investigate a distinctive geophysical survey anomaly, the test trench not only held no midden deposit, but excavations failed to produce any artefacts which could conclusively prove identifiable activities within this area. All contexts (with the exception of the natural clay) dated from Phase V (1828–1872) or later. The area was therefore related to the industrial mining activity in the immediate Hagg area.

Area D

Opened to investigate artefacts eroding from a bridle path on neighbouring National Trust property immediately adjoining the Hagg Cottages, excavations recovered contexts associated with a shallow midden deposit (Figure 2.10). The natural clay of this rising slope had been overlaid with a deposition of artefacts dated to Phase IV – the later occupation of the Hagg Cottages (1872–1940s). Following abandonment of the site (late 1940s onwards), silt and topsoil built up over the disused rubbish midden (Phases III–I).

Figure 2.10 Detail of Area D midden feature, Alderley Sandhills Project, 2003

Artefact and environmental analysis

Recovered artefacts were analysed by a team of specialists contracted through the ARCUS field unit at the University of Sheffield. Due to the sheer volume of collected materials, analysis was not undertaken on 100 per cent of the excavated artefacts. All of the 370 'special finds' were sent for more detailed analysis – these objects had been identified in the field as having the potential to be especially valuable for study, and all had been recorded with three-dimensional co-ordinates.

The bulk of the remaining collection had been recovered from Areas A and B. No artefacts from topsoil contexts were sent for analysis, with the exception of special finds. Within Area A, the main context relating to the abandonment of the houses (context [1004]) contained such a large quantity of artefacts that it was realistic to send only a sample of these for specialist examination. Area A, unit 1, was selected for analysis, as excavation of this area had exposed the greatest extent of the cottage interior. Artefacts from the remaining contexts of Area A and all artefacts from stratified contexts in Area B were also sent to ARCUS for specialist analysis. Due to the lack of clear interpretation of the past activities in Area C, 100 per cent of artefacts recovered from this test pit were sent for analysis. Although representing a midden deposit, Area D only represented a small feature. The relatively low quantity permitted all artefacts from this trench to be sent for further specialist examination.

Prior to analysis, artefacts were separated according to fabric types: ceramic, glass, metals, bone and shell, seed, wood, building materials, coal and charcoal, leather and rubber, and plastic. Once separated, specialists in each field undertook detailed examination of these Hagg assemblages. In addition to these specialised material studies, environmental samples were also examined. A total of sixty-four botanical samples were collected by soil flotation during field excavations. These were sent to ARCUS for specialist archaeobotanical analysis. Finally, soil samples from a range of contexts on the site were subjected to geochemical analysis, with concentrations of cobalt, copper and lead recorded alongside the basic pH of the recovered soils.

This chapter has demonstrated the broader significance of results from the Hagg cottage excavations. The Alderley area was engaged in some of the key historical processes of the modern era. Life for the cottagers can be viewed as a narrative sequence, beginning with an initial rural farmhouse site which developed in a region in which settlement had existed far back into prehistoric periods. The archaeological work carried out at the site allows a critical examination of this small community from the post-medieval community with a clear local social hierarchy, through to the decline of this traditional social system, with the eventual sale of the Stanley estate. Supported by data from the wider historical research and vegetation survey, the excavation results presented in the following chapters allow us to examine this community through the past 300 years, focusing on community and individual identities of the site's residents.

3

Feeding the family

This chapter examines what are commonly called 'foodways' in historical archaeology. Thus far, the term has been utilised to a much lesser extent in British post-medieval archaeology. However, since it encompasses a wide array of related practices and material evidence, the concept provided a useful construct for the purposes of this study. Foodways can include the food people eat, the manner in which this food is prepared, the person who prepares the food, and the symbolic and ideological values understood in both the food itself and the practices surrounding it (Janowitz, 1993: 6). It takes us beyond a simple focus on diet or any single category of artefacts, such as ceramics, and allows us to ask wider social questions of the evidence relating to food consumption at the Hagg Cottages site.

We used various aspects of the Alderley Sandhills Project data to examine food preparation and consumption patterns, including the impact of mass-produced foodways, the increasing commodification of foods, and the social meaning of foods within working households. These themes are also closely linked to the discussions in later chapters of consumerism and commodities that focus upon different spheres of social practice. Some of the key questions and interpretations that have been presented internationally in historical archaeology are also briefly summarised. The shift from home-produced to shop-purchased provisions is tracked and the project also examines the changing scales of product distribution and availability within the local region of north-west England. The chapter culminates in a discussion of how these relate to changes in consumption patterns on an international scale.

The data presented here are not intended to provide a conclusive discussion on the foodways of the rural working classes in eighteenth- to twentieth-century Cheshire. Rather, it allows us to present initial interpretations, and to pose important questions for archaeologists to address in future, as more data become available.

Historical perspectives on diet in the industrial era

Whilst the precise beginnings of both capitalism and industrialisation are topics for some debate (Johnson, 1999), it is nevertheless widely agreed that the 'classic' industrial era began around 1760 (Styles, 2000: 131). An essential consumer commodity, food nourished the entire population, and provided mass employment through agricultural and processing industries. Historians have emphasised how rapidly diet changed over the past few hundred years, both before and after the industrial revolution. Normally food selections and practices of consumption change only when certain conditions occur: with the introduction of new plant or animal varieties, the availability of new foods through commercial or government channels, or the resultant cultural exchange of dietary and culinary practices following the immigration of a group of people to a new area (Pelto and Pelto, 1983: 515). In post-medieval England, changing food patterns were intrinsically linked to the revolutionary expansion of colonialism and capitalism.

Colonialism made new foods available, through channels of capitalist trade. With exploration spreading to all corners of the world, new foods were discovered and returned to Britain to cater to a national palate, growing in diversity. Expanding industrial capitalism meant that foods were increasingly mass-produced and purchased through cash exchanges outside of the household and immediate community. These early changes began to occur just prior to the industrial era, with the 'new exotic groceries' of tea, sugar, coffee, tobacco and chocolate becoming first available in the early modern Europe (Styles, 2000: 127) as a result of colonial intervention in Africa, Asia and the New World.

Modifications to agricultural production on a global scale were linked to changing patterns of foodways in England, with Caribbean sugar plantations a prime example of a manifestation of a rapidly developing mercantile commerce in food products (Mintz, 1985; Pelto and Pelto, 1983: 515). The availability of such store-bought foods increased throughout the post-medieval period, with foodstuffs such as sugar and tea increasingly forming an integral part of English working-class foodways. By 1850 most households in England had become dependent upon professional food suppliers, with new foodstuffs such as potatoes, introduced from the New World, widely incorporated into working-class diets (Burnett, 1989: 8; Thompson, 1980: 374). Basic staples such as sugar and flour were by then primarily available through merchants or shops. At the end of the nineteenth century, developments in mechanised food production, such as the manufacture of metal cans (Rock, 1984), encouraged workers to increasingly rely upon shop-bought goods. Although the initial movement away from regional self-sufficiency with regard to foodstuffs has been argued by historians to have begun from the end of the eighteenth century (Jones, 1993), archaeological data presented within this chapter shifted this transformation towards the second half of the nineteenth century. Buying food, rather than growing or raising it, meant that the average person would have access to a wider range of foodstuffs. Adoption of canned produce also increased the longevity of foods. While this technology made food easier to stockpile, it also left the average consumer at the vagaries of the merchants, as they would have to accept the prices and goods that were offered to them.

These patterns reflect broader international trends within the industrialised world. Nutritional standards of the working classes generally appear to have lowered over the last 250 years as food consumers become linked into an 'ever-increasing and intensifying network of socio-economic and political interdependency' (Pelto and Pelto, 1983: 507). Alongside this reliance on mass-produced foods, entrepreneurial food producers in the industrial era actively marketed their commodities in an attempt to develop established 'brands' for their products. This was particularly crucial during the mid-nineteenth century when adulteration to some degree existed in the majority of manufactured foodstuffs available. Contaminants could include inert substances such as chalk added to bulk flour, but could also include hazardous substances, for example, alum (aluminium potassium sulfate). Such practices in urban areas sometimes made it almost impossible to buy many basic foods in an unadulterated state (Burnett, 1989: 217; Koehn, 1999).

The archaeological evidence for foodways at the Hagg Cottages represented part of this global framework of changing industrial consumption patterns, practised within the local context of food available at the site (Johnson, 1988: 220). It also reveals the nature of domestic labour required for everyday food acquisition, preparation and consumption. The community living in the farmhouses at the Hagg site over the late seventeenth and eighteenth centuries were largely self-sufficient in their food production and procurement. They may not have grown or produced all foodstuffs they utilised on their own farm site. But the post-medieval farm communities of the Hagg site would be expected to buy their remaining foods from local markets selling regional produce. This chapter explores how far it is possible to trace such home and regional food procurement practices through the archaeological evidence from the Hagg site.

Within a broader historical archaeological framework, the question of who was producing foodstuffs at eighteenth- to twentieth-century rural sites has been much studied. Existing debates centre upon the increased utilisation of commercially manufactured foodstuffs, which may have been important to average consumers as early as the mid-eighteenth century (Jones, 1993). Linked to this are questions over which foods were being produced for domestic consumption, and which may have been produced for sale. Practices surrounding dairying (particularly the manufacture of butter and cheese for sale) have been linked to arguments with regard to the importance of women's work in rural households which contributed a cash income (still controlled by women) through the sale of dairy produce (Yentsch, 1991).

While the Hagg site was on the limit of the main Cheshire dairying area, the cheeses produced within this region were sold internationally, even by the eighteenth century. 'Cheshire cheese by the basket or single cheese' was advertised in the *Nova Scotia Gazette and Weekly Chronicle* of June 1785 (Jones, 1993: 29). Such advertisements demonstrate both the regional identity of the Cheshire area as one of high-quality dairy production and the complex links of food production and distribution which developed in the colonial era. Clearly foodways are vital to a detailed interpretation of daily practices and identities of the post-medieval period in which British colonial expansion was occurring. Oral historical evidence supported the idea that there had been continued domestic production of foods at the Hagg Cottages until the early twentieth century and later in the chapter we will discuss this alongside the artefactual data for commercial foodstuffs.

Foodways as social practice

Our twenty-first-century perspectives on dietary practices are informed by a broad knowledge of nutrition that is still an active area of public debate. Today we are constantly bombarded with food and dietary advice to help us make informed choices about the food that we consume. However, the nutritional sciences did not emerge until the 1890s, and both the presence of vitamins in foods, and the relationship between diet and disease were discovered in the twentieth century (Koehn, 1999: 364). Thus most residents of the Hagg Cottages would never have drawn upon 'scientific' facts when thinking about their food. Knowledge of foods, therefore, and choices of foodstuffs to eat, would have formed a contingent part of social practice. This does not mean that food choices were made without knowing of the effects that foods may have had on the body. Throughout history and prehistory there is little doubt of the existence of everyday proverbs and knowledge about food and its effects on the body (Newman, 1946: 39). What is highlighted here, however, is that as well as the changing economic relations of foodways at the Hagg Cottages, food consumption was about much more than just economics and nutrition. Food retained a deeper, more corporeal dimension, intimately linked to social practices of production, distribution and consumption.

In comparison with historical studies, anthropological studies of foodways have tackled a wider range of concerns. Studies have focused on the ecological and market availability of food, the socio-cultural classification of food and the nutritional and medical effects of certain consumption patterns, such as food sharing (Messer, 1984: 205). From these ethnographic perspectives, the way in which foods are viewed as edible or desirable, the preparation of foods and the consumption patterns of individuals and groups all have a shared public role within societies. Tastes in food are learnt at a young age and food consumption and production are entwined with the habits and subjectivities of people. Food itself is culturally defined and is an act of incorporation involving sense, feelings and emotions (Hamilakis, 1999: 39), with its preparation, serving, and consumption providing an important site of social engagement (Stoller and Olkes, 1986). In order to fully appreciate the social role of foodways a more nuanced interpretation of past *cuisines* (i.e. the specific ways in which foods are prepared and how they taste) must be sought (Lyons, 2008; MacLean and Insoll, 1999). As we explore below, specific aspects of the artefact assemblage, particularly the foodways related ceramics, glass and metal food containers and cooking vessels, allow us to formulate interpretations of how cuisines and food consumption practices acted as part of the rich texture of daily life at the Hagg Cottages.

Food and class

Tied to both the social dimensions of food, as well as the economic patterns of foodways in the industrial era, is the underlying relationship between food consumption and class. Deep-rooted socio-economic divisions, forged over the industrial period, became communicated through the realm of food. The major effects of industrialisation have been argued to differ across the well established class divide in England from the second half of the eighteenth century. By the mid-nineteenth century, the gap between food availability and the tastes of rich and poor consumers in England was marked. One result was that the rich of industrial England were beginning to develop cosmopolitan tastes in foods, with famous chefs 'attracted to England by the wealth of the richest country in the world, brought to serve as ornaments to the acquisitive society which industrialism had fostered . . . [placing] the delicacies of the world on the tables of the rich' (Burnett, 1989: 83). The upper classes partook in an internationally shared understanding of cuisines, exemplified by the fashionable spread of French cooking in the early nineteenth century. This was centred on the upper and middle classes of both Europe and the United States forming one of the first 'ecumenical movements in ethnic food adoption' (Pelto and Pelto, 1983; 515). Class divides thus existed between both the foods available and the preferred tastes of foods, with foodways playing a crucial role in the maintenance of group identities. As one major historian of food has argued:

> In nothing was the contrast between wealth and poverty more obvious than in food. House, dress, or manners might be a misleading test of income in 1850, but a man's dinner-table instantly announced his taste and standard of living to the world at large.
>
> (Burnett, 1989: 83).

However, by the end of the nineteenth century this specific socio-economic divide had begun to decrease. With the exception of beer, foodstuffs were one of the last major industries to experience industrial production (Burnett, 1989: 119; cf. Jones, 1993). For the most part, the advent of mass production was inexorably bound up with the improvement of transport links, permitting new food commodities to be distributed rapidly around the country. This modernisation in turn supported ever larger-scale mechanised industries for food production (Burnett, 1989: 118). This was tied to complex food marketing, arguably reaching across social classes, which came about from the second half of the nineteenth century, which further developed the earlier eighteenth-century basic food advertising mentioned above (Koehn, 1999; Pelto and Pelto, 1983: 515). A further question addressed to the Hagg Cottages assemblage is linked with the changing relationship of social class to food. Is it possible to see either the class divide, or the erasure through food of that divide, in the material excavated from the Sandhills site? This question will be dealt with in greater detail in subsequent sections.

Foodways and ideology: perspectives from historical archaeology

Archaeological evidence related to foodways has been a key area of interpretation within historical archaeology. Throughout the industrial era, mechanised processes standardised the way in which people ate, thereby creating similarities between practices in many different areas of the world. Thus, while much of this scholarship has emerged from North America, the underlying interpretations hold international implications. The Hagg Cottage residents formed part of the globalised relations of international capitalism. Before reducing the analysis of food consumption down to the micro level using the evidence uncovered at the Sandhills site, it is useful to consider the main theoretical issues that have been used previously to interpret foodways within the discipline of historical archaeology.

As mentioned before, one of the major areas of change related to an increased purchasing of mass-produced consumer goods. Such changes have been interpreted as a cognitive teleological move towards modernity (Deetz, 1977), as an economic pattern demonstrating the decreasing unit cost of industrially produced ceramics (Miller, 1980) or as a means through which the less fortunate materially emulated their richer neighbours (Leone, 1999). More recent critical interpretations have stressed that archaeological explanations need to go beyond simple estimates of economic value, and instead consider the ideological basis behind consumer choice in ceramics. Crucially, ceramic research must explore the social practices for which these artefacts were utilised (Beaudry *et al.*, 1991; Leone, 1999; Orser 2005).

A central thesis put forward by this socio-economic approach to historical archaeology, is that the use of foodway-related goods provided an active means of creating disciplined workers. The acquisition and use of these goods was a crucial component in the shift from pre-capitalist to capitalist social relations. Two North American sites in particular have considered changing foodways within the social relations of capitalism: Annapolis, Maryland, dating from the late seventeenth century through the early twentieth (Leone, 1999) and Harper's Ferry, West Virginia, ranging from the late eighteenth century through the nineteenth (Shackel, 1996).

In Mark Leone's research, detailed empirical analysis of Annapolis ceramics – by ware type, decoration and form – showed a clear temporal change in the use of foodway-related artefacts from the late seventeenth century. Prior to industrialisation most ceramics used in this region were redwares and slipwares (Gibbs, 2005), with only the elites able to afford imported luxury tin-glazed wares from Europe. Ceramic possessions were limited in both variety and quantity. A seventeenth-century probate inventory from one wealthy Chesapeake resident, for example, recorded just three chamber pots, two old close stool pans, two porringers and a chafing dish (Beaudry et al., 1988: 54). Many eating and drinking vessels in this period were likely not ceramic, with wooden trenchers, pewter containers and shared leather drinking vessels characterising a typical dining assemblage in early seventeenth-century Anglo-America (Beaudry et al., 1988: 55; Deetz, 1977).

The Annapolis data (Leone, 1999) allowed a study through time of town residents who at first appeared to have been using shared vessels for their food consumption patterns. As the eighteenth century progressed the archaeological evidence showed that increasingly modular place settings were used. In these, matching sets of ceramic plates, cups and bowls were interchangeable, manufactured in standardised styles often in the potteries of Staffordshire, or based on designs originating there. Thus, at a table, all of those eating would be utilising the same vessels. Mark Leone has argued that this material trend indicated an ideology of 'individualism' entering the lives of Annapolis residents. This was a central part of the materialism of capitalism whereby:

> [these goods] represented and reinforced the concept of people as individuals. Individuals were defined as having freedom, making progress, and improving their conditions. Individuals could take opportunities and could own property, things and skills that produced actions that purchased rewards.
>
> (Leone, 1999: 211)

Through this argument, the changing patterns of goods at Annapolis are claimed as not merely just a reflection of styles spreading and poorer persons emulating richer persons. The changing dining habits and the ceramics used in these are a means for 'producing' the individuals who conform to the ideological beliefs of a capitalist way of life. It must also be noted here that this argument is not solely based along the lines of food-related ceramics. Clocks are seen as an important aspect of material culture that added to the regulation and ordering of daily life and the eating utensils for individual modular plate settings also formed a coherent part of this same ideological regime.

A similar analysis has been undertaken at the site of Harper's Ferry. Paul Shackel also used a detailed empirical analysis to contrast assemblages from two households – one related to richer master armourers, the other to poorer armoury workers. These assemblages related to the initial industrialisation of the town of Harper's Ferry at the end of the eighteenth century, and more established periods of industrial life in the later nineteenth century. The simple pattern of foodway-related ceramics that Shackel expected from the site was that these would increasingly be mass-produced fashionable wares. Like Leone, this was not a simple argument of ceramics reflecting the economic conditions of their purchasers and users. The use of such goods was tied to the way in which persons came to understand, and participate in, socio-economic practices of the industrial era:

> Early nineteenth-century American industrial behaviour became the norm in urban areas, and households no longer relied upon home production and barter for their everyday needs. Instead, they increasingly relied upon monetary exchange for labour and goods for their everyday necessities . . . Goods that were once generated by the family unit were now purchased, since family providers spent an increasing number of hours labouring to the rhythms and motions of machines as they laboured in factories.
>
> (Shackel, 1996: 112)

Close analysis of the data from Harper's Ferry demonstrated complex temporal patterns. Armoury workers in the early nineteenth century appeared to follow the fashion trends of ceramic use more closely than the master armourer's household, which still showed a significant proportion of coarse earthenwares (Shackel, 1996: 119). In contrast, by the mid-nineteenth century, the armoury workers appeared to use mostly outdated ceramics (Shackel, 1996: 138). Simultaneously, the proportion of coarse earthenware vessels had greatly reduced in the master armourer's household, with fashionable transfer-printed pearlwares, whitewares and edged pearlwares accounting for 74 per cent of food serving and preparation vessels (Shackel, 1996: 121). Thus, at Harper's Ferry, while industrial workers generally began to use modular place settings, and thereby engage with the capitalist ideology of individualism, it was not a simple or straightforward process. Neither type of household directly conformed to the vagaries of fashion. Their choices in the purchase of ceramics were part of their participation in a new industrial culture, but this was mediated through the particular sub-jectivities of different persons within the wider community (Shackel, 1996: 143). As we discuss the Hagg farmhouse and cottage data below we will explore whether these changes, which form an established pattern in North American historical archaeology, are mirrored at a rural English site.

Another area of research in relation to foodways in historical archaeology has been the interpretation of gendered identities and ideologies in relation to changes in ceramic assemblages. Evidence from the Hagg site included a large quantity of earthenwares, particularly those pre-dating the nineteenth century, which may have been produced on a regional scale and which may also have been tied to domestic food production practices. Of particular interest were pancheons, a ceramic hollow form typically used in the prepa-ration of dairy products. Most comparative historical archaeological case studies were concerned with mass-produced ceramics, as these generally form the majority of ceramic artefacts on later historical sites. Nevertheless, this dominant focus has been critiqued. Locally produced, dairy-related ceramics have been particularly marginalised in many archaeological reports. Indeed, Anne Yentsch (1991) observed that in rural east-coast America over the eighteenth and nineteenth centuries, women may have been producing butter and cheese for local sale, and thereby generating an income under their own control. The ceramics which form the central thesis of Yentch's argument are predominantly ordinary coarse earthenware vessels, including redwares. While we would not expect the exact same kinds of regionally produced vessels at the Hagg Cottages (see Gibbs, 2005), it is important to note that these ordinary local earthenwares were crucial indicators for understanding domestic production.

Further gendered perspectives were developed in Diana de Zerega Wall's study of ceramics and the construction of middle-class domesticity in late eighteenth- and early nineteenth-century New York City (Wall, 1994). Wall argued that historical archaeologists should pay attention to women as a group who are often omitted from documentary histories of the period. To explore this hidden past, Wall examined foodway-related ceramics recov-ered from middle-class neighbourhoods, linking teawares, in particular, to the creation of a shared feminine identity. As in the Yentsch study, she directly equated the ceramics with a single gender group, observing, 'So many of the artefacts we excavate are women's goods – the bits and pieces of crockery and glass that make up the rich fabric of domesticity and woman's sphere' (Wall, 1994: 14).

While it is felt that gender is an important aspect of foodway analysis, and that interpreting the creation of disciplined workers in a capitalist system without an inclusion of the gendered aspects has its own difficulties, it is not possible to simply read foodways as intrinsically linked to women alone. At the Hagg Cottages, for example, oral histories recounted how Mrs

Lena Perrin, one of the final residents, had ostensibly moved to the hamlet to help look after her young nephew, George Barber (junior). She was nevertheless remembered as a bad cook and the boy had apparently travelled to cousins at nearby Brynlow Farm in order to eat many of his meals (Mrs Molly Pitcher, ASP interviews, July 2003). The preparation of foodstuffs is too often uncritically assigned a gender designation of 'female', when the relationship between gender and kitchen labour may be far more complex. Indeed, some of the Hagg Cottages were occupied by men alone, including Mr George Barber (senior), who remained at the Hagg site when his son, daughter-in-law and grandchildren moved to Wilmslow at the end of the 1920s. This may have meant that men were preparing and using food by themselves. We will discuss below whether there appears to be any clear material correlate for this in the ASP data.

A final key theme in relation to foodways is the rise of consumerism. This continues the debates of Leone and Shackel, in reiterating that material culture is not simply a reflection of the social status of those who owned and used it. While objects do embody relations between producers and consumers, they do not form a simple mirror to such relationships (Mullins, 1999: 29). The idea of 'consumers' reflects the growing culture of material acquisition from the nineteenth century. Buying the ceramics used in foodways was not simply a way in which the working-class households of the Hagg Cottages became disciplined industrial workers. By drawing on the perspective of consumerism it is possible to think about the ways in which domestic ceramics and commercial products may have been a means for the Hagg Cottage residents to imagine new social possibilities through their food consumption practices. Foodways, particularly over the later Victorian era, may have provided a way for the cottagers to mediate the broader experiences of community life at a number of different scales: the local Hagg community, the parish of Alderley, and the emerging British national community. By purchasing commercial foodstuffs and ceramics, these people may have been utilising purchasing strategies as a way of mediating lived social contradictions and envisaging new social pleasures (Mullins, 1999: 29).

This perspective is of particular importance when we move to look at the late nineteenth-century and early twentieth-century assemblage from the Hagg Cottages, covering a period of dramatically increased marketing of food products to consumers. When thinking about how and why households came to purchase a specific range of commodities, the relative availability of goods, the social status of the households under investigation and the scale of food advertising must all be considered (Purser, 1999: 129). Drawing these perspectives together, it is useful to move towards thinking about the transformations and continuities of foodway practices in relation to a broad range of questions. Firstly, in relation to the changing economic situation of cottage residents, could they afford goods? Secondly, how available were these products? With the development of the new railway commuter village of Alderley Edge, perhaps consumer goods were increasingly available to Hagg Cottage residents. Did archaeological evidence support this premise? Thirdly, we could also consider the influx of workers to the Sandhills site throughout the nineteenth century. Did the increase of mine workers from outside of Cheshire impact the foodway-related evidence recovered during excavations of the Cottages?

Ceramics and foodways at the Hagg Cottages

At the Sandhills site, the dominant category of evidence came from the ceramic assemblage. The data presented within this section provided an excellent baseline on which to begin to consider consumption practices within the Hagg Cottages. In total, foodway-related ceramic vessels formed an estimated maximum number of vessels (MNV) of 1,475 from the analysed ceramic data. (See Chapter 2 for a discussion of post-excavation sampling methods.) Proportionally, 93 per cent of ceramic sherds from the site fell within this sub-category, with the remainder consisting of ornamental ceramics, sanitary wares and flowerpots. In all excavated areas, foodway-related artefacts comprised the dominant ceramic category: 85 per cent of ceramics from Area A (MNV 294), 93 per cent of those in Area B (MNV 967), 94 per cent in Area C (MNV 60) and 90 per cent in Area D (MNV 154). While Area B contained ceramic assemblage primarily dated to the nineteenth century and earlier, the ceramics recovered from Areas A and D mostly dated to the late nineteenth through the early twentieth centuries. This result facilitated the structure of a ceramic 'timeline' that revealed interesting temporal patterns in ware types, vessel forms, and functional categories.

Domestic ware types and date ranges

Literature on domestic post-medieval ceramics in Britain has maintained a strong emphasis on chronology and dating. The particular trajectory of post-medieval ceramic studies in the United Kingdom has had a significant impact on the way in which later ceramics are approached, recorded and interpreted. Largely, this scholarship developed from the work of the Society for Post-Medieval Archaeology. With its traditional AD 1500–1750 focal period, this research produced several studies of the medieval to post-medieval ceramic transition (Barker and Majewski, 2006: 206; for more detailed studies see for example Gaimster, 1997; 1999; Hurst *et al.*, 1986; Miller, 1980; 1991). The main trend in ceramic assemblages from this date range is the change from regionally produced earthenwares, including redwares and slipwares, to mass-produced wares.

The manufacture of these mass-produced wares was mostly centralised in Stoke on Trent, Staffordshire, with areas of secondary importance developing in areas such as south Derbyshire and Glasgow. It could be argued that the latter part of such a transition is visible in the Alderley assemblage, as the shift from open vessels and coarsewares, through to creamwares and other wares in more refined forms, is a part of these wider social changes. Concluding the most recent comprehensive review of ceramics in historical archaeology, Barker and Majewski (2006: 230) drew attention to the fact that most scholarship has thus far focused on the trade and economic status of ceramics, with less attention paid to the social meanings related to their use.

Most importantly, these studies have generated an essential chronology for British post-medieval ceramics. One of the most common forms of ceramics produced in Europe from the seventeenth century were earthenware vessels termed 'slipwares' (Barker and Majewski, 2006: 213). These ubiquitous artefacts were first decorated with a dilute clay slip of a contrasting colour – either applied in trailed, combed or marbled patterns, or dipped as a single layer and incised in patterns to reveal the original colour of the body beneath – and then lead-glazed (Gibbs, 2005). Over the eighteenth and nineteenth centuries, when slipwares were extensively used at the Hagg Cottages, north Staffordshire had emerged as Britain's industrial centre for ceramic production. The manufacture of slipwares also changed with the increasing mass production of ceramics, with later slipwares often being decorated by coloured slips in banded and mocha patterns (Miller, 1991: 6). Alongside the production and design innovations of these slipwares, continuities in manufacture persisted of local coarse utilitarian earthenwares, often for local markets.

Eighteenth-century ceramic development was driven by demands for teawares, as increased accessibility of tea and growing popularity of tea drinking in Europe stimulated production of home-produced teawares, rather than expensive imported Chinese porcelains. White salt-glazed stoneware was the earliest of such high-end domestic ceramics, perfected by Staffordshire potters in the 1740s (Barker and Majewski, 2006: 214), and comprised less than 1 per cent of the Alderley assemblage. With the simultaneous development of new clay bodies and glazes by Josiah Wedgwood, creamware quickly emerged as the dominant elite domestic ware of the later eighteenth century. An earthenware made with a pale body and glazed with a yellowish tint, it was often elaborately moulded during the mid-eighteenth century (Barker and Majewski, 2006: 215; Miller, 1991: 5). By the early nineteenth century, creamwares were in turn superseded by pearlwares. This later ware type represented a further evolution of the technological refinement of earthenware production. The bodies of pearlware ceramics were whiter than those of creamware and they were decorated with a clear glaze

Figure 3.1   Utilitarian brown glazed coarseware, Alderley Sandhills Project, 2003

with a bluish tint, most commonly decorated with some form of underglaze decorative pattern (Barker and Majewski, 2006: 215). A range of decorative techniques were used on these ceramics, with transfer-printed decoration appearing from the beginning of the nineteenth century. The cheapest varieties of pearlwares were simple rim-moulded and painted 'shell-edged' tablewares (Miller, 1991).

From *c.* 1830 'whitewares' became the predominant form of English manufactured ceramics. Whitewares had a highly refined white body, similar to that of pearlwares, but without the bluish tint to the glaze. The final innovation in ceramic production was that of porcelains, particularly bone china. In later ceramic production, this was a key ware type, in which Britain had a significant interest on the international market. Bone china was produced from a mixture of china clay, china stone and calcined animal bone and displayed a translucent white finish. Due to these features, it was quickly adopted by both higher and lower ends of the domestic ceramic market. It is commonly found as simply decorated teawares and tablewares in late nineteenth- and twentieth-century deposits (Barker and Majewski, 2006: 219). This type of ceramic appeared extensively within the Alderley assemblage.

Brown-glazed coarsewares were found alongside pearlwares, creamwares and slipwares, particularly in Area B (Figure 3.1). These were common utilitarian earthenwares, usually produced at country potteries, as opposed to the industrial centres of production, where white salt-glazed stonewares, creamwares, pearlwares and slipwares were made. Brown-glazed course-wares were in production from the late seventeenth century, although the majority of sherds recorded from the Sandhills site date from the eighteenth and nineteenth centuries.

Almost one-sixth of all ceramic sherds from Area B (15 per cent of the foodway-related vessels) were brown-glazed coarsewares. This concentration was significant, as the Area B assemblage related to the earlier phases of site occupation. In contrast, the assemblages from Areas A and D both dated almost exclusively to the late nineteenth through early twentieth centuries and contained much lower quantities of brown glazed coarsewares: only 1.2 per cent from Area A, and 0.3 per cent from Area D.

Another utilitarian ware in use at the site was brown salt-glazed stoneware, which had a wide manufacturing base across the English Midlands. Brown salt-glazed stoneware sherds formed only 1.8 per cent of the ceramic vessel assemblage from Area A, 1.3 per cent of those from Area D, and a more significant 3.1 per cent of those from Area B, where the earlier deposits had been excavated. Interestingly, a similar concentration of regionally produced utilitarian ware types seemed to characterise seventeenth- and eighteenth-century sites in the eastern United States (Beaudry *et al.*, 1988; Gibbs, 2005; Shackel, 1996; Yentsch, 1991), and appeared in nineteenth-century sites in colonial Australia (Brooks and Connah, 2007; Casey, 1999).

Juxtaposed against this early use of more coarse earthenwares was the later adoption of mass-produced wares. The major changes in manufacturing techniques and ceramic fashions described above were clearly apparent in the Hagg Cottages assemblage. A distinct difference in the status of the wares could be comparatively distinguished among the excavation areas. Eighteenth-century ceramics included finds of fashionable tablewares – such as white salt glazed stonewares. Quantities of such wares were small, however, with only 0.5 per cent of the Area B ceramics coming from this category. The later fashionable creamwares (dating from the mid-eighteenth century) and pearlwares (dating from the later nineteenth century) were much better represented within the Hagg assemblage, particularly in Area B. A full 30 per cent of foodway-related sherds from Area B were recognisably creamwares, contrasting with only 2.5 per cent of those from Area A, and 1.7 per cent of those from Area D. Similarly, pearlwares (Figure 3.2) were located in Area B in much greater proportions than in Areas A or D. While 16 per cent of foodway-related ceramics from Area B were shell-edged, feather-edged or transfer-printed pearlwares, this type constituted only 2 per cent from Area A, and less than 1 per cent of Area D.

A range of late eighteenth- through nineteenth-century slipwares were recovered from the Hagg site. These include banded wares (a factory-produced slipware), inlaid slipwares, marbled slipwares and slip-banded wares. The most significant quantities of such wares were recovered from

Figure 3.2   Pearlware, Alderley Sandhills Project, 2003

Figure 3.3   Whiteware, 'Willow' transfer-printed, Alderley Sandhills Project, 2003

Area B, where proportionally 7 per cent of the MNV of vessels fell within the slipware category. Only 1 per cent of Area A ceramics were slipwares, and no sherds were found in Area D.

Later ceramics were characterised by whitewares – identified as a stand-ardised, refined industrial earthenware and dated from the nineteenth and twentieth centuries (Figure 3.3). There was also evidence of late nineteenth- and twentieth-century porcelain/bone china. Whitewares constituted the most significant ware type overall, with 35 per cent of all foodway-related ceramic sherds from the site falling within this category (MNV 1,665). It also provided the majority of foodway-related ceramic evidence from both Area A (62 per cent) and Area D (83.6 per cent). These high proportions of a single ware type are clearly characteristic of the increasing homogeneity and dominance of mass-produced inexpensive wares over the nineteenth century.

In contrast, while whitewares still served as a significant ware type in Area B, it was proportionally far lower, representing only 15.9 per cent of the total MNV of ceramics from that trench. Although porcelain/bone china was a less significant ware type overall, comprising only 5.5 per cent of foodway-related ceramics (MNV 259), similar proportional trends could be distinguished among the different areas of the site. Porcelain/bone china accounted for 16.7 per cent of foodway-related ceramics in Area A and 5.3 per cent in Area D. Much lower quantities were recovered from Area B, where porcelain/bone china vessels accounted for only 2.2 per cent of the assemblage. Thus, from the simple characterisation of the main ware types across the two areas, significant differences in the date ranges of the ceramics were visible.

In summary, a clear transition emerged in the types of ceramic vessels used at the Hagg site over time. In the earlier phases of Area B – deposits associated with the tenant farmers of the eighteenth and early nineteenth centuries – regionally produced coarse earthenwares accounted for a significant proportion of foodway-related vessels. These utilitarian wares were supplemented by modest proportions of finer mass-produced tablewares, primarily creamwares and pearlwares. In later occupation phases, represented by deposits from Areas A and D, coarse earthenwares had almost disappeared from the assemblage. No longer fashionable, creamwares and pearlwares had been largely replaced by the ubiquitous whitewares. Smaller quantities of fine bone china augmented these assemblages by the late nineteenth century.

Not only does this pattern illuminate changes in manufacturing techniques, it also appears to demonstrates temporal changes in the status of the Hagg residents. The earlier phases represent stronghold tenant farmers, who supplemented their everyday local earthenwares with a range of finer Staffordshire tablewares. In contrast, later cottage residents were mostly purchasing mass-produced wares, with the bulk of their ceramics consisting of inexpensive whitewares. These working-class cottagers appear to have ceased using regional wares for daily tasks, supporting an interpretation that they were increasingly reliant on national consumer commodities, rather than regionally manufactured products.

Vessel forms

For the purpose of vessel form analysis, we have removed the category of 'unidentified' vessels before calculating proportions of various forms. Overall 69 per cent (MNV 3,292) of foodway-related ceramics fell under this category. The remaining 31 per cent of the assemblage are discussed in this section. Removing this unidentified category before calculating relative proportions of vessel forms permits a more statistically relevant analysis of use-related activities.

Overall, flatwares formed the largest category of vessels. Those identified simply as flatwares (with no ascription to large or small plate forms and saucers) accounted for 17 per cent (MNV 243) of identifiable vessels. Plates (Plate I) also accounted for 17 per cent (MNV 248) of the assemblage, a further 3 per cent (MNV 41) were identified as small plates, and 3 per cent (MNV 49) were saucers. When these categories were combined, flatwares proportionally accounted for 40 per cent (MNV 581) of foodway-related ceramic vessels from the Hagg Cottages site. Drawing upon arguments from North America (e.g. Deetz, 1977; Shackel, 1996) these flatwares would most likely have been used for individual servings of food and drinks. The use of these may have also have been supplemented, as was the case in the seventeenth- and eighteenth-century Chesapeake region, by pewter or wooden vessels which would not have survived in the archaeological record (Beaudry *et al.*, 1988: 55).

In contrast, hollow wares (excluding drinking vessels), constituted a slightly smaller, but nevertheless significant, category. Those identified simply as hollow wares, with no ascription to particular bowl or dish forms, accounted for 7 per cent (MNV 104) of the total identified vessels. Bowls represented a further 6 per cent (MNV 94), and dish forms (including both dishes and saucers) constituted 4 per cent (MNV 61). A further set of hollow wares were pancheons, or large open vessels used for food preparation tasks. Similar to North American and Australasian vessels identified as 'milk pans' (Beaudry *et al.*, 1988; Brooks and Connah, 2007; Casey, 1999), these artefacts proportionally formed 6 per cent (MNV 89) of the assemblage. When indeterminate jar/pancheon vessels (MNV 32) and open vessels (MNV 17) were included within the 'pancheon' category, the total proportion of these vessels rose to 10 per cent (MNV 140). Thus hollow wares constituted 27 per cent (MNV 397) of identifiable ceramic vessels from the Hagg Cottages assemblage. Representing the most frequent hollow ware vessel, the pancheon was probably used for a variety of daily food preparation activities, including both cooking and dairying.

A final set of vessel forms related to the consumption of beverages. These were primarily comprised of two forms: cups (7 per cent, or MNV 102) and mugs (6 per cent, or MNV 91). Teapots formed a further 2 per cent (MNV 28) of identifiable foodway-related ceramics from the Hagg Cottages. In total. then, vessels for the consumption and serving of beverages total 15 per cent (MNV 221) of vessels from the site. These results suggest that ceramic drinking vessels (Figure 3.4) were widely available throughout the site's occupation. The prevalence of teapots demonstrates that tea drinking served as an important aspect of daily life for Hagg cottage residents.

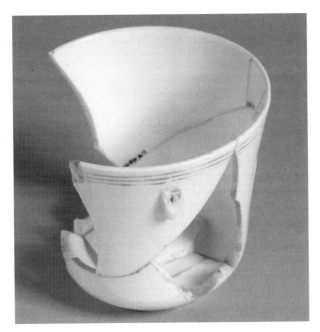

Figure 3.4   Whiteware teacup, Alderley Sandhills Project, 2003

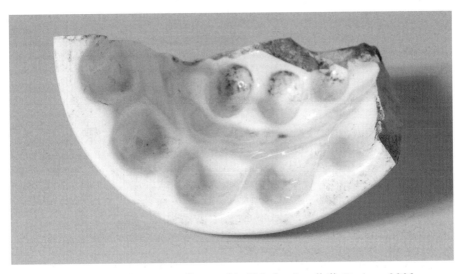

Figure 3.5   Whiteware jelly mould, Alderley Sandhills Project, 2003

The remaining 18 per cent (MNV 262) fell into various miscellaneous categories, including bottles, cake plates, eggcups, jelly moulds (Figure 3.5), jam jars, shallow jars, small jars, unidentified 'tablewares', lids and tureens. Ultimately, the majority of the analysed ceramic assemblage consisted of flatwares, with hollow wares forming the second largest group, and beverage-related vessels as the third. To illuminate further use patterns, this section now turns to consider the various vessel forms for each major ware type.

Slipware vessel forms

Of the total slipware vessels, 58 per cent (MNV 168) were undiagnostic and of indeterminate form. Of the diagnostic sherds, the main form in use was that of bowls, dishes and hollow wares, which in total comprised 43 per cent of slipwares (MNV 48), with a further 6 per cent (MNV 7) in the form of open vessels. The other half were a mixture of flatwares and plates, which comprised 32 per cent (MNV 36), mugs were also common and formed 19 per cent (MNV 21) of the slipwares. The remainder included forms such as teapots (2 per cent, MNV 2), jugs (2 per cent, MNV 2) and jars (2 per cent, MNV 2). These late eighteenth- to nineteenth-century vessels tended to support foodways which required hollow wares and drinking mugs, although a significant portion also appeared to involve flatware forms. The majority of the slipware forms seemed to reflect food consumption activities – plates, saucers, mugs, teapots and many of the bowls would certainly have been used for the purposes of dining.

Other slipware forms may have been utilised in tasks of food production and storage, particularly the open vessels and dishes, jugs and jars. Slipwares were not the finest of tablewares and may have been explicitly manufactured for these purposes. Mrs Edna Younger remembered that, over the 1920s, the cottage residents regularly purchased dairy products direct from a local farmer. Mrs Younger would be sent to neighbouring Whitebarn Farm with a jug to collect fresh cream, 'beastings' and buttermilk (Mrs Edna Younger, ASP interviews, August 2003). From the eighteenth century, slipware jugs and jars could have been used for the collection and storage of local milk, cream and butter. Prior to the increased commercialisation of dairy farming in the industrial era (Winstanley, 1996) dairy products would have been purchased locally, especially within dairy farming regions like Cheshire. Jugs may also have been used to decant and store alcoholic beverages, such as beers, ales and whiskey (Karskens, 1999: 164), although these leisure activities are considered in greater detail within Chapter 5. The slipware category is comprised of proportionally more vessels which may have been used for food storage and preparation than some of the finer ware categories, and therefore may be an important class of ceramic data for understanding such practices.

Creamware and pearlware vessel forms

Creamwares, as previously discussed, were produced slightly earlier in the eighteenth century than pearlwares, although the two were not chronologically distant and overlapped somewhat in their use. Creamware vessels were mostly recovered from Area B, with a total MNV of 964 – a significant quantity of vessels. These were fragmentary, with 80 per cent (MNV 769) of unidentifiable form. Diagnostic vessels were comprised of almost equal quantities of flatwares and hollow wares. Flatwares (including plates) accounted for 54 per cent of identifiable vessel forms (MNV 106), with bowls, dishes and other hollow wares constituting 40 per cent (MNV 77). The remainder of the creamware vessels were cups (2 per cent, MNV 3), mugs (1 per cent, MNV 2) and jugs (3 per cent, MNV 6).

Since both creamwares and pearlwares were interpreted as 'fine' table-wares within the excavated deposits, their vessel forms were comparatively examined, and similar patterns did indeed emerge. Pearlware sherds were slightly less fragmentary than the creamware sherds, with only 72 per cent (MNV 363) of undiagnostic form. Flatware forms, including feather-edged plates, constituted under half of the recognisable vessels, at 42 per cent (MNV 61). Bowls, dishes and hollow wares formed a slightly higher proportion at 45 per cent (MNV 65). Cups appeared more commonly as pearlwares than creamwares, forming 7 per cent (MNV 10) of the former type. Unfortunately, the sample size was too small to determine whether this difference repre-sented any expression of consumer choice. The remaining vessels consisted of mugs (2 per cent, MNV 3), saucers (5 per cent, MNV 7), serving dishes and tureens (2 per cent, MNV 3), and jars, jugs and lids (3 per cent, MNV 5).

Marked differences were clear between the forms of slipwares and those of creamware and pearlware vessels. The relative proportions of flatwares were higher for both creamwares and pearlwares than those of slipwares. These results suggested that creamware and pearlware vessels served primarily as tablewares, with the plates indicating food service through individual place settings. When large open vessels were included in analysis, slipwares also occurred more commonly in hollow ware forms than did either creamwares or pearlwares. The utilitarian category of 'large open vessel' was completely absent from either of these finer assemblages, suggesting that they were not typically used for food preparation activities. The quantity of mugs was also significantly smaller in creamware and pearlware forms than in slipwares, perhaps suggesting that the finer wares appeared as teacups rather than beermugs. Further discussions on the role of beer consumption are presented later in Chapter 5.

Pearlwares in particular showed evidence of food service activities, with serving dishes and tureen forms appearing within this ware type. If pearl-wares are considered as a late eighteenth- to early nineteenth-century ware type and compared with earlier slipwares and creamwares, it could be argued that a gradual incorporation of neatly mannered dining occurred over time at the Hagg Cottages. Perhaps diners began to be served from tureens or serving dishes as they sat around a table together for family meals.

Brown-glazed coarsewares, pancheons and open vessels

In contrast to the fine wares, the utilitarian vessels, particularly brown-glazed coarsewares, formed a significant part of the Area B assemblage. They dated from the seventeenth century to the nineteenth, although the majority of these sherds were eighteenth-century or later. Over two-thirds of this ware type (71 per cent, MNV 352) were of undiagnostic form. The remaining 29 per cent offered a very different pattern of vessel form than that of the creamwares and pearlwares. Only 2 per cent (MNV 3) were dishes or hollow wares. The remaining vessel forms related to food preparation and serving practices rather than the genteel dinner settings represented by the finer wares. They may also indicate different spheres of activity within the household. Coarser earthenwares were likely purchased for food preparation and storage practices when the finer wares were purchased for table display purposes. Open vessels accounted for 6 per cent (MNV 9), jugs 4 per cent (MNV 6), jars 6 per cent (MNV 8).

Pancheons were clearly the most common form of this ware type, comprising 57 per cent (MNV 81) of identifiable vessels within the brown-glazed coarseware category. A further 24 per cent (MNV 34) were indeterminate jar/pancheon forms. When vessels identified as pancheons (MNV 89 in total from the Hagg site) were analysed by ware type, 91 per cent (MNV 81) were brown-glazed coarsewares. The remainder were yellow-glazed coarsewares (6 per cent, MNV 5), redwares (MNV 2) and black-glazed coarsewares (MNV 1). Vessels identified simply as 'open vessels' (MNV 17), a form not dissimilar to that of pancheons, followed a similar pattern. Brown-glazed coarsewares accounted for 53 per cent (MNV 9) of these vessels, redwares were 5 per cent (MNV 1), and slipwares were 42 per cent (MNV 7). While the sample size was too small to draw any firm conclusions, the use of slipwares for open vessels suggested that the ware type was more closely allied with the manufacturing output of country potteries producing locally available utilitarian wares, in contrast with the industrialised Staffordshire potteries, that focused their production on the finer creamware and pearlware vessels. This would again demonstrate the way in which food preparation and purchasing may have been more closely tied to a local economy. Regional Cheshire potters were best able to produce the necessary vessels for specific food preparation tasks that were required by regional dairy specialities. Thus two distinct foodway economies appeared to emerge from the ceramic assemblage of the eighteenth and nineteenth centuries. While homogenised polite dining habits may have been easier to manufacture on a mass-produced national scale, local food preparation implements may have been more efficiently produced by regional potters.

Whiteware vessel forms

Whitewares formed the largest body of ceramic data by ware type. It is perhaps unsurprising then that the greatest formal variety was found within this category. A relatively smaller proportion of these whitewares were undiagnostic, comprising 68 per cent (MNV 1,139) of the total. Of diagnostic vessels, flatwares (including plates) formed the largest vessel class, representing 54 per cent (MNV 283). Hollow ware forms, including bowls and dishes, formed a much smaller proportion than was the case with earlier tablewares, comprising only 18 per cent (MNV 95). Cups accounted for 12 per cent (MNV 62), and saucers 6 per cent (MNV 29), perhaps indicating the importance of teawares alongside flatwares for household consumption practices. Teapots were also represented, although they formed less than 1 per cent of the whitewares (MNV 3). Mugs accounted for 7 per cent (MNV 39), and serving dishes and tureens together comprised 1 per cent (MNV 7).

Nineteenth-century whitewares represented an inexpensive commodity, mass-produced in bulk quantities. Their low unit cost made them accessible to most households over the nineteenth and early twentieth centuries (Miller, 1991). Appearing in the later contexts of the Hagg site, these artefacts linked to the four working-class households that occupied the subdivided cottages over the nineteenth century. Thus, while the earlier creamwares and pearlwares may have reflected the relative affluence of eighteenth-century Hagg farmhouse residents, the generic whitewares seemed to belong to the service workers of the Hagg during the later industrial era.

Porcelain/bone china vessel forms

Porcelain/bone china vessels formed the final ware category under analysis. These artefacts also fell into the later nineteenth- and twentieth-century occupation of the cottages, and were roughly contemporaneous with the whiteware vessels. A lower proportion of porcelain/bone china sherds were of undiagnostic form, comprising 57 per cent (MNV 148) of the total. Of the remainder, teawares seemed to have been a favoured form, with cups representing 29 per cent (MNV 32) of the diagnostic vessels and saucers 13 per cent (MNV 14). When combined, these two forms accounted for 32 per cent of the porcelain/bone china assemblage. In contrast, hollow wares were only a small component of this assemblage (7 per cent, MNV 8), and flatwares a slightly larger proportion at 32 per cent (MNV 35). The remainder of porcelain/bone china vessels were mugs (14 per cent, MNV 16), and eggcups, jugs (Figure 3.6) and lids (5 per cent, MNV 6). As the finer ware type of the later nineteenth- to early twentieth-century period, these bone china vessels seemed similar in function to the earlier creamwares and pearlwares. Given

Figure 3.6   Porcelain/bone china milk jug, Alderley Sandhills Project, 2003

the high proportion of teawares and flatwares, this category likely formed the 'best' china of the later Hagg cottage residents.

The ceramic data from the Hagg cottages demonstrated a range of foodway-related practices. The importance of home-prepared foods, particularly in the earlier phases of site use, was evidenced through the frequency of pancheons and large open hollow vessels. These utilitarian vessels occurred only in the coarser and cheaper forms of earthenware, and were likely manufactured by smaller regional potteries, rather than the large-scale operations of the Staffordshire factories. Local food procurement may also be visible through the use of coarseware jugs, jars and other storage vessels which may have been used to acquire foods such as milk, cream and butter direct from nearby dairy farms.

Changes in dining habits were visible through both the gradual increase in plates and serving vessels and simultaneous decrease in hollow ware forms. The use of coarsewares and pancheons ceased prior to the early twentieth century. By this last phase, as cottage residents increasingly joined the service economy of Alderley Edge village, less food processing and preparation may have taken place in the cottages themselves. This change in food procurement and preparation practices is further explored below, as this chapter continues by examining evidence for the glass bottles, jars and tin cans representing the purchase of commercial foodstuffs.

Glass artefacts and foodways at the Hagg Cottages

Glass artefacts also formed a coherent part of the food preparation, storage and serving practices at the Hagg Cottages. Only a small number of glass vessels were tablewares, used for serving food and condiments. Where these artefacts appeared, they represented a small number of finer items. The majority of foodway-related glass evidence represented bottles, particularly those for commercial sauces and condiments. A much smaller number of glass artefacts were jars used to contain foodstuffs. Overall, as will be discussed, the foodway-related glass evidence provided a key area of research for understanding the use of commercially bought foodstuffs at the cottages.

Tablewares

Several glass tableware items were found in Area A. The most superior was a complete facet-cut pepperpot, with an electroplated nickel silver top, which appeared to have been made in Birmingham between 1920 and 1940 (Plate II). A better-quality piece than other glass finds from the site, it would not have been costly and, therefore, does not indicate luxury glassware in use by cottage residents during the early twentieth century. The remaining glass tablewares from Area A were all twentieth-century press-moulded items. These included a small matching salt and pepper pot, an eggcup, an oval bowl and the stem from a cakestand.

In Area B, inexpensive press-moulded wares include the sugar caster from the top of a cake or patisserie stand. While the piece had been broken on the stem at some point in its history, the break had been subsequently ground flat and thereby recycled as a dish. The archaeological evidence for modifying such glassware to keep it in use demonstrates the importance of such objects to the Hagg Cottage residents.

Condiment, sauce and pickle jars

The majority of glass finds discussed here in with regard to consumption patterns mostly relate to early twentieth-century material. Quantification of glass objects at the Hagg site was based upon minimum numbers of vessels, with diagnostic fragments drawn upon to provide positive identification. Although this approach has the disadvantage of potentially underestimating the true number of vessels originally deposited, the vessels recovered offered an important line of evidence on local foodways. They related specifically to key dietary practices of the Hagg Cottage inhabitants, particularly the growing use of mass-produced commoditised foods, the standardisation of culinary taste and the expression of food preferences among the Hagg households.

Food jars accounted for 13 per cent of the glass container finds from Area A, dating mostly to the beginning of the twentieth century. These include jars for a wide variety of products, marked with trade names such as Horlick's, Bovril, Shippam's and Ye Olde Farm Pickles. Condiment and food constituted 24 per cent of the glass containers, including a milk bottle embossed with 'White Barn Dairy, Worthington' and a vinegar bottle embossed 'Genuine Malt Vinegar'. Sauce bottles accounted for a further 22 per cent of glass container finds from Area A (Figure 3.7), although these were spatially concentrated in the southern half of the conjoined Area B cottage, occupied by the extended Barber household. Embossed labels on these bottles included Fletcher's Sauce (Selby), Mason's OK Sauce and Hazlewood & Co. In contrast, only 3 per cent of glass bottles from Area A consisted of sauce bottles.

While post-depositional conditions and slightly differing bottle date ranges may have influenced these results, proportional difference between the two excavation areas suggested culinary difference between the Barber and Barrow households. The quantity of the sauce bottles in Area A was also considered as a proportion of non-alcohol, medicine or cosmetic food containers – in other words, as a proportion of non-recreational or medicinal glass containers. This produced a figure of 37 per cent, again demonstrating the importance of the quantity of these containers to residents of the Hagg cottage in Area A.

Vessel shards from Area B were generally smaller and less easy to determine product brands than those of Area A. Nonetheless, it was still possible to assign such shards to broad functional categories. Of the glass containers use in Area B, 14 per cent were food jars, 44 per cent were non-alcohol, medicine, cosmetics or sauce containers and only 3 per cent were sauce bottles. The remainder were related to alcohol consumption, as will be discussed further in Chapter 5.

Area D consisted of a rubbish midden related to both Area A and B cottages. As a result, the functional proportions of glass vessel container shards appeared to fall between those of the two other trenches. From Area D, 7 per cent of glass containers were food jars, 7 per cent sauce bottles – including Lea & Perrins Sauce – and 26 per cent were non-alcohol, medicine, cosmetics and sauce containers, including a Bovril jar. The remaining 60 per cent were bottles related to alcoholic beverages.

A double-ended banana-shaped glass baby feeding bottle was also recovered from Area D. Embossed 'The Hygienic Feeder' (Figure 3.8), the unique

Figure 3.7   Clear glass sauce bottle, Alderley Sandhills Project, 2003

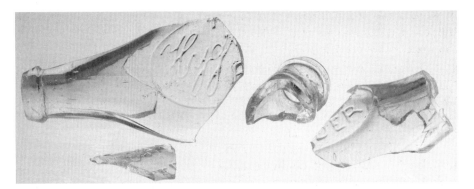

Figure 3.8   Clear glass baby-feeding bottle, Alderley Sandhills Project, 2003

shape of this artefact was intended to prevent the baby gulping air with the milk. Although reminding us of the broad age range represented by residents of the Hagg Cottages, other health-related aspects of this artefact are discussed later within Chapter 4.

A significant proportion of the glass containers in all areas represented functional categories such as alcohol, cosmetic and medicine containers, linked with adult practices at the Hagg site. Yet a major strand of interpretive evidence for this material came from the oral histories of former residents – all of whom were small children when they occupied the site. The baby feeding bottle thus illuminated the presence of these minors at the Hagg Cottages. It indicated changing familial relations over the nineteenth and twentieth centuries, when bottle feeding began to supplant traditional breast-feeding. Such changes in nursing practices for babies were tied to both the economic position of middle- and working-class women who could not nurse their own children full-time and could not afford wet-nurse services for their babies (Levenstein, 1983: 78). This single artefact thus also provides an important point of reflection for gender and familial practices over the early twentieth-century phase of occupation.

Metal artefacts

A diverse range of recovered metal artefacts represented foodway practices at the Hagg Cottages. The majority of this assemblage was recovered from Area A, home to the extended Barber and Perrin family. While the assemblage was dominated by structural artefacts, a significant number of objects reflected food consumption and preparation practices. These latter materials were subdivided into two further categories: tablewares and canned goods.

Structural

One particular example of structural metalwork offered an indirect source of evidence on food preparation activities. In Area A, unit 1, two large square spikes, 0.26 m in length, had been driven into the floor, and were surrounded by cuts into the flagstone for the purpose of reflooring the room with red quarry tiles (Figure 3.9). A small rectangular zone of intact flagstones remained in conjunction with these metal spikes. The feature was interpreted as the location of a large cast-iron metal cooking range, as this common nineteenth-century kitchen appliance would have been too large to move during retiling.

This excavated feature placed the kitchen of the Perrin household in the rear room of the western cottage in Area A. Such a range may have been a focal point for many of the food preparation tasks of the household. Mrs Molly Pitcher recalled that her mother bought a cast-iron range when she

Figure 3.9 Detail of kitchen floor, with location of cast-iron range, Area A, Alderley Sandhills Project, 2003

moved to the Hagg Cottages at the beginning of the 1920s (Mrs Molly Pitcher, ASP interviews, August 2003). This modern appliance was central to her mother's domestic work within the household, particularly as Mrs Barber was responsible for preparing food for herself, her husband, two children, her father-in-law and relatives in the adjoining Area A Perrin household. Thus, even as the Hagg Cottage residents were increasingly purchasing commercial foodstuffs, a great deal of labour was still required to prepare the everyday meals of this extended household. This structural evidence of a cast-iron range offered a material testimony to the labour involved in early twentieth-century domestic foodways.

Tablewares

From the metal tableware artefacts recovered, a total of sixteen were cutlery and flatware (Figure 3.10), eighteen were kitchenware and thirty-one other domestic objects. Area B (home to the Ellam and Barrow families) produced much smaller quantities of metal artefacts: only three metal cutlery and flatware objects, a single kitchenware item and three other domestic metal artefacts. Small numbers of metal objects were also recorded in the midden

Figure 3.10   Cutlery and metal flatware, Alderley Sandhills Project, 2003

dump of Area D. Although no cutlery and flatware objects were recovered from these deposits, two kitchenware metal items and five other domestic metal items were found. All of these metal artefacts appeared to date to the early twentieth century and provide a very specific lens on some of the practices surrounding foodways in the latter period of the cottages' occupation.

The excavation produced a total of nineteen cutlery and flatware objects. These related to a range of consumption practices and economic values. By fabric, Hagg tablewares separated into four categories: silver, electroplated nickel silver (EPNS), stainless steel and carbon steel. Area A, unit 1, contained several EPNS spoons and forks, including two undecorated forks, a small mustard spoon, a tablespoon, a fiddle-pattern table fork and a fiddle-pattern dessert fork, marked 'BUSS Manchester', possibly a reference to its factory of origin. The excavation unit also contained a single serrated kitchen knife blade, stamped out of a stainless steel strip, and representing an inexpensive, mass-produced item of cutlery.

Excavations also recovered a Birmingham silver endcap from a stag handle, possibly part of a carving set. Marked with a letter 'r' to indicate its production during 1891, this relatively high-status artefact was found in Area A, unit 2. An EPNS teaspoon with a fiddle pattern was also located in this same unit. Area A, unit 3 contained five nickel-silver teaspoons,

Figure 3.11 Green enamel saucepan, Alderley Sandhills Project, 2003

including one with fiddle pattern and one with an Old English pattern. Spoons were also found in Area A, unit 4: a dessert spoon bowl, a stainless nickel dessert spoon marked 'Debesco' and a teaspoon marked 'Turners Encore'. One carbon steel carving fork was also found in this unit.

Overall, Area A, unit 1 yielded most items consistent with a kitchen used for cooking and eating. Since it also contained the structural evidence of a cast-iron range, the room was interpreted as the Perrin household's kitchen. Equipment recovered from this area indicated a standard and quality of design generic to working-class homes, with the most refined metal item represented by the EPNS mustard spoon.

Like ceramics, metal objects were frequently used as cooking vessels for food preparation activities. Unit 2 of the Area D rubbish midden contained a hollow saucepan handle, with part of its trivet marked in the shape of an Isle of Man icon. Area A, unit 1 contained a white enamel dish or plate with a blue edge, 130 mm in diameter, and a green-painted wall-mounted steel plate or bottle rack. Several cooking implements were also found. These included a curved hollow pot handle, a 220 mm diameter frying pan, a black saucepan or frying pan handle, a late nineteenth-century hearth support for a kettle or pan, a cast-iron two-pint white enamel saucepan and a repaired cast-iron single-pint green enamel saucepan (Figure 3.11). A blue enamel kettle lid was also found in Area A, unit 4.

In a similar echo of the ceramic assemblage, metal objects also reflected the consumption of tea. Teapots were also strongly represented within the metal finds. From Area A these artefacts consisted of a brown enamel teapot lid with a diameter of 100 mm, possibly a four-pint teapot, and a black enamel teapot lid, also 100 mm in diameter. An EPNS tea strainer was also found in Area A, unit 3.

Far fewer cutlery and flatware items were recovered from Area B. Implements included a small nickel silver spoon with an Old English pattern, which would have been used for salt or mustard and dated to 1920s, a steel 3 in. blade kitchen knife dating to the 1920s, a fork with a wooden handle, dating to around 1900, an EPNS teaspoon bowl and a blue enamel saucepan handle.

Canned goods

The increasing adoption of mass-produced food at the site was reflected in the evidence for canned goods. While artefacts related to the consumption of this commercial form of food came from Areas A, B and D, it was not possible to determine specific brands and types of foods consumed from these cans. The one exception was 'sardine can' ring pulls, found in all but Area C. Area A, unit 2, contained a tin with wired edges and a folding handle boss, possibly from a snap (food) tin. Tin-can pieces and part of a sardine tin with key and a ring pull were found in Area A, unit 4. A tin opener made from a flat metal strip was found in Area A, unit 4. An intact tin can, part of a sardine tin and the lids of two additional sardine tins were recovered from Area D. One single food tin was also recorded in Area B, unit 5.

These cans related to the food acquisition practices of the later Hagg cottage residents. Developments in food canning technology took place throughout the nineteenth century, with the key and pull sardine can type manufactured by 1866 (Rock, 1984: 100). The 'sanitary can', or standard cylindrical food can, was first manufactured in 1904 and rapidly reached universal adoption (Busch, 1981; Rock, 1984: 101). With these early twentieth-century developments, canned foodstuffs became most widely available, as cans were inexpensively manufactured through a fully mechanised process. Through the evidence of the incorporation of canned foods into the diets of the early twentieth-century Hagg cottage residents we can clearly see their increasing participation in the commercial food economy.

Faunal evidence: meat, poultry and fish

Only a small amount of evidence was recovered to indicate the kinds of meat consumed by the Hagg residents. Normally faunal remains constitute an important element of understanding past foodways on historical archaeological sites (e.g. Reitz, 1994; Reitz *et al.*, 2006), and faunal remains have been highlighted as a key line of evidence in understanding changes in dietary patterns through archaeological analysis of modern periods (Mrozowski, 2006: 30). The relative paucity of faunal remains was therefore surprising. A total of 241 fragments of animal bone were recovered from Area A (149 fragments), Area B (91 fragments) and Area D (one fragment; small, burnt and indeterminate). No faunal remains were found in Area C. Given the small sample, it has proved difficult to extrapolate detailed information about animal populations at the site. Thus questions cannot be posed to consider the ages of the animals butchered, or the proportion of different species utilised by Hagg Cottage residents over time.

From Area A ninety-five fragments (64 per cent) of animal bone were recovered from contexts disturbed by rabbit and rodent activity. The remaining sample appeared to mostly reflect joints of meat consumed on or near the cottage site. Although predominantly cow, sheep and goat, a single fragment of rabbit rib bearing cut marks suggested that Area A occupants drew upon their local environment to supplement their diet. No fragments from this area could be firmly identified as pig. However, the absence of identified pig bone did not necessarily indicate an exclusion of pork products from the diet of Area A residents – particularly given the presence of food tins, which may well have contained processed pork products.

The faunal remains of Area B differed from those of Area A. Four fragments were located in deposits underlying the structures, and all exhibited evidence of chop marks. These fragments were associated with the earliest seventeenth-century occupation at the site. Unfortunately, the small sample size available inhibits the possibility of reaching any detailed understanding of early dietary patterns at the Hagg site. As with Area A, most faunal evidence from Area B was identified as cow, sheep and goat, with a single canine (dog) bone also present. Earlier structural phases of Area B contained a number of burnt and calcinated cow-size ribs and other small bone fragments that displayed saw marks. This may indicate a change in butchery processes over time at the site. Nevertheless, the small size of the sample prevented any conclusive interpretations.

Frustratingly, the lack of faunal evidence also hampered any detailed consideration of the use of wild species as dietary supplements. When discussing their lives as children in the cottages during the 1920s, all oral history participants remembered either wild or domestically raised animals and birds as a component of food consumption. Mr Roy Barber recalled specifically that they used to collect 'peewit' (lapwing) eggs from birds living in the hedges near the cottages. These would be eaten along with bantam eggs as well as the bantams themselves, reared in the Barber family garden (Mr Roy Barber, ASP interviews, August 2003). Mrs Edna Younger, as previously discussed, recalled that they used to get dairy products from nearby White Barn Farm. These foods differed from commercially available foodstuffs, and included 'things you can't get now, such as "beastings" – a dairy product used to make custard (Mrs Edna Younger, ASP interviews, August 2003). As previously observed, the archaeological presence of jugs and pancheons may similarly indicate the importance of local dairy farming in the Hagg Cottage diet.

As well as products bought legitimately from the farm, and raised within the confines of the cottage garden, the residents also benefited from animals claimed from the neighbouring Alderley estate. The last gamekeeper of the estate used to allow the cottagers to keep any of the birds from shooting parties on the estate that landed within the confines of their gardens, and our participants made frequent use of the widespread local rabbit population (Mrs Edna Younger, ASP interviews, July 2003). Unfortunately, little archaeological evidence of any of these practices was present within the Hagg assemblage. Future excavations of midden deposits associated with the cottages may add further depth to this important aspect of the Hagg residents diet.

Changing food consumption patterns at the Hagg Cottages

This chapter has so far considered the changing foodways practised by residents of the Hagg Cottages. The most obvious transformations can be traced through the ceramic data. Initial use of pancheons and jars over the eighteenth century was followed by the gradual decline of these vessel forms over the subsequent century. Regionally produced utilitarian wares similarly disappeared from the archaeological record over this period. However, evidence for production of food within the home continued to appear, albeit in a changed form. Over the later phases of site occupation, enamelled saucepans and the large cast-iron range within the Perrin household attested to the centrality of this essential household activity. Obviously, coarse earthenwares, produced to local designs and styles, and mass-produced enamelled saucepans, demonstrate radically different modes of food preparation. Perhaps this material transformation supported the rapid nationalisation of English cuisine over the industrial era. To fully understand these broad changes, detailed comparative studies of regional and national patterns in late post-medieval utilitarian earthenwares are urgently required.

Tentatively, it is possible to begin to trace some changing foodways through tableware assemblages at the Hagg site. In the initial seventeenth- and eighteenth-century occupation period, slipwares were used alongside fancier creamwares and pearlwares. Flatware forms constitute only a small proportion of slipwares, with more mugs, dishes and hollow wares, jugs and jars than were represented in the finer wares. Bought through cash exchanges, slipwares may have formed a constituent part of emerging capitalist lifeways. Or perhaps the mug and open vessel forms of these wares supported the continuation of regional foodways, even in a domestic world increasingly shaped by mass-produced goods.

By the later eighteenth century, the archaeological presence of creamwares and pearlwares may indicate a standardisation of interior fashion as Britain embraced industrialisation. Over half of these were flatwares, suggesting their use within modular place settings at the dining table. Matched and specialised serving vessels also began to appear upon these domestic tables. As industrial mining grew over the nineteenth century, workers had wages that could be used to augment their household possessions. The purchase of tablewares, and their associated dining practices, may have helped cement the social status of miners as industrial workers. Clearly this was not a simple linear progression, as these changing foodways may have simultaneously reflected both the growing availability of mass-produced goods and the shift in the residents' status from locally established farmers to non-local waged workers (see also Brooks and Connah, 2007; Karskens, 2003). The intricacies of the adoption, cessation and use of different ceramic wares over the eighteenth and nineteenth centuries offer an important direction for future research at the Hagg.

The final late nineteenth- through twentieth-century occupation phase demonstrated that refined whitewares continued to use patterns first established with the earlier pearlwares. Since proportions of these whitewares closely mirrored those of the pearlwares, the similarity was interpreted as a substitution of ware type. Flatwares continue as a dominant form, with mugs and serving dishes also well represented. The crucial difference appeared as a slight increase in teawares, with both cups and saucers represented. The most visible changes in tableware forms may have therefore occurred over the eighteenth and early nineteenth centuries, with food serving and consumption etiquette well established by the later nineteenth century. Porcelain and bone china continued this tableware pattern, with an even larger increase in teawares. Ultimately, tablewares at the Hagg Cottages seem to support an argument of increasingly standardised and international patterns of food-serving practices over the industrial era.

The utensils used to consume food also seem to reinforce these international patterns. As tables were laid out for meals, not only were ceramics used, but implements such as forks and spoons, pepperpots and saltpots and condiments such as mustard were all presented and served in the correct way. These material goods linked table manners and food consumption patterns at the cottages over the nineteenth and early twentieth centuries. These may all have helped Hagg Cottage residents practise class through the symbolic medium of polite mealtime manners. The use of knives and forks to accompany individual modular table settings in polite dining practices of the industrial era has been argued to have been as important in the changes in ceramic use for cementing new industrial-capitalist appropriate food consumption habits (Paynter, 2001; Shackel, 1996). By the later phases of occupation, eating with a full complement of cutlery and table settings was normal practice for the Hagg Cottage residents.

Foodways in later historical England

Comparative data on British foodway practices currently serves as an area of emerging research. A key document for comparison is the not long published North West Regional Framework for Archaeological Research (Brennand, 2006, 2007). In this two-volume assessment of major research trends for the post-medieval period, the general absence of data on domestic ceramic use is highlighted (McNeil and Newman, 2006a: 157). Thus the Hagg Cottages collection represents a key assemblage for interpreting foodways in the north-west of England during the recent past.

Towards regional patterns

A few North West sites offered comparative perspectives on the Hagg Cottages assemblages. Located in Cheshire, the Old Abbey Farm site in Risley, to the west of the Sandhills site (Heawood *et al.,* 2004), provided one local collection, although the limited analysis of these ceramics made detailed comparison difficult (Howard-Davis, 2004: 111). No quantification was available for specific ware types. With a total sherd count of 2,940 for the site, the 'large majority' of the ceramic assemblage was of late nineteenth and twentieth-century date (Howard-Davis, 2004: 109). Nevertheless, important points can be drawn even from this brief discussion.

Locally produced wares appear to have dominated the Old Abbey Farm assemblage throughout the eighteenth century, with continuing use of similar blackwares to those available during the previous century (Howard-Davis, 2004: 111). Tankards continued to be used throughout this period, and only a few sherds of tin-glazed ware, stoneware and slip-trailed wares were recovered. To facilitate greater accuracy in comparison, more rigorous investigation of previously excavated material will be necessary. The most significant results were drawn from Old Abbey Farm ceramics dated to the later eighteenth through twentieth centuries. A similar pattern of use appears to have existed:

> Black-glazed redwares and yellow wares remained in production well into the eighteenth century and, although there was a general trend towards confining their use to the larger domestic vessels such as storage jars and pancheons and a general trend towards softer fabrics, they remain abundantly represented in this assemblage, alongside a range of brown-glazed vessels in similar forms, occasionally decorated with simple slip-trails. There appears to be a significant lack of later eighteenth-century tablewares, with little, if any, diagnostic material obvious among the assemblage. After this point however, white-glazed tea and tablewares, especially the ubiquitous blue and white under-glaze transfer printed cups and plates, become abundant, and it is clear that the deposition

of pottery in and around the dwelling did not cease until the house was
abandoned, shortly before these excavations.

(Howard-Davis, 2004: 111)

Certainly, in the earlier periods represented in the Hagg Cottage assemblage, there appear to have been comparable trends. The deposition of
pancheons over the eighteenth century seems particularly important. When
compared with national trends in ceramic use, these vessels appeared to
demonstrate a pronounced regional pattern potentially related to the dairy-
producing Cheshire region surrounding both the Hagg Cottages and Old
Abbey Farm sites. Their continued presence into the nineteenth century
may have indicated active engagement with local food practices, which
may in turn have reinforced a sense of rural community, when faced with
the rapid industrialisation of the food market. Comprising 2 per cent of all
foodway-related ceramics at the Hagg site, soft-fired black-glazed redwares
(or 'late blackware') were also an important component of the Old Abbey
Farm assemblage. At the latter site, these were found as 'large domestic
vessels', and represented the continuation of vessel forms from seventeenth
century black-glazed redwares into the eighteenth and nineteenth centuries.
Significantly, such large coarseware vessels 'were not disseminated widely
from their place of production, and thus these are all likely to have been
made relatively locally' (Howard-Davis, 2004: 113).

These food production ceramics appear to have been locally made well
into the nineteenth century. In addition to illuminating foodways at the
Hagg site, they also highlight broader economic changes such as improved
transport links, market growth and capital investment. These factors
transformed the local industries of north-west England from the eighteenth century onwards (McNeil and Newman, 2006a: 156). As discussed
in Chapter 2, it was over the first half of the nineteenth century that the
Alderley region linked into new technologies of transport, firstly via the
canal and then the railway. The appearance of mass-produced whitewares
at the Hagg Cottages likely indicated the lowering cost of such commodities
as this distributive infrastructure improved.

Such changes were also obviously linked with the north-west region's
place within broader global economic transformations. Particularly given
the Alderley region's proximity to both Manchester – a burgeoning centre
of English textile production – and Liverpool – a major Atlantic trade port,
and production centre for tin-glazed wares and porcelains (McNeil and
Newman, 2006a: 157) – the industrial economy reshaped the material world
of this rural district. Unfortunately, a lack of archaeological investigation
into regional post-medieval ceramic production sites (McNeil and Newman,
2006b) prevents any detailed analysis of the local coarsewares excavated
from the Hagg Cottages. Nonetheless, from the eighteenth century onwards,

canal transport enabled these numerous 'country potteries' to trade across both Cheshire and Lancashire (McNeil and Newman, 2006a: 161).

An unpublished assessment report on the Kingsway Business Park site, Rochdale, also highlighted the need for detailed regional studies of post-medieval domestic settlements, including quantitative ceramic analysis (Oxford Archaeology North and John Samuels Archaeological Consultants, 2006: 63). Test excavations at this rural domestic site collected a significant quantity of ceramics dated to the seventeenth through twentieth centuries. Representing 76 per cent of the total assemblage, approximately 2,377 ceramic sherds were recovered in both fine and coarse wares (Oxford Archaeology North and John Samuels Archaeological Consultants, 2006: 49). The first group consisted of slipwares, porcelain, creamwares and whitewares, and appeared in the form of tablewares, children's tea sets, dolls and other toys. Coarsewares primarily consisted of black-glazed red earthenwares, although reasonable quantities of stoneware were also present. These utilitarian vessels largely took the form of bottles and storage jars. While both finewares and coarsewares from the Kingsway excavations were similar to the Hagg Cottages assemblage, it may be significant that coarse earthenware vessels at the former site appeared as bottles and storage jars, in contrast to the open hollowares recovered at the Hagg. Perhaps different food preparation and storage tasks occurred at these two settlements. Since the Kingsway site was located north of Manchester, in the Pennine uplands, the alternative forms of coarse earthenwares might indicate spatial variations in foodways, even within the north-west region. This avenue of comparative regional analysis suggests another fruitful area for future research.

Another comparative regional excavation was located at New Islington Wharf, in the Ancoats district of central Manchester (Oxford Archaeology North, 2005). This nineteenth-century site contained back-to-back cellar dwellings occupied by industrial workers. Although comparable chronologically to the Hagg Cottages, this urban residential site offered an important contrast to the rural context of Alderley Edge. Ceramic evidence from the site was somewhat sparse, with only 211 sherds collected in total (Oxford Archaeology North, 2005: 42). Such a small quantity characterised many urban sites in the North West, where garbage collection was increasingly centralised from the early nineteenth century. In general, ceramic use patterns at the New Islington Wharf site appeared to closely mirror those of the Hagg site, with residual early fragments:

> dated to the late seventeenth to early eighteenth century. The remainder of the pottery vessels comprised large quantities of coarsewares (principally black-glazed red earthenware kitchen vessels, such as crocks and pancheons, and stoneware bowls and storage jars) and tablewares (creamware, pearlware, white earthenware and bone china). The patterns represented on the

white earthenware and pearlware included 'Willow', 'Asiatic Pheasants', 'Broseley', and 'Cracked Ice and Prunus' transfer-prints and blue painted and relief-moulded shell edge. Other forms of decoration were also present (sponge-printing, painting, relief moulding, factory-produced slip decoration). The types of creamware, pearlware and white earthenware represented were mainly dinnerware and teaware, with little bedroomware.

(Oxford Archaeology North, 2005: 43)

In addition to the domestic foodway-related ceramics, the New Islington Wharf assemblage also included ceramic and glass food containers. These included a Daddies ketchup glass bottle, a glass bottle marked 'A. Heald Ltd, Ford Bank Farm, Didsbury' and a W.P. Hartley stoneware jar from the English jam/marmalade manufacturer (Oxford Archaeology North, 2005: 43). These objects suggested some differences in the foods between central Manchester and the rural Hagg site. The milk available for urban workers was purchased from Didsbury, approximately three miles south from the city centre. Unsurprisingly, this indicated a far greater transport distance than was the case at the Hagg Cottages, where milk could simply be obtained from a neighbouring farm. Although Daddies sauce was not a brand specifically represented within the Hagg assemblage, the ketchup was in widespread use as a flavouring source over both the late nineteenth and early twentieth centuries. Overall, there appeared to be a general increase in the purchase of manufactured foodstuffs, particularly mass-produced sauces and condiments, across both rural and urban sites of this period. However, at the Hagg Cottages, residents were able to locally purchase farm produce unavailable to their urban counterparts.

A final comparison comes from Cotehouse Farm and Lawn Farm, two late post-medieval sites at Berryhill, Stoke on Trent (Boothroyd, n.d.(a); n.d.(b)). Located less than 100 miles to the south of Alderley Edge, in the West Midland region of England, these farm sites were situated on the edge of a rapidly expanding industrial town in the Potteries district. They have been excavated over a period of years as a part of an ongoing community archaeology project with the Stoke on Trent Archaeology Service (Friends of Berryhill Fields, 2007). Similar to the working inhabitants of the Hagg Cottages, these inhabitants would have engaged in both wage labour in Stoke on Trent as well as small-scale agricultural production on the farms themselves. The majority of artefacts excavated at both sites dated to the first half of the twentieth century, roughly overlapping with the last phase of occupation at the Hagg site. Cotehouse Farm was a fifteen-acre smallholding, accommodating short-term tenants from the eighteenth century through 1959. Foodway-related artefacts from this site included a range of cutlery, including spoons, a fruit knife and a whisk. Food containers also constituted a significant assemblage at the site. Of the 153 container fragments recovered, the majority were tin cans. Jar and bottle lids to food and drink containers were also recorded. With five examples, the most common brand was Heinz 57 ketchup.

Lawn Farm was a similar site, located in the same Berryhill district on the outskirts of Stoke on Trent. Foodway-related artefacts from this second site represented food preparation – enamelled saucepans, a nutcracker; food serving – four spoons, a table knife, an enamelled plate and a sugar bowl, and foodstuffs themselves – a tin opener, tin-can fragments, bottles and bottle stoppers. Since this data is undergoing analysis, it is difficult to draw quantitative comparisons between these sites and the Hagg Cottages. Nevertheless, the material is noteworthy for its importance in demonstrating the growing body of work that specifically addresses domestic assemblages of England's recent past.

Like the Hagg site, the Berryhill data demonstrated increased reliance on commercially produced foodstuffs over the early twentieth century. Both the Berryhill sites and the Hagg Cottages adopted nationally branded products, including canned and jarred foods. Meals were prepared in mass-produced standardised cooking vessels, such as enamelled saucepans, rather than the locally produced coarse earthenwares utilised in earlier centuries. These results suggested an increasing homogenisation of English foodways from the late nineteenth century. Standard condiments (HP sauce and Heinz ketchup), beverages (Horlick's), spreads (Shippam's meat paste) and food supplements (Bovril) and tinned foods were commonly utilised in the rural and urban households of Cheshire, Manchester and Stoke on Trent. Demonstrating a growing commercialisation of food production (Pelto and Pelto, 1983), this archaeological evidence contrasted with oral histories from our former Hagg Cottage residents. They described local foods (peewit and bantam eggs, rabbits and dairy products) as an important component of the rural Cheshire diet. Perhaps the use of branded glassware and tin cans made commercial foods appear more prominent in diets than was the actual case. Ultimately, while mass-produced commercial foods were enthusiastically adopted by rural English workers, they continued to traditionally supplement their diet with both local farm produce and edible resources from their local environment.

National comparisons

As Brooks (2003: 127) noted, 'the comparative, interpretive analysis of material culture has been somewhat neglected in the literature of British post-medieval archaeology'. Nevertheless, social questions have begun to emerge as a central comparative focus for the national field. One comparative research project involved the ongoing excavation of seventeenth- to twentieth-century sites in Coalbrookdale, at Ironbridge Gorge (Belford,

2003; Belford and Ross, 2004). Focused on a region of international significance for industrial heritage, the study has examined nineteenth- and twentieth-century tenement homes occupied by industrial workers (Belford, 2003: 61). While existing reports from the project have yet to provide detailed comparative ceramic data, other assemblages from the site offer evidence for the foodways practised within the Coalbrookdale tenement dwellings. Of particular interest was a stash of mid-twentieth-century bottles recorded from the tenement cellar. These included vinegar bottles and soft drink bottles branded Tizer and Ribena. Although national brands, it was observed that these particular products were manufactured in Bristol, the Forest of Dean and Worcester. Thus, while these finds superficially indicated changing consumption and distribution patterns to fit a national commercial framework, the drinks and vinegars of mid-twentieth century Coalbrookdale residents were still sourced from a 'traditional hinterland supply along the River Severn' (Belford and Ross, 2004: 224).

Although currently undergoing completion, the Spitalfields Project offers a few preliminary comparative patterns. Directed through the Museum of London Archaeology Services (MOLAS) from 1998 to 2004, the study focused on a block of town houses in the Spitalfields district of London. From the late seventeenth century the area was linked with the silk-weaving industry, and by the early nineteenth century these urban dwellings supported extended merchant households. With the bulk of recovered assemblages dated to this period, post-excavation analysis has focused on the nature of domestic consumption within these early Victorian urban households (Nigel Jeffries, 2007: pers. comm.). Like the Hagg assemblages, the Spitalfields collection was dominated by ceramics. However, the socio-economic status of these residents differed greatly, and increasing quantities of matched tablewares have been interpreted as material indicators of an emergent bourgeois-merchant identity within urban London society. Despite these contrasts, preliminary results have also illuminated a distinct material fluidity between work and domestic life – an overlap that characterised daily activities at the Hagg Cottages. Thus the forthcoming completion of the Spitalfields volume promises exciting directions for future comparative research.

Alisdair Brooks (1997, 2003) adopted a similar social approach in his analysis of domestic wares from eighteenth- and nineteenth-century Welsh sites. Interpreting tablewares as an important material component in the construction of Welsh identities (Brooks, 2003: 127), he argued that plates, bowls, teacups and saucers were important in the construction of specific nationalist ideologies over this period of the empire. His work drew a contrast between bowls, used for the traditional preparation and consumption of Welsh stews, and fine teawares, which he tied to emerging British food practices, increasingly considered superior (or more 'cultured') to traditional Welsh behaviours (Brooks, 2003: 134). Significantly, the pancheon and mug forms – so important for the Hagg Cottage residents of Cheshire – are also heavily represented in these later post-medieval rural Welsh assemblages.

Interpretive directions

As this chapter has demonstrated, the role of post-medieval artefacts is pivotal when exploring changes to food and food-preparation practices throughout the late historical period. Unfortunately, the analytical potential of these artefacts is often overlooked during excavations, with precedence given to earlier assemblages, but as appreciation for later post-medieval artefacts grows, new research directions have begun to consider the fundamental themes of identity, empire, consumption and community that shaped domestic life over the industrial era.

The British 'cuppa' and colonialism

Foodstuffs and consumption patterns at the Hagg Cottages strongly represented themes of colonialism. These links were particularly visible in the fine tearwares, with evidence for tea drinking found in every occupation phase at the site. Teapots (Plate III) appeared to have been one ceramic form continually in use from the eighteenth century. These ranged from black basaltware teapots (mid-eighteenth/nineteenth century), a marbled slipware teapot (nineteenth-century), slip-banded ware teapots (nineteenth/twentieth centuries) and whiteware teapots (nineteenth/twentieth centuries), including lustre ware and transfer-printed variants. In total, an MNV of twenty-eight can be calculated for teapots across the site. Enamelled metal teapots were also found in early twentieth-century contexts, in addition to a nickel silver tea strainer. As already discussed, teawares provide an increasingly common form of ceramic, with a third of diagnostic porcelain/bone china sherds representing either cups or saucers.

This evidence for tea drinking suggests an almost cliched aspect of the national British identity, forming a structuring element of many people's daily routine. The roots of this practice lay firmly in colonial history. While tea, the tablewares used to drink it, and even the concept of drinking it, were all non-European in origin, this caffeinated beverage was 'co-opted into a unified vision of a European mercantile world' throughout the industrial era (Jamieson, 2001: 287). From its initial adoption by upper-class Europeans in the seventeenth century, by 1850 tea had become a drink available to all social classes in England (Burnett, 1989: 15). Tea consumption rose from 1.6 lb per head in the period 1841–1850 to 5.7 lb per head in 1891–1900, thereby signalling its position as the 'national drink' (Burnett, 1989: 114). This embrace of tea consumption went alongside changes in domestic ceramic production, with manufacturers such as Wedgwood responding to the growing popularity of tea drinking (Styles, 2000: 166). Thus the increase in teacups and saucers at the Hagg Cottage site and prevalence of teapots in all phases of the site linked these local foodways with the entrenchment of colonial products in working-class homes. The material construction of a nineteenth-century British colonial identity is further explored in Chapter 5, in relation to tobacco pipes and commemorative figurines.

The social significance of tea consumption at the Hagg Cottages should not be understated. In addition to forging an important aspect of a national identity in Britain, tea-drinking practices may have helped cement group solidarity among the Cottage residents, while sustaining hierarchies of gender, class and status between them. The everyday practices around tea drinking could, however, vary greatly. Tea could be drunk from a range of ceramic vessels and in a variety of social settings. Teawares in nineteenth-century middle-class New York City have been archaeologically interpreted as part of emergent feminine domestic identities, where ladies chose delicate ceramic vessels to display at their afternoon tea parties (Wall, 1994: 123).

Teawares from the Hagg Cottages appeared more haphazardly selected than the matched delicate Chinese landscape and floral decorated teawares found in New York contexts (Wall, 1994: 141). The Hagg cups and saucers are made in a variety of wares and with no clear patterning in their decorative styles. The teapots found do not appear to match the cup and saucer sherds in ware type and decoration. As discussed above, these were manufactured from a variety of wares, including cheaper slipwares, and utilitarian metal enamel teapots were also used. Indeed, in her study of The Rocks, a working neighbourhood of nineteenth-century Sydney, Australia, Grace Karskens argued that the mixed variety of colours and styles may have reflected a distinctive aesthetic preference, rather than simple economic necessity (Karskens, 1999). The data relating to tea drinking from the Hagg cottages could similarly indicate the way tea drinking formed part of distinctive working-class sensibilities. Tea drinking was a fundamental part of the daily diet and if a working-class family could afford it, then tea would most likely accompany every meal. The Hagg Cottages teawares may therefore demonstrate a pattern of British working-class consumption radically different from that of the feminine salons of New York City. While tea drinking was constitutive of national, colonial, class and gender identities, the specific material attributes and historical contexts of the teawares must be carefully understood.

A bit of sauce: food marketing and consumer choices

The use of sauces and other mass-produced consumer foods at the site is another way through which we can examine the increasing globalisation of foodway practices at the Hagg Cottages. In her undergraduate dissertation study of the Hagg Cottages bottle glass assemblage, Alice Hall (2004) conducted oral historical interviews with a sample of persons over fifty-five years old in Greater Manchester, London, Gloucester and Bath. She asked for memories about the range of brand names, with food-related examples including Shippam's, Bovril, Garton's, Lea & Perrins, Mason's OK Sauce and 'Genuine Malt Vinegar'. Respondents reported that Garton's was tomato or brown sauce and was remembered nationally. Lea & Perrins sauce was also remembered widely – a North West respondent commented that it was a bit of a 'luxury item' (Hall, 2004: 67), and that it was used to spice up dishes. The Mason's OK Sauce bottle prompted the recollection of advertising slogans; 'Mason's OK Sauce for the saucy boy' and 'Here we come with OK Sauce' (Hall, 2004: 69). It was noted that malt vinegar was a product that often came in lots of local brands (Hall, 2004: 72) rather than one particularly favoured national brand.

Other non-sauce products were also remembered for their specific uses, in addition to their promoted nutritional benefits. Bovril was recalled by most respondents as a beef extract commonly used in drinks, gravy and soups (Hall, 2004: 66). Horlick's, a malted barley milk supplement, was described as a luxury product. One of those questioned commented that their rich schoolmates used to pay 3*d* per week to get a mug of hot Horlick's, but that not all children could afford this enrichment. A similar memory came from a man who had grown up in Gloucestershire, who commented that Horlick's could be bought by the cup in the winter months at school. An advertising slogan for this malted milk drink was also recalled: 'Get a good night's sleep with Horlick's malted milk' (Hall, 2004: 71).

The recollections of these brands can be compared with historical evidence for the way in which commercial foods were marketed over the nineteenth and early twentieth centuries. Results also reflected the range of branded products found at sites contemporaneous with the Hagg Cottages, in both national and international contexts. In Britain, as already mentioned, vinegar bottles formed a part of the finds from Coalbrookdale tenements of the twentieth century (Belford and Ross, 2004: 224). Sauce bottles with branded names also formed part of the finds from the Berryhill site, Stoke on Trent, including the Heinz ketchup (Boothroyd, n.d.(a)), one ubiquitous international brand not represented at the Hagg Cottages.

As globally marketed commodities, some of the same products were found at contemporary North American sites. For instance, at the Mascot Saloon site, in the turn-of-century Gold Rush town of Skagway, Alaska, a similar array of mass-produced products were recovered (Holder Spude, 2006: 15). Artefacts consisted of vinegar, mustard and potted meat containers in addition to a Horlick's jar, dated to between 1912 and 1924 (Hurst, 2006[1987]). Similarly, Lea & Perrins' Worcestershire Sauce bottles were also recorded at a supposedly isolated late nineteenth-century ranch site in Paradise Valley, Nevada (Purser, 1999: 128).

With pre-packaged sauces increasingly distributed from the 1840s, the presence of such food products was characteristic of the later nineteenth century (Alexander, 1970: 115). Ketchup, of many varieties, including the traditional flavours of walnut and mushroom, had been used in Britain as flavouring for fish, meat, vegetables and gravies since the early eighteenth century (Koehn, 1999: 373), but from the 1840s pre-packaged sauces entered mass production through new technologies of bottling, sterilisation and preservation. British companies such as Crosse & Blackwell (sweet pickles and gherkins) and Lea & Perrins (Worcestershire brown vinegar sauce) found markets for their commodities across both the empire and North America. A transnational process, American companies such as Heinz simultaneously exported their food products to British and European markets by the late nineteenth century (Koehn, 1999: 391). This commodity exchange thereby reflected an increasingly 'shared' international culinary palette as brands became transatlantic favourites.

These products also revealed wider technological changes in the nature of food production. After 1868 can making became increasingly mechanised and foods began to be preserved in metal tins as well as glass jars, bottles and sealed ceramic crocks (Koehn, 1999: 389). The changing nature of food storage was visible at the Hagg Cottages site, with evidence for canned foods and mass-produced products such as potted meats present within twentieth-century deposits. Crucially, the rise of a global market signalled a new 'delocalisation' of foods, with production and distribution of foodstuffs increasingly removed from its consumption (Pelto and Pelto, 1983: 507; Rock, 1984). While commercially marketed and distributed foods may have entered the British market as early as the mid-eighteenth century (Jones, 1993), archaeological evidence from the Hagg site clearly shows the developing importance of mass-produced non-local foodstuffs, such as canned goods, potted meats and bottled sauces. By the early twentieth century, these commodities were clearly staples of the everyday diet for these cottage residents. This represents significantly different foodways from those of both the eighteenth-century farmers and the early nineteenth-century mineworkers, who were far more reliant on foodstuffs prepared in coarse earthenwares within the household itself. These assemblages also suggest a shift from regional 'tastes' and cuisines to those dictated by national preferences and global markets.

Although mass-produced foods were increasingly purchased by households at the Hagg Cottages, they also relied upon traditional patterns of local food acquisition. While products such as the Shippam's meat paste jar signalled the influence of industrialisation and food delocalisation, they were not straightforward commodities. At the beginning of the twentieth century, jars like these were frequently recycled as containers for home-made foods. For example, during oral historical interviews, the Parkinson sisters, neighbours of the Hagg Cottages, remembered how Miss Burns or Miss Short – with some debate over the precise name – ran the sweetshop in

Alderley Edge village, and would collect jars to fill with jams or jellies (ASP interviews, July 2003). Thus some products packaged in branded glass containers actually came from alternative local sources. Another archaeological example derived from the milk bottle sourced to a local dairy. During interviews, the Parkinson sisters also described the way foods were not always fresh in homes not served by electricity: 'The milk tasted different in summer, because it had gone just, or not quite, off' (ASP interviews, July 2003). Even in the industrial era of advancing technologies for packaging and preserving foods, sour milk still formed an acceptable taste prior to mass refrigeration.

On metropolitan and countryside foodways

When rural and urban patterns of food consumption practices over the late nineteenth and early twentieth centuries are compared, similarities are immediately apparent. By the turn-of-century, nationally marketed commodities, such as HP Sauce, Horlick's, Bovril, OK Sauce and Heinz Ketchup were utilised across a range of English sites. Canned goods offered a common food storage option in workers' larders. Tea served as a national drink for all socio-economic classes. Perhaps the differences in foodways did not enter the archaeological record. Oral history evidence demonstrated the continued importance of locally procured foodstuffs to rural cottagers, even over the inter-war decades. As further archaeological research explores later post-medieval sites in both urban and rural English settings, significant comparisons may emerge. While some of these rural foods (home-made jams, dairy products, baked goods) may not be archaeologically visible, careful quantitative analysis of domestic ceramics and metal objects may show differential use of storage vessels in urban versus rural sites.

What is clearly apparent from the discussions of this chapter is that similar consumer practices influenced the foodways at both metropolitan and countryside settlements. By the late nineteenth century, both increasingly relied upon branded and commercially produced foodstuffs. Working households across England appeared to participate in similar foodways. Thus the relationship between commercial foodstuffs and class identities offers another interesting avenue for future research. Were the neighbouring elite households of the Alderley Edge villas equally incorporating branded commercial foods, or were canned foods and mass-produced sauces particularly characteristic of working-class diets? Future archaeological research may be able to answer this crucial question.

Food as community life

The acquisition and consumption of foodstuffs at the Hagg site were an integral aspect of local community life. While details of this shared identity are discussed within Chapter 6, foodways articulated with the maintenance of community at both the Hagg Cottages and wider Alderley parish. From oral historical evidence we know that Mrs Barber prepared meals for their Perrin relatives in the adjoining Area A household (Mrs Molly Pitcher, ASP interviews, July 2003). Similarly, as a girl Mrs Edna Younger shared meals at both the neighbouring Ellam household and her maternal grandmother's, who occupied a nearby cottage (Mrs Edna Younger, ASP interviews, July 2003). During the early years of the Second World War, Mrs Molly Pitcher would return by bicycle to the Hagg to deliver food from her mother in Wimslow to her elderly great-aunt, Mrs Lena Perrin, final occupant of the Area A cottage (ASP interviews, August 2003).

Clearly the sharing of foodstuffs between households offered an important way of creating and maintaining tight bonds of community at the Hagg site. Wider community links may also have been created through the habitual purchase of foods from nearby Whitebarn Farm – the social transaction providing quite a different mode of exchange than a visit to the shops in Alderley Edge village. While oral histories articulated the social importance of foodways for early twentieth-century Hagg Cottage residents, these are difficult to trace through archaeological data. Chapter 6 will consider the complex relationship between these two sources of evidence, and how they illuminate the materiality of community life at the Hagg.

Conclusion

Tentative changes in foodway patterns have been interpreted from the material assemblages recovered from the Hagg site. In particular, an obvious increase in mass-produced ceramics and foods can clearly be charted from the late eighteenth century. By the 1920s Hagg Cottage residents may have tucked into a dinner of rabbit stew, caught from the back fields, flavoured with American-produced Heinz Ketchup, and washed down with a mug of warm Indian-grown tea mixed with slightly sour milk bought from the neighbouring farm.

While the households discussed here clearly placed increasing value on the global market of ceramic and food commodities, they did so in a specific local context. Future directions of research in British historical archaeology may further illuminate the ways in which these general patterns of mass production and commercialisation articulated with local, regional and national trends. Foodways may also have contributed to class, age and gender identities, and to shared family and community ties. As we turn to discuss evidence for the way in which 'home' was created by Hagg Cottage residents from the seventeenth century we will explore these social themes in further detail.

4

Keeping the home

The touching picture of country people leaving neat and pretty thatched cottages for the sins and slums of the cities is easily dispelled by a closer look at the pretty cottages.

(Gauldie, 1974: 21)

From house to 'home' in rural England

This chapter is concerned with the way in which space and objects at the Hagg Cottage site were used to create a place of 'home'. Over the industrial era, as city slums accommodated ever-increasing numbers of urban workers, rural life became idealised in English popular culture. In particular, romanticised images of rural cottages proliferated throughout the late nineteenth century (Sayer, 2000). Such representations created a myth of country cottages as the pinnacle of community life (Figure 4.1), a bucolic image that in turn supported wider discourses on the nature of the Victorian 'home'. Within these nostalgic and paternalistic constructions of rural life, images of these cottages as generically neat and clean 'became indicators of the moral superiority, physical health and industriousness of the inhabitants' (Sayer, 2000: 43). Indeed, such popular images fuelled a nostalgic middle-class desire for the mythical country home. Memories shared by Mrs Edna Younger, a former resident and oral history participant, appeared to support this rustic theme. She spoke of her childhood at the Hagg Cottages as an idyllic time and nostalgically recalled household practices and rural lifestyles absent from today's society. Life in the cottages, despite the material privations, was fondly described as 'a beautiful time to live' (Mrs Edna Younger, ASP interviews, July 2003).

In contrast, Mrs Molly Pitcher described her memories of daily life in at the Hagg Cottages differently. While she felt that growing up in the cottages had indeed been an idyllic childhood, her mother had experienced quite a difficult time at the isolated site. Before her marriage, Mrs Pitcher's mother

Figure 4.1   Massey family wedding at the Hagg, 1910s

had lived in the nearby town of Wilmslow – described as an 'inhabited place', in contrast to the Hagg site, which was barely a 'little village'. Mrs Pitcher passionately detailed the hardships of the site during interviews, suggesting a rather ambivalent sense of material life within the Area A cottage. Even over the early twentieth century, household maintenance was not easy. She recalled that the southern half of the Perrin–Barber cottage had been 'going into the manse' (i.e. subsiding into the hill) even as they lived in it. Utilities consisted only of cold running water supplied to the kitchen. She explained how her mother had been expected to take on domestic responsibilities for the extended local family – including her grandfather (the elder George Barber) who still occupied their half of the Area A cottage, and her great-aunt and uncle (Lena and Jack Perrin), who occupied the adjoining northern half. 'And with two little children,' Mrs. Pitcher added, 'It must have been wicked. No electricity, lamps and all the stuff had to be brought up. Outside lavvies, you know, two to a seat' (Molly Pitcher, ASP interviews, July 2003).

In the spaces between these nostalgic and pragmatic memories, archaeological and historical evidence illuminates how a material sense of 'home' was sustained at the Hagg Cottages through the everyday domestic practices of site inhabitants. American historical archaeology has interpreted buildings and domestic architecture to understand the social and economic ideologies of the recent past. However, in both structuralist (Deetz, 1977) and Marxist (Leone, 1988, 1992) approaches, material culture continued to be understood as reflecting one singular cultural or socio-economic reality. As a result, those studies focused on interpreting the architectural form, rather than the *use* of domestic space by different persons (King, 2006: 302).

This chapter offers an alternative example of 'household archaeology' in that it explores what actually created a sense of social dwelling. This area of archaeological research has often been assumed to primarily reflect adult female members of a household. Nonetheless, by drawing on perspectives from practice theory, household archaeology can attempt to reconstruct the activities of daily life for every member of a household (Hicks and Horning, 2006: 284). Sites such as the Hagg Cottages may appear at first to simply represent a homogeneous social group – a cluster of working-class households. However, built into everyday life at this site were complicated patterns of dissonance and multiple meanings. It is clear from the recollections of Mrs Pitcher and Mrs Younger that their mothers (who were both of a similar age and who had children of the same age) experienced life at the Hagg cottages quite differently, despite their comparable material circumstances. By recognising such discordant experiences within a single site, we can avoid peopling the past with 'faceless blobs' (Tringham, 1991: 94) and instead look at the plural and changing identities that characterised material life within these rural homes.

Alongside this archaeological evidence, relevant historical backgrounds and comparable case studies are presented. By comparing documentary, archaeological and oral historical perspectives on workers' housing in the industrial and post-industrial eras, this chapter will highlight changing perceptions of domestic comforts, in the context of general conditions of English working-class homes. The nature of interior decor is considered, with changes to decorative elements revealing both issues of both idiosyncratic taste and shared aesthetic values. Finally, an increasing emphasis on, and commercialisation of, domestic cleanliness and sanitation are examined to illuminate the complex realities of what 'keeping the home' entailed on a day-to-day level.

Post-medieval farmhouses

Most artefactual and oral historic evidence for home life at the Hagg Cottages, dates from the nineteenth and twentieth centuries. These resources situate our understandings of these homes firmly within the late industrial to post-industrial period. Yet the buildings themselves pre-date this period by at least 100 years. Historical documents suggest that the original Area A farmhouse was constructed during 1747. Additionally, as demonstrated in Chapter 2, the early brick entrance porch from the Area B building dated to as far back as the mid-seventeenth century. Thus a full range of post-medieval household activities can be interpreted from archaeological research at the Hagg site.

Significantly, the industrial era began earlier in Cheshire than in many other regions of England. Silk entrepreneurs, relocated from the Spitalfields district of London (McNeil and Newman, 2006b: 159), constructed their earliest northern mills in Macclesfield during 1743 (Pevsner and Hubbard, 1971: 26). Their arrival began to transform the regional economic base, with later mill developments occurring at the village of Styal, located just a few miles from Alderley. In general, these changes had important effects on the vernacular architecture of Cheshire, with the construction of mills, workers' housing and institutions such as churches, chapels and almshouses (Palmer and Neaverson, 2005: 112; Pevsner and Hubbard, 1971: 27). Both architectural and archaeological evidence at the Hagg site has been dated to the mid-seventeenth century, well before the first industrial mill complexes were built in Cheshire. Further, while the Hagg Cottages originated as farmhouses, the surrounding Alderley landscape was always linked to industrial processes. The mining of metal ores and the quarrying of stone are thought to have been occurring locally throughout the medieval and post-medieval periods (Timberlake *et al.*, 2005: 143). Therefore, even the farmers of the Hagg would not be entirely divorced from industrial activities.

The earliest date for evidence of building at the site is from Phase VIII, dated to between *c*. 1650 and 1747 AD. According to the classification of Brunskill (1982: 56) both original buildings appear to fit into the categorisation of 'small rural houses'. These were mostly farmhouses, separate from functional farm buildings and can therefore be classed purely as domestic buildings. Evidence from excavations does not suggest separate farm buildings (e.g. barns, blacksmiths or dairies) and none appears on any of the site maps. The development of small houses from medieval to post-medieval forms reflects a national trend from open buildings to those with increased segmentation and division of public and private areas (Johnson, 1993). This transformation was varied over the country, and considerable regional differences are manifest in British houses in plan, section, the entrance door, means of access between storeys and the nature and location of the principal heat source (Brunskill, 1982: 57). Regional differences are also presented in the building materials used and the styles employed by builders. This is particularly true for the periods preceding the seventeenth century, when builders relied on local craft traditions and used local distribution networks when acquiring construction materials (Johnson, 1993).

In general, whilst rooms became increasingly segmented in formal domestic post-medieval buildings, they were still commonly sequentially or simultaneously multi-purpose in small rural houses (Brunskill, 1982: 58). Dining, sleeping, storage, dairy and other work activities might all take place in the living rooms and parlours of these vernacular dwellings (Brunskill, 1982: 58; see Glassie, 1975, for comparative North American examples). The original structure in Area B appears to represent a lobby (or 'baffle') entrance house, with back-to-back fireplaces and two 'units', or two rooms, on each floor of the house. This layout would have related to an initial construction of a multi-storey house, with historical photographs indicating a ground floor and first floor, but not suggesting any upward extension of the original house. The two main rooms formed living units for the household, with an internal staircase and a chimney stack emerging through the roof in the centre of the house (Brunskill, 1982: 73). This traditional English house form was remarkably similar to a contemporary North American vernacular style identified as 'hall and parlor' (Deetz, 1977). Represented a typical 'closed house' in Johnson's (1993) analysis of post-medieval houses within Suffolk, the design was widespread and varied little around a plan with the lobby entry backing directly on to the chimney stack (Johnson, 1993: 42). Brunskill (1982: 73) provided a date range of AD *c.* 1600–1700 for these common domestic dwellings, with a very wide distribution over most of lowland England (including Suffolk).

Archaeology of the Area B farmhouse

The floor plan of the structure in Area B was confusing, since the original layout had been substantially altered through sequential building modifications and recycling activities over its 300 year use-life (see Figure 2.9). The initial construction appeared to have been the chimney and fireplace structures, followed by a brick and stone southern (front) wall and side wall. The next structure erected consisted of a porch to the southern entrance-way of the house, also part of the original building. Due to the extensive modifications of this early feature, contiguous foundations were impossible to follow. Wall cut trenches were visible, in addition to the original sandstone and brick foundation plinth of the porch. Various fill contexts had been packed in around these walls during its construction. Crucially, one of the key artefacts for accurately dating the house's construction was found within this packing material – a small clay-pipe bowl with the date range of *c.* 1650–1670 (see Chapter 5). This essential artefact placed the Area B farmhouse firmly within the appropriate chronological range for the post-medieval 'baffle' entrance vernacular design.

Following demolition in the 1950s, the original building fabric was extensively recycled. As a result, the interior spatial uses could not be reconstructed through specific artefact patterns within the seventeenth-century farmhouse. It was possible, however, to marry some of the archaeological features in Area B with architectural histories of spatial use in comparative two-unit lobby entrance houses (Figure 4.2).

During the initial seventeenth- and early eighteenth-century occupation period, the house was oriented with its entrance on the southen facade, through the original brick entrance porch. All that remained of the two

Figure 4.2 Typical seventeenth-century two-unit lobby-entrance house (after Brunskill, 1982)

fireplace jambs were two excavation features of brick construction, interpreted as the surviving remnants of the chimney foundations. These would
have been arranged so as to form two fireplaces, back to back, in the centre
of the building. The side of these would have been opposite the front door,
creating the lobby or 'baffle' – a feature which protected the two main rooms
from draughts and provided a small entry space within the front door. In the
Area B structure the brick porch would have provided extra protection from
draughts, insulating the interior (Figure 4.3). Archaeologically it seems that

Figure 4.3   Detail of porch feature, with bricked-in doorway, Area B, Alderley
Sandhills Project 2003

there would have been a step up from the brick-built farmhouse porch to the
lobby entranceway of the house.

One ground-floor room would have been larger than the other. This
was likely to provide a more public living room (or a living room/kitchen).
The smaller of the two would have served as a more private heated parlour
(Brunskill, 1982: 70). Alternatively, following North American nomencla-
ture, the rooms could be comparatively identified as a hall and a parlor
(Johnson, 1993: 93; see also Deetz 1977; Glassie 1975). Stairs may have
been found in one of two locations – either at the entry, in front of the
fireplace jambs, or tucked behind these, to the rear of the house (Brunskill,
1982: 71). No clear archaeological evidence survived to identify the specific
layout of this cottage. Wherever located, these stairs would have led up to
two further rooms on the first floor, one or both of which might have had
further fireplaces to heat them.

Brunskill (1982: 20) has argued that small vernacular rural houses tended
to be occupied by 'ordinary farmers' or working families of similar standing. Residents of the Area B farmhouse over the seventeenth century thus
appeared relatively affluent in the social strata of English post-medieval
society, especially given the extensive use of expensive brickwork in the
original structure. Such a well-off family would also have maintained servants, who would have lived within this building and helped sustain a sense of
home. While we cannot be sure of precise interior uses, the dwelling clearly
provided enough room for this farming family, and their servants, to have
clear spatial segregation between public and private activities.

Additional domestic activities could be interpreted from exterior spaces around the home. A brick-and-stone box drain projected from the exterior wall of the Area B house, running diagonally towards the south-west. A single complete brick with surface lead glaze was also recovered from Area B. Comparisons with bricks from East Yorkshire (Tibbles, 2000: 29) and Lincolnshire (Tibbles, forthcoming) suggested that this may represent the residual elements of a pottery kiln floor of sixteenth- to seventeenth-century origins. As an isolated example it seemed likely that the brick represented a recycled import to the Hagg site. Nonetheless, it demonstrated the range of productive industries occurring in the wider landscape over the post-medieval period. It also highlighted the high economic value of this particular building material over the seventeenth and eighteenth centuries. Despite the relative affluence of the initial Hagg farmhouse residents, they were still utilising bricks for their home improvements.

Eighteenth-century homes at the Hagg

History is almost entirely silent for residents of the Hagg during this period. A single mention of the 'Hagg tenements' listed a date of 1735. Recorded within a late eighteenth-century notebook of Lord Stanley, this evidence suggested the existence of a farmhouse at the Hagg, leased from the Stanley family. The next documentary mention of the Hagg site related to the eighteenth-century construction of the second (Area A) farmhouse, around 100 years after the original farmhouse construction. Although locally termed a 'Stanley cottage', this 'double pile' domestic floor plan was used widely over England from the second half of the eighteenth century through the end of the nineteenth (Brunskill, 1982: 90).

Over this second period, the Hagg site residents become more historically and materially visible. Initially built for a man named Daniel Dean, the Hagg site was continuously occupied by the Dean family through to the close of the eighteenth century. The Hagg farm was recorded as consisting of two farmhouses, established just before the final enclosure of Alderley, fifty years prior to major commercial expansion of copper mining along the Edge. This newly expanded farm would have supported a range of income-generating activities, including local agriculture and mining and even textile industries, with the arrival of silk mills in neighbouring Macclesfield. Given this economic diversification, the period appeared as a transitional phase, with all members of the Hagg farm increasingly impacted on by the changes wrought through gradual industrialisation.

Order and privacy: the Area A farmhouse

In contrast with Area B, the absence of extensive post-depositional recycling allowed quite a detailed building sequence for the double-pile house in Area

A (Figure 4.4). Initially the external brick walls were built, followed by the internal dividing walls, and a drain at the bottom of the cellar (located centrally to the rear of the farmhouse). Brick cellar walls were inserted and yellow bedding sand was laid down across the ground floor surface. The fireplace in the front parlour was then built, and the home was finished with the laying of sandstone flag flooring.

In keeping with regional architectural traditions, it is perhaps unsurprising that this outwardly symmetrical farmhouse – constructed squarely in the middle of the Georgian period – was brick-built, since bricks became more frequently utilised as building materials throughout Cheshire over the later eighteenth century (Pevsner and Hubbard, 1971: 47). Simultaneously, flagstone flooring had begun to commonly replace earthen floors in even the poorest quality of rural homes (Gauldie, 1974: 56). The drain, built into the foundation of the cellar, offered a clear indicator of the careful construction of this Area A farmhouse, as until the late nineteenth century sanitary arrangements for rural housing were minimal. Surface drains were normally the only means of removing waste from houses. Underground drains, such as that in the cellar of the Area A farmhouse, were thus a rare luxury and may have reflected either particular drainage problems at the Hagg site (Gauldie, 1974: 57). Or alternatively, the enclosed basement drain might demonstrate unusually progressive estate improvements on the part of Lord Stanley, the local squire. Throughout occupation of the Hagg Cottages, the basic physical condition of these houses would have been dictated by the landlord, who kept a tight hold over those who rented his land (Rule, 1986: 79). Estate owners effectively held control over such aspects as building new houses, improving drainage and maintaining the basic integrity of their housing stock (Gualdie, 1974: 27). It appears that a seemingly benevolent Lord Stanley, responding perhaps to strong economic conditions (Hoskins, 1955), funded the improvement of workers' housing across his estate lands. These works included the historically documented 'modern' farmhouse of good-quality constructed for the Dean family in the mid-eighteenth century. Despite maintaining their own servant, the Deans were still part of a complex social hierarchy. Within the late feudal traditions of post-medieval England, they may have had little control in the way in which their tenant farmhouse was designed or constructed.

As with the early occupation of the Area B, it is difficult to precisely infer spatial use of the eighteenth-century Area A farmhouse interior from archaeological evidence. Nonetheless, comparative historical and architectural studies suggest general patterns of household activity. There were four separate rooms on the ground floor of the farmhouse, and a half-cellar (Brunskill, 1982: 88). From the entrance, the largest of these rooms (see Figure 4.4) was most likely the living room, which excavations revealed to be approximately 4.5 m × 4.5 m (around 15 ft × 15 ft). This living room

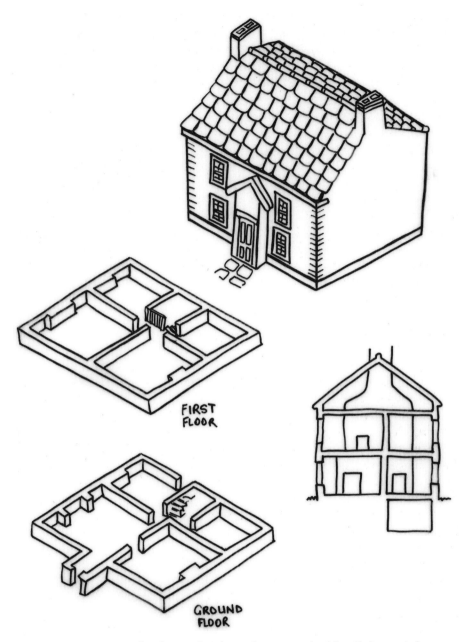

FIRST
FLOOR

GROUND
FLOOR

Figure 4.4   Example of typical eighteenth-century double-pile house (after
Brunskill, 1982)

had a fireplace built into the southernmost wall. As one entered the house into the living room, an internal door to the left allowed access to the next largest room, that was probably used as a parlour. This room would have had a fireplace against the northernmost wall. Although this is out of the excavated area, historical photographs (see Figure 2.4) show the building to have had symmetrical chimneys at each gable end of the house.

Behind the living room and parlour were two further rooms, used as kitchen, scullery and possibly also dairy rooms. The most south-easterly of these (see Figure 2.8), the largest of the three, measured approximately 2.5 m × 3 m and was (as with the rest of the ground floor), floored with sandstone flags. Brunskill's traditional plan (1982: 88; Figure 4.4) did not indicate any original fireplaces in these rear rooms. While a fireplace structure was recorded in the south-east room of the house, this feature seemed to date archaeologically to the subdivision of the house into two separate adjoining residences. The cellar was located between the two rear rooms and measured approximately 2 m × 1.8 m. It had only three steps leading down and would have provided a simple means for cool storage. Given the high presence of coarseware pancheons and slipware vessels recovered from this structure (see Chapter 3) and the general importance of dairy farming in Cheshire, the cellar may have been linked with dairying activities. Demolition deposits excavated from Area A included stair balustrades in the fill of this cellar, indicating that the main stairway to the first floor ran up the centre rear of the house directly above the cellar. On the first floor, four bedrooms would have been provided (Brunskill 1982: 80).

A dwelling modified: the Area B farmhouse

From the mid-eighteenth century, the availability of rural housing typically depended upon existing stock, rather than on the addition of new buildings (Rule, 1986: 76). Construction of the Area A double-pile house was accompanied by extensive structural changes to the lobby entrance house of Area B. Indeed, archaeological analysis of the Hagg Cottages demonstrated on-going adaptations and alterations to the original dwellings. Undertaken to transform the houses into 'homes', these architectural modifications reflected the changing desires, needs and status of their inhabitants rather than the formal designs of a professional architect or builder.

The first major alteration involved a reorientation of the Area B cottage. To connect both houses along the same Hagg Lane access route, the seventeenth-century Area B farmhouse orientation was flipped from a southern to a northern entrance. Now obsolete, the once elite brick porch entranceway was bricked in (see Figure 4.3) and divided by a second brick wall down the centre of the original structure. Recycled as a pair of rear store rooms, the floor level was infilled with a number of rubble and clay contexts to raise the inner ground surface to the same level as the rest of the house, thereby improving groundwater drainage on the southern exterior.

Evidence of this reorientation event was found external to the building. The ground level around the southern and eastern sides of the building was also raised to improve access. A new sandstone path was laid to the north of the building, thereby elaborating access to the relocated 'front' (or main entrance) door of the house. A post hole filled with a dark sandy soil adjacent to the path suggested a possible gatepost along this entrance path. A single-course brick retaining wall was also built, running parallel to the path along the eastern side of the cottage. This wall feature presumably functioned to protect the new path and entrance area from groundwater runoff from the sharply rising land to the east.

On the specialisation of domestic interior space

How can we link the Hagg farms to the broader socio-economic transformations of home life? The study of post-medieval buildings in Britain has previously been critiqued for drawing broad conclusions from small non-random data samples (Johnson, 1993) and it is not the intention here to claim that the data from the Hagg Cottages site can be used to make any firm interpretations about widespread trends in vernacular architecture. Nevertheless, it is possible to place excavated structures in their social context and to interpret living patterns within this rural community. The general trends visible through the architecture of the Hagg farmhouses highlight the role of post-medieval archaeology for enriching our knowledge of traditional English rural architecture.

Archaeological evidence for this first period of occupation at the Hagg site suggested underlying changes in spatial arrangements between the early yeomen or husbandmen farmers (Johnson, 1993: 194) and the later industrial-era cottage residents. Over the seventeenth century a limited range of rooms were available to the household – an extended and mutually dependent group that included the immediate family of the farmer, in addition to agricultural labourers and domestic workers. Downstairs rooms of the Area B cottage would have been used by all residents for a wide variety of tasks. Householders would have divided their accommodation among the three upstairs rooms. By the mid-eighteenth century, the double-pile farmhouse of Area A, with its fireplaces, divided rooms and glazed windows, signalled the local arrival of a clearly 'modern' form of vernacular Georgian architecture (Hoskins, 1955: 159; see also Glassie, 1975; Deetz, 1977).

A number of regional studies do exist which look at such farm buildings through both excavation and buildings survey (Barnwell and Giles, 1997; Heawood *et al*, 2004; Oxford Archaeology North and John Samuels Archaeological Consultants, 2006). As this literature increases, the construction and modification of post-medieval farmhouses will become comparatively sequenced, supporting the further development of regional frameworks for understanding vernacular rural settlement (see McNeil and Newman, 2006a: 149–150).

From farmhouse to cottage: a different way of life

Dating from 1808 to 1828, the subsequent occupation phase of the Hagg site (Phase VI, construction period III), offered crucial insight on the material effects of industrialisation on rural settlements in north-west England. From 1805 the Alderley Mining Company began to lease the Hagg region from the Stanley family for the purpose of mining. Although it is now known that this initial phase of nineteenth-century industrial mining struggled to be profitable – eventually ceasing in 1815 – within the economic climate of the Napoleonic Wars it presumably seemed a viable business venture. In 1808 Stanley family estate records indicate that the small farms of the Hagg were transformed into cottages.

This shift in documented reference from 'farmhouse' to 'cottage', while superficially a slight semantic change, actually illuminated a profound socio-economic transformation. Rural 'cottages' of the early nineteenth century referred to a very precise kind of residence – dwellings specifically inhabited by the lower levels of rural society. Those who lived in cottages were farm labourers, miners, quarrymen, industrial workers, craftsmen, widows and the poor generally (Brunskill, 1982: 90). In other words, with the conversion of the two farmhouses into four cottages, the Hagg site had evolved into a working-class settlement.

Following the conversion in 1808, non-local transient mining families increasingly replaced the established farming leaseholders of the pre-industrial centuries. Despite popular romantic images of bucolic dwellings, many rural workers in the nineteenth century occupied housing in an even poorer state than their urban industrial contemporaries (Gauldie, 1974: 58). As apparent at the Hagg, housing utilised by nineteenth-century rural workers had typically been in existence since the eighteenth century or earlier. Although some improvements in rural housing stock occurred at the very end of the eighteenth century, very few were carried out over the subsequent Victorian era (Gauldie, 1974: 42). By the mid-nineteenth century, most agricultural labourers still lived in single-room cottages of an extremely meagre quality (Rule, 1986: 81; Gauldie, 1974: 24).

The archaeology of workers' housing

Such low-quality housing was widespread across the British rural landscape from the late eighteenth century onwards. Coal miners in Durham, in the north-east of England, often had large families, crammed into overcrowded tiny cottages. Their only mitigation against the physical hardships of domestic life was virtually free coal, allowing them to have a good fire – a rarity for nineteenth-century working-class homes (Rule, 1986: 87). In the Welsh town of Swansea unusually high standards of workers' housing were actually built for the coal miners and copper smelters, with some buildings of a high enough standard that they continue to be occupied today (Hughes, 2000). Similarly, eighteenth-century workers' housing in the Gwynedd region of Wales consisted of solid single-storey, front-entrance stone cottages, with numerous examples in active use (Gwyn, 2006: 182–183). Nonetheless, other forms of workers' accommodation fell short of this standard. Short-lived timber houses were built for the early work force employed on the Severn Tunnel at Sudbrook in Monmouthshire and wooden houses were built for coal miners in the Rhondda Valley (Hughes 2005: 139).

Housing was also partly determined by the nature of the labour taking place. In the textile areas of south-west England, weaving was often carried out within the household in the eighteenth and early nineteenth centuries (Palmer and Neaverson, 2004, 2005). The materials of which weavers' housing in this region were built varied from those built of cob, with thatched roofs, to those built of brick with tiled roofs (Palmer and Neaverson, 2005: 95). All of these structures had to incorporate the space for looms as well as for other basic domestic requirements (Palmer and Neaverson, 2005: 94). The occupation of weaving within houses also altered the architecture of many workers' cottages in the Pennine upland regions of England, particularly in Lancashire and the West Riding of Yorkshire, where weaving was similarly carried out within the home. Features such as long-mullioned windows in upstairs storeys, used to let in the light, in order for weavers to see their work, are a typical feature of this kind of working-class vernacular architecture, driven by local industrial requirements (Caffyn, 1983). Similarly, the weaving industry influenced the design of urban housing within the Spitalfields district of eighteenth-century London, with these purpose-built multi-storey houses retaining distinctive rectangular 'loom shop' windows and lit staircases that rose immediately inside the entrance door (Guillery 2006: 118–119). Workers' housing varied not only according to the economic conditions under which they were built, and through the materials available for their construction (Gwyn 2006: 183), but also through the home workshop requirements of a given industry.

In British urban industrial areas, working-class housing was also of limited quality. Research has identified a clear hierarchy of housing for these urban dwellers (Timmins, 1998, 2005). This ranged from common lodging houses (at the lowest end of the scale), through cellar dwellings, singly rented rooms, two-room rented units and through terraces (Rule, 1986: 98). Archaeologically, workers' housing has begun to gain increasing attention over recent years, particularly in northern English cities such as Manchester (e.g. Oxford Archaeology North, 2005) and Sheffield (Symonds, 2002, 2006). Cellar dwellings, in particular, often survived in cities beyond twentieth-century redevelopment. Although the above-ground portion of these domestic buildings were largely demolished as part of post-war slum clearance programmes, the cellars frequently remained, sealed beneath car parks and roadways. While almost no artefactual evidence remains from these sites – as a result of early centralised rubbish collection – the features provide structural evidence with which to compare nineteenth-century urban and rural working-class housing.

Excavations of nineteenth-century cellar dwellings in Sye's Court, central Manchester, revealed tiny household spaces, with rooms of around 4 m × 5 m serving as a single dwelling (Oxford Archaeology North, 2006: 21). These were lit by cellar light windows and heated through back-to-back fireplaces, which would also have been used for the purposes of cooking. The cellars were floored by flagstones, but laid only on a thin bedding of sand, or directly on to previous building rubble (Oxford Archaeology North, 2005: 24). Some features demonstrated modifications for comfort or interior decoration, such as slate shelves built around a number of the excavated fireplaces. One of the fireplaces also displayed the remains of decorative fire-surround tiles, placed there in modifications between 1850 and 1882 (Oxford Archaeology North, 2006: 26). Even with shelving and tiling around a fireplace, these are the lowest end of housing provided for Manchester's textile workers and would have offered a far lower level of domestic comfort than was experienced by the Hagg cottage residents of the nineteenth century.

Creating the Hagg cottages

How do these comparative data relate to the Hagg Cottages? Returning to our site narrative, detailed archaeological data can be provided, through which interpretations of the physical conditions of 'home' during the nineteenth century at the Hagg Cottages can be examined. In Area B, no archaeological evidence existed for the subdivision of the single farmhouse into two separate cottage households. Historical records supported the fact that both farmhouses were converted into cottages in the same year (1808). From historical photographs, oral histories and plans, the dividing wall was most likely located on the western end of Area B. While extensive post-war demolition and recycling events of the 1950s obscured the remains of interior features, the absence of physical evidence could also indicate that the dividing wall lay outside the western trench boundary. Either way, no evidence for it was archaeologically recovered.

In contrast, the subdivision of the Georgian double-pile house in Area

Figure 4.5   Northern section of Area A, detailing interior wall divisions, northern kitchen and cellar, Alderley Sandhills Project, 2003

A was clearly visible through the structural remains. The first stage of this subdivision involved the addition of brick walls (Figure 4.5) to block the hallway and cellar of the southern household (formerly half of the scullery, kitchen and possible dairy area of the eighteenth-century farmhouse) from the rear room of the northern cottage household. Interestingly, to the front of the house, the western end of the central dividing wall was *not* blocked up at this time. The fact that an unlocked door remained between the two Area A cottages was also mentioned in one of the oral history interviews, demonstrating a special interconnection between the two households of Barber kin.

In the newly subdivided space of the southern cottages, a smaller brick fireplace was built on to the exterior wall of the rear room. Presumably, this area was now the kitchen for the southern cottage, and a second fireplace was installed, possibly to separate cooking activities from the original front parlour fireplace. Unfortunately, the exterior northern wall lay outside of the excavated area. Future research will determine whether this extra fireplace modification was mirrored in the northern half of the subdivided cottage. A further recorded change in the northern cottage was the placing of a large sandstone door sill between the front and rear rooms. This door sill was mortared into place, and small square cuts were made for the installation of a wooden door frame. Finally the walls of both cottages were replastered, with the plastering across the newly built walls being contiguous with that along the older walls.

The impact of industry: cottage modifications, 1828–1872

Following the subdivision of the cottages, significant building modifications continued throughout the nineteenth and early twentieth centuries. As discussed in Chapter 2, the industrialising and modernising processes in which Hagg cottagers' lives were entwined were by no means static during the Victorian period. This time was defined by rapid changes to the regional socio-economic landscape. In 1828 formal mining activity temporarily ceased at the Edge. By 1831 the Macclesfield Canal had been completed, built to provide a link between Manchester and the Potteries, connecting through Macclesfield and other important Cheshire towns (Macclesfield Canal Society, 2007). The railway reached the district by 1844, taking residents to central Manchester in less than an hour. Within a few years the village of Alderley Edge was created, transforming the social landscape of Alderley with the influx of wealthy bourgeois villa residents. Simultaneously, from late 1857 through the early 1870s mining was resumed on a new industrial scale by the re-established Alderley Edge Mining Company (Derbyshire Caving Club, 2007). The acid-leaching extraction process adopted by the re-established industry produced several thousand tons of copper and mounds of waste sand that came to characterise the immediate surrounds of the Hagg Cottages.

Archaeologically, this industrial phase of occupation was primarily manifested through the major reconstruction works on the Area B structure. Historical records from the Stanley estate mentioned that the front wall and roof of this structure were rebuilt in 1828. The reasons behind this rebuild were unclear – local mining activity had ceased only eleven years before, and several decades would pass before the late Victorian phase of industrial mining was to begin. Since the Alderley Edge railway line was fifteen years away, no artisans or labourers associated with its construction would have been residing at the Hagg from such an early date. Thus, by the early nineteenth century, the 150-year-old cottage may have been in such a poor state of repair that major structural renovations were simply essential to maintain basic habitation.

Since excavations in Area B did not locate an original foundation for the north wall of the seventeenth-century farmhouse, the 1828 reconstructed north wall (see Figure 2.9) may have utilised the same foundations as its original predecessor. One interesting feature of this rebuild was discovered along the eastern facade. Here, instead of recycling the original foundations, a new exterior wall directly abutted (and architecturally replaced) the seventeenth-century feature on the western interior side (Figure 4.6). These extensive structural modifications suggested that the building may have been quite unstable before renovations commenced. A small demolition context associated with this rebuilding activity was found beneath later path features

Figure 4.6   Detail of nineteenth-century kitchen addition, abutting original
seventeenth-century eastern wall, Area B, Alderley Sandhills Project, 2003

to the exterior of the Area B cottages. This largely consisted of sandstone
and brick rubble fragments, with some artefacts such as ferrous pipe fragments intermixed. This again suggested that the Area B subdivided cottage
dwellings were not particularly comfortable places to occupy over the early
nineteenth century, given their potentially dilapidated state.

At the same time as these basic structural renovations, an extension was
also built on to the excavated eastern half of the Area B cottage. An entrance
was created through the east side wall of the house and immediate external
garden and access ways to the eastern cottages also appear to have been partially remodelled. A cobblestone path was laid, oriented north–south along
the eastern side of the cottage. A series of post-hole cuts into this path suggested fencing, although the exact date sequence for this feature remained
ambiguous. A new brick box drain was also installed on the northern (front)
exterior, running east–west. An additional path of small pebbles was also
recovered within the northern side of the Area B excavations. This feature
may have formed the edge of Hagg Lane itself, as early twentieth-century
photographs record the lane running quite close to the Area B cottages.

Archaeological evidence provided a clear picture of extensive mid-
nineteenth-century activity towards the rear (south) of the subdivided Area

B cottage. Around the original porch structure, to the south-eastern corner of the structure, on-going fill activities were undertaken to raise and maintain the ground level. This presumably facilitated the use of this area for work or storage activities. Behind the western cottage, a new household work space appeared to have been constructed. A series of small brick walls (see Figure 2.9) were created, in addition to a brick-paved area that filled the excavated rear yard of the western Area B cottage. The remains of a metal gatepost suggested that this area might have been enclosed for animals or machinery, possibly recycling half of the seventeenth-century porch as a covered area for yard work.

In Area A, significant modifications also took place to extend and improve the cottages over the mid-nineteenth century. The most significant of these was a decoratively floored extra room, added to the southern side of the internally subdivided cottage. A double-course brick wall was added. Abutting the exterior wall of the cottage, but recessed slightly from the front wall, the new wall actively maintained the symmetry of the eighteenth-century Georgian facade. A doorway was cut through the southern wall of the cottage to access the new extension, and no evidence suggested the extension included a door to the outside. Thus access to the new extension was gained by passage through the cottage interior. Perhaps the space was designed for private family use, rather than functioning as a public parlour or separate entrance lobby. Two sandstone blocks were placed on either side of the doorway to strengthen the extension. Additional internal plasterwork was added to refinish and seal the doorway. An exterior drain was constructed against the new extension structure, running down from its roof and guttering. To complete the room, red and grey quarry tiles were laid upon the floor, creating a decorative diagonal chequerboard pattern of alternating colours (Figure 4.7).

Given the range of mid-Victorian English workers' accommodation, the southern conjoined house of Area A represented a relatively commodious dwelling. In comparison with the contemporary cellar dwellings of industrial Manchester, the single-room rural miners' cottages of the North East or perhaps even the crumbling seventeenth-century cottage across Hagg Lane in Area B, the Area A structure offered both living space and quality of construction. The residents enjoyed three downstairs rooms, allowing a greater degree of spatial separation among household activities. One room extension was attractively floored with quarry tiles; with the railways providing greater ease of transport for heavy (yet fragile) architectural ceramics, such decorative flooring emerged as an increasingly fashionable feature of mid-nineteenth-century homes.

Furthermore, both the southern and northern subdivision of the Area A cottage retained two rooms on the first floor. The decorative southern extension was built at the same time as the neighbouring bourgeois villas

Figure 4.7   Detail of nineteenth-century extension, Area A,
Alderley Sandhills Project, 2003

were under construction in the new rail commuter suburb of Alderley Edge. Such elite dwellings offered many more comforts to both their primary householders and domestic staff. Therefore, the Hagg Cottages formed a part of a complex regional typology of workers' housing over the mid-nineteenth century, with a careful distinction made between residential and self-accommodated domestic service.

Extension, repair and rennovation: cottage modifications, 1872–1940s

With the shift to turn-of-the-century (Phase IV) occupation, interpretation of the site was enriched by the availability of a rich artefact collection of household discards. For the first time, material evidence of interior furnishing and ornamentation supplemented the architectural data gathered from construction and modification of the Hagg Cottages. In the northern subdivision of the Area A structure a number of modifications were made to the rear ground-floor room – a kitchen area, as discussed earlier in Chapter 3. While the exact sequence remained ambiguous, the adaptations related to the installation of a cooking range and the reflooring of the room with red quarry tiles (see Figure 3.9). A number of metal pegs and spikes were driven into the sandstone, as well as into the newly tiled floor, and a brick-and-metal plate was cemented to the southern wall of the kitchen. A further cut was made into existing eighteenth-century sandstone flags and new bedding sand and plain red quarry tiles were laid. A slightly uneven corner of sandstone flagging was left in place in the southern back corner of the room, suggesting an object too heavy to be moved – possibly a cast-iron range or boiler. This structural evidence fits with the description Mrs Molly Pitcher provided of her mother bringing along 'a great big black range' when her marriage to George Barber moved her to the Area A cottage (Mrs Molly Pitcher, ASP interviews, August 2003). Although the northern cottage was actually home to the Perrins, the new cast-iron range may have been fitted in the northern kitchen because this half of the subdivided cottage did not contain a second fireplace for cooking activities. Indeed, if her mother's cooking range was placed inside the Perrin half of the subdivided Area A cottage, the regular sharing of cooking activities would demonstrate a significant pattern of connection between this extended multi-generation household. These questions of community life, extended kinship networks and communal preparation of foods are explored further in Chapter 6.

Other decorative additions took place in the Area A cottage during this later occupation phase. In the first instance, a blue plaster render was added to most of the interior walls of both subdivided dwellings. A number of alterations also took place to the fireplace in the front room of the southern cottage. Particular decorative attention was paid to the front sitting room of the southern cottage. A metal plate was mortared into the front of the fireplace, the purpose of which seems to have been to support a new wooden surround to the fireplace. A series of small red rectangular glazed tiles were also cemented on to the front base of the fireplace. Later, a green plaster render was added to the walls of this front room and wooden skirting boards were affixed to the walls.

In contrast to these decorative changes, more utilitarian renovations were also undertaken. According to former residents, the Area A cottage appeared to have been subsiding towards the south-east. Shifting foundations eventually caused the decorative quarry tile floor of the southern extension to become uneven. Cement was used to repair this floor, presumably to mitigate against the effects of structural distortion (see Figure 4.7). The use of Portland cement suggested a late nineteenth-century date for the repair work, for although this type of mortar had been granted a British patent in 1824, it became a mass-produced and affordable building material only during the latter half of the century (Stratton and Trinder, 2000: 133). Patches of cement were laid at the southern end of the front room, the entrance doorway to the extension and covering the quarry tiles in the eastern section of the extension itself (see Figure 2.8). The cement repairs were not the only change to take place in this southern extension room. During this late occupation phase, two single-course brick walls were also built directly on top of the quarry tile floor, with the end of each abutting the western exterior wall. According to oral history (Mr Roy Barber, ASP interviews, September 2003), these brick features served as the base of a workbench. Thus the decoratively floored extension had eventually been reused as a domestic workshop. Its new function as a utilitarian space may have demonstrated a change in auxiliary economic activities undertaken to support the household over this final occupation period.

Externally, paths and flower beds were constructed around the Area A cottages in the late nineteenth century. Running alongside the extension in an east–west direction was a sandstone path with sandstone edging (see Figure 2.8). From oral history interviews it appeared to head towards a privy, shared by all of the cottages. Behind the Area A cottages a cobblestone path was built leading from the back door. Abutting this was a brick paved area, set further away from the cottages to the east. Between the cobblestone path and the house was a flower bed, filled with a dark silty soil and decoratively bordered with a sandstone edging.

A significant number of alterations were also in evidence for this last phase of occupation in the Area B structure. The first of these was a further extension of the mid-nineteenth-century kitchen within the eastern subdivided cottage. This took the form of a small boiler room, abutting the original side wall of the house (Figure 4.8). Older half-bricks and sections of bricks were used for this later addition, suggesting that recycled materials were used for

Figure 4.8   Detail of Area B. *Foreground* Nineteenth-century boiler room extension (under tree). *Background* Original seventeenth-century southern wall and brick porch, Alderley Sandhills Project, 2003

this new boiler room. A circular cut was made into the ground inside this room, probably providing a base mount for the copper boiler. In the north-west corner of the structure, a dark charcoal-rich layer had built up, most likely from the use of charcoal as the primary power source.

Most structural evidence from Area B over this last occupation phase related to the exterior of the cottages. As in previous occupation periods, these features appeared to modify external work areas. This is most clear in the area that formed the brick-paved yard to the rear of the western Area B cottage. This rear exterior work yard had been elaborated by a brick-and sandstone-paved area running westward. Two small brick walls were excavated, likely related to an unidentified square structure recorded in the 1872 Ordnance Survey map (see Figure 2.2). A coal-rich deposit had built up in this area and was later overlain by a separate deposit of fine grey mortar. Further sandstone flagging had also been laid, extending westwards from the cottage in the south-west corner of the Area B excavation trench.

A number of path and drain features were also constructed around the Area B cottages, further indicating that continuous management of ground water, soil movement and rising damp characterised life at the Hagg. To the front of the cottages a new ceramic drain was laid, potentially supplanting the earlier brick box drain in function. An additional ceramic drain and metal grate, possibly dating from the 1930s, abutted the kitchen extension wall. A third concrete drain was also assembled to the east of the cottages. In addition to these drainage features, early twentieth-century sanitation features included a privy structure. This 'night soil' privy had a brick foundation plinth rather than pit drop, thereby aiding collection and removal of human waste. The brick walls of the privy were built directly onto the foundation plinth, then plastered externally and painted blue. A range of recycled bricks, brick rubble, sandstone rubble and large sandstone blocks were used to construct a solid path between the privy and the back door of the eastern Area B cottage.

Other paths were also laid around the Area B cottage during this final phase of occupation. These included a yellow compact sand path to the front of the structure. Edged on either side with a black sandy silt, the entrance path may have been elaborated by either a wooden fence or decorative plants along the entrance pathway. As with the extended Barber–Perrin household of Area A, archaeological and photographic evidence indicated that the Barrow family of Area B established formal flower beds around their cottage, domesticating the front of their home with ornamental floral species. A distinct cut and dark, humic sandy-silt fill were placed between the front wall of the cottages and the entrance path. Additionally, along the eastern pathway to the shared privy, sandstone edging suggested a second decorative flower-bed feature.

Following these final building modifications, both sets of cottages were gradually abandoned, and subsequently demolished (Phases III and II). Over 300 years of occupation, the structural development of the Hagg Cottages reflected wider technological and socio-economic transformations of north-west England. Further, daily household practices both shaped, and were choreographed by, this vernacular residential landscape. This chapter now turns to consider the delicate transformation of bricks and mortar into a living 'home'.

Decorating the home

A range of artefactual evidence related to the furnishing and adornment of the Hagg Cottages. Most relevant data were recovered from the Area A cottage, because of post-depositional recycling, but very little information survived from Area B. Nevertheless, these archaeological materials formed an integral part of 'home' for cottage residents. This chapter will consider two particularly illustrative strands of structural and artefactual data.

Floorcoverings

Fragments of various floorcoverings were recovered from the front room of the southern half of the subdivided Area A cottage. Retrieved with the help of conservators from the Manchester Museum, these artefacts offered unique archaeological example of late nineteenth- and early twentieth-century domestic interiors from English working-class homes. Three distinct layers of flooring surfaces were identified and seriated. Since they were all quite fragmentary, it was impossible to discern whether they would have covered the room wall to wall or demarcated separate interior spaces within the room. The earliest of these was a floorcloth – a material produced throughout the nineteenth century that pre-dated the invention of linoleum in 1860. As a textile, few examples of floorcloth survive archaeologically, even in fragmentary form. Representing the first and most important floor-covering of the industrial era, it was adopted by a wide spectrum of social classes. The pattern on this first fragment echoed an encaustic tile – a type of ceramic floor tile decorated and glazed with different colours of inlaid clays. Decorated with a 'Greek key' pattern, this first example was characterised by regular repeats of interlocking right-angle and vertical lines (Plate IV). Dated stylistically to the early 1870s, it was laid during the pivotal transition between Occupation Phases V and VI at the Area A cottage, shortly after the construction of the southern quarry-tile floored extension. Perhaps it demonstrated a desire for decorative unity, with cottage residents attempting to make their front room appear fashionably tiled in the manner of their new decorative side room.

A second layer of floorcovering consisted of 'Congoleum'. An imported

American innovation, Congoleum was first produced around 1911 as a cheaper alternative to linoleum that could still be printed with a high standard of design. A loose illustrative style decorated the fragment found within Area A at the Hagg Cottages. While a precise date could not be established, the pieces were reminiscent of the French decorative style for interior furnishings in use during the 1920s and early 1930s. The topmost layer of floorcovering was made of linoleum. Decorated by a simple floral design, its use spanned from the mid-nineteenth century through the 1930s.

Furniture

Evidence for furniture was provided by a variety of artefactual remains, mostly of metal and glass objects. From demolition deposits in Area A, three press-moulded glass handles with screw threads were recovered, likely remnants of wooden cabinet doors. The same demolition context contained several fragments of bevelled window glass. These pieces measured only 60 mm across, and as such appeared too narrow to represent the remains of a looking glass. These artefacts were therefore interpreted as mirror panels from an early twentieth-century cabinet. Together, these glass artefacts suggested the presence of a decorative cabinet, one used to display ornamental items such as fine pottery, figurines and family mementoes.

The existence of decorative furniture items was also suggested through the metal object assemblage. In Area A these included a variety of fastenings and handles, such as a brass-ring drawer handle attached to a disc, a decorated brass disc which came possibly from bedroom furniture and a small brass furniture hinge. Several metal curtain rings were also found in Area A, as was part of a metal fire grate and a thin non-ferrous metal magazine or letter rack, decorated with a fleur-de-lys motif. Similar brass ornamental furniture items were also recovered from Area B. These objects consisted of a decorative disc with a pierced floral design and a rectangular strip stamped with a pattern of flowers and leaves. A single curtain ring was also part of the Area B assemblage. This range of artefacts indicated that all cottage residents, certainly by the early twentieth century, utilised a wide range of decorative furniture items to help create a sense of domesticity.

Alongside these ornamental furniture elements, a range of more functional furniture items was recovered from demolition deposits. In Area A, one of the most compelling items consisted of a cluster of metal artefacts identified as components of a metal-framed bedstead. Nicknamed 'Mrs Perrin's bed' by excavators, elements included mattress springs, spiral wires and a chain-linked mesh. Other artefacts related to bedroom furnishings included a wardrobe hook and a hot-water bottle stopper. In Area B a single cast-iron rod was recorded which may have formed part of a second bedstead.

From these intimate assemblages, we interpreted the personal comforts that created a sense of everyday home life.

Other metal artefacts provided evidence of furniture elsewhere within the Hagg Cottages. Excavations in Area A recovered a wall-mounted green tinned-steel rack designed to hold plates, a steel shelf bracket, metal bars for shelf brackets or supports and a cupboard door catch. A green enamel chamber stick, used for supporting candles, provided a reminder that, despite the presence of comfortable furnishings, these cottages were never served by electricity. In Area B a small number of other furniture-related metal objects were also recovered. These included a large 'chest-type' handle, a drawer handle with a back plate as well as a rectangular swing handle. Hagg Cottage residents thus maintained a range of furniture, covering both mundane domestic needs and decorative display functions.

Ornamentation and display

As previously observed, some of these Hagg Cottage furniture items would have been used for the explicit purpose of display. Other objects were used to augment the domestic interior. One particularly polyvalent object, the household clock, held significance as both a timekeeping instrument (Leone and Shackle, 1987) and an ornamental artefact (Lawrence, 2000). A brass clock key, an alarm clock key and alarm clock back and casing formed part of the Area A assemblage. Similarly, a non-ferrous clock plate was recovered from Area B.

The largest component of display artefacts came from glass and ceramic assemblages. Overall, 3 per cent of ceramics (ENV 134) from the site were ornamental. In Area A, this category formed a particularly significant 11 per cent (ENV 117) of the total ceramics. Conversely, ornamental items constituted a much smaller portion of the Area B assemblage, forming less than 1 per cent (ENV 14). When compared across trenches, spatial distributions suggested a clear depositional pattern. A total ENV of 134 was recorded from the analysed ceramics. Of these, 88 per cent were from Area A, 10 per cent from Area B and 1 per cent each from Areas C and D. Thus a distinct concentration was observed within the northern Perrin household of the internally subdivided Area A cottage.

Of these ornamental ceramics, only 3 per cent were identified as possibly eighteenth-century. Approximately 80 per cent were dated across the nineteenth and twentieth centuries. A further 9 per cent could be securely dated to the nineteenth century, and 6 per cent were placed within the twentieth century. The remaining 2 per cent were of unknown date range. Thus ornamental ceramics recovered from the Hagg site appeared to temporally cluster. Even given differential survival rates between earlier and later ceramics at the site, this evidence suggested that ornamental ceramics served as a decorative phenomenon between the later half of the nineteenth and early part of the twentieth centuries. The majority (71 per cent) were whiteware, 14 per cent were stoneware and 11 per cent bone china/porcelain. A small proportion (4 per cent) were also specialised ornamental wares, consisting of 'encrusted' ware (3 per cent) and jasper ware (1 per cent).

Providing the most common form of these ornamental ceramics (58 per cent), vases were decorated in a colourful variety of styles and techniques. Several sherds were quite simply decorated, with overglaze painted flowers outlined with gold lines. Floral designs served as a popular motif and were added to vases as both an overglaze transfer print and an applied ceramic decoration (Plate V). Gold paint lustre was another common decorative technique, serving as a floral outline and linear highlight around the foot, rim and/or handles of vessels.

Figurines constituted the second most common decorative form. Appearing in both human and animal forms, figurines totalled 18 per cent of the total ornamental ceramic assemblage. Zoomorphic examples included the body and tail of a moulded swan and a horse-like figurine – its underglaze painted with parallel black stripes to identify it as an exotic zebra (see Figure 5.7). Human figurines were found in a variety of styles. They included a small unglazed porcelain androgynous figure with long hair wearing a bicorn hat; two glazed whiteware conjoined figures of a girl and a boy sat on a tree stump; three whiteware conjoined female figures in eighteenth-century dress supporting a dish-like receptacle; and a male figure with a blue coat. One particularly spectacular figurine depicted a white infant hand supporting an egg-shaped orange object, encrusted with fine chips of ceramic and applied polychrome flowers (Plate VI). Dated by its base registration stamp to 1870, the wrist of this hand was also encrusted, and adorned with a floral wreath. A highly similar ornamental vase – its exterior described as 'textured frit chipping finish, [with] applied ceramic roses and leaves' was identified as a turn-of-the-century family heirloom in Grace Karskens' study of The Rocks, a working urban neighbourhood of Sydney, Australia (Karskens, 1999: 142). Further research would potentially track the global distribution of this rather dramatic decorative style over the Edwardian era.

Remaining ornamental ceramics included those of unidentifiable form (18 per cent), ring trees (1 per cent) and various bowls, jars and plates (5 per cent). This latter category included a commemorative vase for the coronation of Queen Victoria (see Plate VIII), a commemorative mug for the coronation or silver jubilee of George V and souvenir vessels from the Isle of Man and Blackpool (see Plate VII). While purely decorative items, these polysemic objects also operated as souvenirs and commemorations of specific holidays or recreational activities, as discussed within Chapter 5. Overall, these ornamental ceramics form a vital line of evidence with which to interpret the homes of late nineteenth- and early twentieth-century Hagg Cottage residents. This interpretation becomes clearer when combined with a further aspect of the decorative artefacts from the site.

Ornamental glass

The final type of evidence related to an ornamentation of the Hagg Cottages came from glasswares. Again, the most significant concentration of these was recovered from Area A, although preliminary analysis did not yield quantitative data for calculation of precise proportions of ornamental glasswares within the assemblage. Some of these objects were increasingly common in early twentieth-century homes, such as the two clear glass press-moulded vases – inexpensive and well suited for floral displays. Another example consisted of two opaque white vases, each decorated with a horizontal band of red paint and dated to the early twentieth century. One particularly unusual glass display item from Area A was a pedestal bowled 'lustre', a popular late Victorian sitting room ornament, designed for mantelpiece display as a matched pair (Willmott, 2004: 117; Karskens, 1998: 156). The single Hagg Cottage example was moulded from an opaque blue glass and decorated with a worn banded gilding. Eight cut and faceted drops would have hung from small holes drilled into it, with seven of these recovered. This object was dated to 1860 through 1880. Given the twentieth-century date of the majority of artefacts in this Area A demolition zone, this Victorian 'lustre' appeared a particularly unusual object for its time of deposition.

Two glass vases were also recovered from the Area B cottage. The first of these was clear glass, formed into a tapering pedestal shape and decorated with rolled multicoloured blobs of glass. The second was a rim shard from a late nineteenth-century clear glass vase, cased on the outside with swirled red glass. The distribution pattern for decorative glass objects generally appeared to match that of ornamental ceramics. High quantities were found in Area A, representing both a wide variety of styles and a fairly broad date range. Far fewer examples were recovered from Area B, yielding an obvious concentration of display-related artefacts within the northern half of the Area A cottage.

Garden wares

Domestic ornamentation did not stop at the front entrance. Hagg Cottage residents modified their gardens as an integral part of the domestic space that formed their homes. We have already discussed the remnant structural evidence for flower-bed features around both cottages. Further evidence for the elaboration and decoration of cottage gardens came from flowerpot sherds, specialist-identified as 'horticultural wares' (a low-fired coarse red

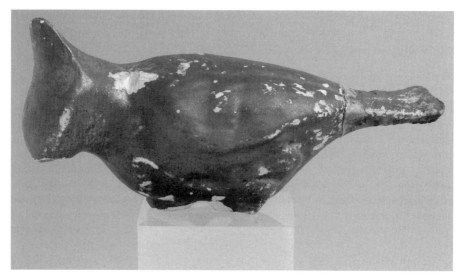

Figure 4.9   Ceramic bird figurine, Alderley Sandhills Project, 2003

earthenware). The majority of garden-related ceramics (53 per cent, or ENV 33) were recovered from Area B, perhaps reflecting a particular interest in gardening expressed by the early twentieth-century residents of the southern cottage. Despite the highly ornate interiors of Area A, much smaller numbers of horticultural wares (ENV 14) were recovered from excavations. A small quantity of these wares appeared within the midden of Area D (ENV 15), including a ceramic bird figurine (Figure 4.9). Modelled in a distinctive crude style, it seemed likely that this red-painted bird would have graced one of the Hagg Cottage gardens.

Consumerism

Archaeological perspectives on consumerism embrace both the material realities of objects and the social process of acquiring, using and discarding these commodities. From the early nineteenth century, home decor was transformed through the production and availability of new consumer goods. As mass production and improved transport reduced the basic unit price of household commodities, a diverse array of domestic products became available to working households. Complex motivations directed this process of domestic consumption, with marketing and advertisements promising a fulfilment of desires that transcended any perceived utilitarian or psychological 'need' (Mullins, 1999: 31). Through their active engagement with new commercial goods, Hagg Cottage residents gradually joined the modern consumer economy.

Industrial-era goods

The Victorian era witnessed rapid advances in the processes of manufacture, and numbers produced of mundane and decorative household goods (Briggs, 1988). This was in some ways tied to a maturation of the industrial revolution, with an evolution in technology making the mass production of a wide range of goods increasingly possible. The complexities by which new goods came to be manufactured and availability to consumers of different classes, was most clearly illustrated at the Hagg site through the floorcoverings assemblage. During the eighteenth century, the poorest members of society were lucky to have their dirt floor interiors improved with flagstones (Gauldie, 1974: 56). However, for the middle classes the eighteenth century witnessed a 'consumer explosion'. As opportunities for purchasing goods increased, luxury goods became recast as basic living 'necessities' (Shackel, 1994: 161). Along with carpets, basic polychrome floorcloths were in manufacture throughout the century and were frequently laid within homes of the English middle classes (Sarin, 2004) – including the yeoman farmers of the eighteenth-century Hagg Cottages.

Floorcloths were technologically transformed by the invention of linoleum in 1860. Manufactured with high-quality multi-coloured designs on an easily cleaned oil-coated finish, linoleum had superior qualities to floorcloth. For several years, this advanced floorcovering was restricted to the middle and upper tiers of English society. However, by 1888 there were over twenty linoleum manufacturers in Britain. It was over this period of widespread manufacture that the lower end of the market became targeted, particularly by Jas Williamson & Son of Lancaster, in the north-west region of England. The subsequent decade witnessed a major international trade in floorcoverings. Initially these were manufactured in Britain and exported across the Atlantic. However, by the end of the nineteenth century America supported a well established linoleum manufacturing industry of its own. Indeed, the next development in floorcoverings was an American innovation. Like linoleum, Congoleum had a easily printed yet hard-wearing finish, but was cheaper to produce. Close international links between companies meant that, after being introduced in America in 1911, Congoleum was quickly manufactured across the Atlantic.

This shift in late industrial floorcoverings fits with general trends in the manufacture of finished commercial goods. Until the mid-nineteenth century, many of these finished goods remained in smaller-scale and non-mechanised manufacturing processes (Rule, 1986: 11). Lines of comparison have been drawn between linoleum manufacturing and sales and those of other goods in the late nineteenth and early twentieth centuries, with Gooderson (1996: 36) arguing that the Lancaster firm of Jas Williamson & Son 'became as important to the nation as Lever, Cadbury and Wills as practitioners of aggressive pricing policy'. Gaudily patterned linoleum gradually became valued as one of the brash possessions that prosperous working-class households came to use as one of the 'ultimate symbols of respectability' (Johnson, 1988: 37), along with other flamboyant items of furniture and ornamentation. In doing so, the workers of the Hagg Cottages were not mimicking domestic interiors of the genteel classes, but exerting their own aesthetic through interior decor.

The floorcoverings used in the late nineteenth and early twentieth centuries by the southern Area A cottage form an interesting chapter in the creation of these homes. They can be argued to be utilitarian in nature, tied to an inherent Victorian preoccupation with hygiene. With hardened slick surfaces, linoleum and Congoleum were particularly easy to clean and therefore supported efforts towards hygienic domestic interiors. An important aspect of consumer behaviour was also enacted in the purchase and use of these commercial goods. As mining activity ceased at the Edge the new floorcoverings may have displayed relatively modern flooring – certainly better than uncovered stone flags. Thus, for mining families newly emigrated to the Hagg from the south-west of England, floorcoverings laid in the front parlour may have created a comfortable domestic interior. Later, over the early twentieth century, ever reducing prices made linoleum and Congoleum increasingly available. Hagg Cottage residents perhaps exercised increasing consumer choice in the continued decoration of their front rooms with the updated floorcoverings. The later layers of these may therefore represent the particular rendering of domestic fashions of the later Barber family.

On the Victorian domestic interior

To fully understand the creation of 'home' at the Hagg, the acquisition of decorative commodities and their embedded social meanings must be explored. Different types of commodities sustain alternate systems of provision, production, taste, price, habit, distribution, retailing and meaning (Fine and Leopold, 1993: 5). Thus consumer goods retain many levels of interpretation – they do not simply have a singular meaning, but may mean different things to different people, dependent on the particular setting. These meanings are further circumscribed by broader discourse, material form and social structures (Mullins, 1999: 30). What were such discourses and structures for nineteenth- and twentieth-century Hagg Cottage residents? To truly understand the archaeological remains from these excavated households, we must explore these social questions.

From the early origins of industrialisation, people adopted mass-produced goods in order to communicate their own personal and social identities (Orser, 1996: 173). Over the later nineteenth century the Hagg Cottage residents formed part of a wider transcultural network that linked producers, distributors and consumers of a particular commodity or set of commodities (Appadurai, 1986: 27). Before the Second World War, a defining aesthetic for their material world would have been 'Victorianism': a transatlantic phenomenon, it emerged as a central ideology of late nineteenth-century life. By the 1850s Victorianism was well established in Britain, and represented 'an expression of the rejection of the attitudes of the aristocracy for a new set of values, drawn from the commercialisation of the middle class' (Praetzellis and Praetzellis, 1992: 75).

The taste of Victorianism was widely shared, and originally adopted to define the etiquette and equipage of middle-class society. This shared taste exemplified the way in which members of a social group actively chose similar material items from a repertoire of mass-produced goods in order to construct the group's social boundaries from shared symbols (Shackel, 1994: 165). The tastes of Victorianism were particularly manifest in knick-knacks and other fancy domestic display artefacts. One commentator in the 1860s observed, 'It decorates the finest modern porcelain with the most objectionable character of ornament' (Briggs, 1988: 225). An interesting twist in the Hagg Cottages ornamental ceramic assemblage, however, was the fact that over two-thirds of the ornamental items were inexpensive whitewares, rather than 'finest modern porcelain'.

By the mid-nineteenth century, domestic aesthetics were internationally popularised by a range of publications intended for the middle-class householder. Victorian housekeeping manuals devoted to cooking and interior decor began to appear in the second half of the nineteenth century. Topics included furniture, wallpapers, carpets, domestic furniture, cabinetwork, textile fabrics and pottery (Briggs, 1988: 217). Publications included C.J. Richardson's *The Englishman's House* (1870), Loftie's *A Plea for Art at Home*, R.W. Edis's *Decoration and Furniture of Town Houses* (1881) and Rosamund Marriott Watson's *The Art of the House* (1897). Periodicals were also available which further supported this formal guidance of home decor, with the *Furniture Gazette* first printed in 1872 and *Furniture and Decoration* in 1890.

While this literature was squarely aimed at middle-class audiences (Briggs, 1988: 231), by the end of the nineteenth century a concern with decoration had spread beyond this social boundary. At this time books began to appear in print, concerned with furnishing and decorating the home, but aimed at the working classes. First printed in 1897, *Cassell's Book of the Household* explicitly aimed at a mass readership. Thus, by the end of the nineteenth century, Victorian values and tastes permeated beyond the middle classes.

Inexpensive mass-produced goods of the nineteenth century were not manufactured within closely defined 'schools' of decorative styling. Instead goods for the lower end of the market represented popular products and left precise stylistic interpretation of these objects to the consumers themselves

(Mullins, 2004: 88). This did not mean that those purchasing these popular goods interpreted them in entirely fanciful ways – they were still linked into the wider ideologies and aesthetics of social class – but these meanings were not as commercially defined as they were for upper- and middle-class households.

Additionally, socio-economic status did not necessarily determine turn-of-the-century consumer behaviours. In his study of excavated household possessions from Oakland, California, Paul Mullins (2004) discussed how neighbouring households of similar economic means demonstrated alternative choices in bric-a-brac and interior adornments. Hagg Cottage residents of the late nineteenth and early twentieth centuries would have been exposed to advertisements for household products in not only the village shops of Alderley Edge, but also the market venues of nearby Macclesfield and Manchester. The elegant interior of Alderley Park, the Stanley family's stately home, would have been experienced during annual attendance at the tenants' Christmas party. They would also have been aware of the interiors of the wealthy bourgeois villas of Alderley Edge – either through their work as domestic servants and gardeners, or through descriptions socially diffused throughout the local community. Cottage residents would also have visited the homes of neighbouring working families and known of their public domestic interiors. As they selected goods for their own homes, Hagg residents tapped into a range of aesthetic styles, making conscious, yet financially prudent, choices for the presentation of their homes.

Class and consumption

Issues of class identity complicated the ornamentation of domestic interiors, particularly as the middle classes initially dominated the expression of Victorian values and aesthetics. Indeed, in North America it has been explicitly argued that the middle classes served as primary consumers of the knick-knacks and furnishings that defined this interior style:

> Although not necessarily the creators of fashion, the middle class played a leading role as its generators. During this period [the late nineteenth century] its members largely controlled the production, distribution and marketing of mass-produced consumer goods. They also comprised an important section of the buying public, and served as a source of emulation for the aspiring members of the lower classes.
>
> (Praetzellis *et al.*, 1988: 202)

So what then of working-class consumer practices? Data presented earlier in Chapter 2 demonstrated that all nineteenth-century male residents of the Hagg Cottage were engaged in labouring, mining and industrial support professions. The most directly skilled of these occupants were John Martin, a blacksmith, who lived at the cottages in 1871, and George Barber, a pharmacist's assistant from the early twentieth century and father of oral history participants Molly Pitcher and Roy Barber. How did Hagg Cottage consumers fit into the broader class hierarchy of the village of Alderley Edge? Were they simply participating in emulative behaviour, or were they taking part in more complex meanings of consumer desire? (Karskens, 1998: 142). Did they successfully construct an alternative consumer aesthetic? At the Hagg Cottages, both consumer behaviours and domestic spaces were shaped by complex social, economic and gendered interactions (Mullins, 1999: 27). Despite their trades, despite their domestic accessories, these were still working-class households. Since fewer archival data (catalogues, advertisements, household manuals, etc.) were available for lower-status groups (Scholliers, 2004: 257), a detailed understanding of turn-of-the-century consumer patterns requires archaeological study.

Working-class consumers

The concept of a 'working-class' household itself required further analysis, particularly given the diverse range of working-class accommodation available in nineteenth-century Britain. At the top of this socio-economic scale, just below the middle class, were artisans, engaged in highly skilled trades, such as printing, precious metal work, bookbinding or skilled construction work. Artisan families frequently occupied suburban districts. Female members of these households closely resembled those of the middle classes and possessed genteel social skills (Stearns, 1972: 101). These artisan households contrasted with the 'traditional poor', who formed a quarter of the urban working class and lived on the margins of subsistence (Stearns, 1972: 102). Rule (1986: 37) similarly observed that only *skilled* mid-Victorian workers (the 'aristocracy of labour') could access enough money to buy furniture or domestic knick-knacks.

International comparisons illuminate aspects of consumer behaviour at the Hagg Cottages. One useful case study examined the working-class immigrant neighbourhood of Five Points in New York City. Knick-knacks recovered from this site were argued to be important for understanding the ways in which past residents expressed their distinctive tastes in the public arena. Drawing on Mullins (1999, 2004), Brighton (2001: 25) observed that even if proportionally low, decorative artefacts deserved close examination as key social symbols. This particular case study examined poor Irish immigrant tenement dwellings over the nineteenth century. In the metropolis of New York, working families had the opportunity to purchase ceramics from street auctions, yard sales and junk shops (Brighton, 2001: 21). The display of ceramics in these urban households may have been motivated by social traditions of domestic display assembled from Irish domestic aesthetics and Victorian consumerism – infused with the desire to present a 'respectable' front to established Protestant missionaries while gaining access to civic employment and educational opportunities. Crucially, the Five Points consumers were doing far more than blindly emulating the middle classes. While their social understandings of the artefacts drew upon Victorian bourgeois values, these workers maintained their own ethnic and classed identities through their material world. Although consciously using these objects to create a home environment that supported negotiations with the Protestant missionaries, the Five Point residents made their consumer choices based upon aesthetic patterns relevant to their working community.

At the Hagg Cottages, occupants of Area A were ornamenting their homes to a remarkably greater degree than the residents of Area B. The Perrins, George Barber's uncle and aunt, occupied the northern half of the Area A cottage. Mrs Lena Perrin lived with her widower brother Ernest, having moved into the house in 1912, ostensibly to help look after her brother and nephew. Both the spatial concentration of excavated ornamentals and oral histories shared by former residents linked the bulk of the knick-knacks and decorative items with this Perrin household. Mrs Perrin was renowned within the Hagg community for her slightly eccentric attachment to decorative items – her costume jewellery, vases, figurines and other knick-knacks. In contrast to initial expectations, historical research showed Mrs Perrin to have been surprisingly affluent. She owned several local properties, and had the financial wherewithal to have enjoyed a much better standard of living than provided by her simple four-room semi-detached cottage at the Hagg. This disjuncture generated a search for more complex meanings to Mrs Perrin's consumer behaviour (Whitehead and Casella, forthcoming).

Most of these ornaments held extended links with certain people, places and times, materialised through specific ceramic and glass forms. The various persons involved in their manufacture, sale, display and consumption all infused these objects with their own economic, sentimental, aesthetic and ethnocultural meanings (Chaimov, 2001: 63). Mrs Perrin may have constructed particular individualised meanings around these artefacts. Her nephew, Mr Roy Barber (ASP interviews, August 2003), remembered that she 'went and bought at sales, auctions. That sort of thing.' This was where she not only bought her houses, but also where she likely bought the majority of her ornaments, particularly those that dated back to the nineteenth century. While these goods reflected an idiosyncratic taste, they were also sentimental reminders of the sales she had attended and the family she had purchased for. She kept various commemorative objects which she later passed on to her niece, Molly Pitcher (ASP interviews, August 2003). The ornaments thus created a personal and meaningful sense of home for Mrs Perrin. While slightly eccentric, these objects drew on her personal aesthetic and interpretations of prevailing fashions. They symbolised her social mobility, indicating her access to sales and auctions. Some may have been personal reminders of family members, including her deceased daughter. Thus these constructed a powerful set of symbols within a single parlour and were far more than simply an unfulfilled emulation of her middle-class neighbours.

Hearth and home

The large quantity of ornamental items found at the site may thus represent an anomaly, created by a single known occupant. Returning to a more general scale of analysis, we can think about how the structural and artefactual data presented above related to the ways in which Hagg Cottage residents forged a sense of home. Over the industrial era, the general architectural ideology of homes involved the creation of functionally specific rooms (bedroom, washroom, kitchen, pantry, hallway, etc.) with a specific and standardised behaviour for each space (Shackel, 1994: 15). Such elaboration of interior space was obviously not accessible to all. The most common plan for nineteenth-century rural workers' cottages was simply a single ground-floor main room, two bedrooms upstairs, and a pigsty and privy outside (Gauldie, 1974: 46). Working households may have tried to delimit parlour space along Victorian lines of gentility, but most often household activities combined in multi-functional rooms (Briggs, 1988: 244). Given the trend for overcrowding in nineteenth-century rural housing, the Hagg residents lived in relatively abundant space (Rule, 1986: 78). Nonetheless, with household sizes at the Hagg cottages ranging from five to seven occupants, was there any way to clearly segregate certain spaces within the home?

The front-room fireplace in the southern Area A cottage (Figure 4.10) provided a particular space of domesticity, drawing on ideas of comfort and modernity in a repertoire of Victorian values. For most working households, the central fireplace provided both cooking and heating. Only the better class of workers' homes contained copper boilers and cast-iron stoves (Gauldie, 1974: 57). As previously discussed, both Area A and B cottages showed archaeological evidence for the installation of stoves and boilers. Thus the fireplace in the front room of Area A was not a focus of domestic tasks such as cooking or boiling water. Rather, over the nineteenth century this 'hearth' became imbued with a new social significance. It may have functioned as a central point for family-oriented social interaction in the home – an activity area which new stoves and ranges could not replace (Briggs, 1988: 136). As early as the 1860s 'even in working-class homes the hearth was prominent, and working-class families were prepared then and later to spend considerable sums on the appearance of the fireplace' (Briggs, 1988: 240). Similarly,

Figure 4.10   Detail of southern fireplace, Area A, Alderley Sandhills Project, 2003

Cassell's *Book of the Household* (1897) mentioned that tiled hearths had become fashionable interior decor, alongside wooden chimneypieces and overmantels (Briggs, 1988: 238).

The installation of a tiled surround and mantelpiece around the front-room fireplace within the Area A cottage may have therefore indicated an elaborated sense of home life by this extended household. It is also interesting to note how quickly the side extension appears to have transferred out of domestic use, particularly given its decorative mid-Victorian ceramic tiled floor. While this shift may have related to the fluid socio-economic requirements of these working households, and seamless blend of home and work spaces, it may have also merely reflected the lack of a fireplace in the extension. Given the increasing importance of 'hearth' to a sense of home, perhaps a room without a fireplace seemed an unattractive option for household socialising.

Furniture and home

As with so many other categories of material goods, the amount of furniture available to the working classes changed rapidly over the course of the nineteenth century. An 1840 Report on the Sanitary Condition of the Labouring Population described the homes of the poorest workers as having only the most rudimentary furniture and no decorative items at all. In contrast, houses of better-off workers contained wooden furniture, beds, tables, chairs, chests and earthenware dishes (Gauldie, 1974: 57). As manufacturing reduced the price of goods, both functional and luxury items of furniture became increasingly affordable for the working classes. 'Kitcheners' (ranges with attached boilers) were one example of this material hierarchy. Developed in the 1820s, by the late nineteenth century they were widespread, installed even within working-class homes (Briggs, 1988: 240). Similarly, pianos – in no way an 'essential' part of home furnishings – became increasingly common by the later nineteenth century. During 1890 twice as many were produced in England as in 1850. 'What is a home without a piano?' questioned one advertisement noted on a wall in London's poorest East End (Briggs, 1988: 248). Mrs Edna Younger recalled how her parents (in the eastern half of the Area B cottage) had squeezed a piano into the tiny front parlour despite their cramped living space. Mrs Younger described the downstairs layout of her former home:

> You see, it [the living room] looked quite big to me, in those days, but it must have been so tiny. And then, of course, the stairs out the back of the living room. The stairs were part of it. They were in the living room, and then a curtain at the end, and then we used to walk up.
>
> (Mrs Edna Younger, ASP interviews, August 2003)

Household goods such as pianos thus became enmeshed with notions of the comfortable home.

Goods were not merely objects of desire. Rather, they provided a 'medium that reinforces social relations' (Shackel, 1994: 12). In the purchasing of these decorative ornaments, furniture, paint, tiles and floorcoverings, Hagg Cottage residents were neither buying necessities for life nor emulating their socio-economic betters. Residents of these homes actively drew upon contemporary fashions to enhance the comfort of their dwellings. Consumer goods were mobilised to transform the cottages into homes. Fireplaces, floorcoverings, painted walls and ornaments supported everyday practices of domesticity – an ideal aesthetic increasingly globalised over the nineteenth century. Hagg residents enjoyed the comfort of sleeping in a springy bed, of sitting by a cosy hearth, of filling their homes with music and colour. Simultaneously, their homes may have been damp and subsiding, with buckling floors and mouldy, cracking walls. Despite their relative comfort, these homes were a world apart from the wealthy villas in the commuter village of Alderley Edge.

Cottage gardens

A final example of 'home' creation occurred outside the Hagg Cottages. Today the 'cottage garden' has come to be viewed through art and literature as an idealised rural space, one increasingly linked with the domestic sphere (Sayer, 2000: 79). As at the Hagg, flowerpots were found at nineteenth-century Irish tenement households in New York's Five Points district (Brighton, 2001). In his ceramic analysis, Steve Brighton identified these nineteenth-century utilitarian vessels as an ornamentation of the households, with the grooming of plants and gardens representing an extension of the domestic interior to the outer world (Brighton, 2001: 26).

The Hagg Cottage gardens consisted of two areas. Wider sections of land were used for growing vegetables and disposing of rubbish. Additionally, small tightly delineated spaces around the structures formed the 'cottage gardens'. Mrs Edna Younger described her family's plot in Area B as a small garden, with not much space between the hedge and front wall. To delineate their space, these publicly visible front gardens underwent extensive modification over the late nineteenth and early twentieth centuries, with new flower beds cut, paths laid, decorative borders planted and fences built. In contrast, rear exterior spaces, not immediately visible from Hagg Lane, were left as non-ornamental work yards, as discussed in Chapter 6. Thus both the material elaboration of gardens and the deposition of flowerpots demonstrated that the material constitution of 'home' did not merely occur inside the cottage walls.

Health and hygiene

Alongside the architectural modification and interior ornamentation of the Hagg Cottages, the creation of 'home' reflected changing perceptions of domestic sanitation and personal hygiene. From the mid-nineteenth century, these ideologies extended from the physical condition of cottages to the sanitary cleansing of bodies and commercial use of medicines – thereby reflecting a popularisation of scientific knowledge on the relationship between sanitation and health (Ford, 1994: 49).

The Hagg Cottages were particularly well provided with drainage facilities, perhaps reflecting their topographical position on the down-slope hillside. From the earliest seventeenth-century phases of Area B, external box drains were installed to channel ground water. Surprisingly, a cellar drain was installed during original construction of the eighteenth-century Area A farmhouse. Additionally, extensive works were undertaken over the nineteenth century to improve the sanitary conditions of the cottages. Within the ceramic assemblage, 'structural' items were classed in a separate group that incorporated tiles, pipes and drains. Of these, 69 per cent were sewer or drainage pipes related to the sanitation of the cottages. All dated to the nineteenth century or later; these artefacts reflected a rise in the use of sanitary wares. Additional evidence for increased provision of drainage came from metal artefacts, including a cast-iron gutter stay with semi-circular support, a broken piece of cast-iron gutter and fragments of cast-iron drainpipes. As previously indicated, numerous late nineteenth-century and early twentieth-century drains were in evidence throughout the Hagg site building sequence.

The concern with sanitation and hygiene was not simply about improving the property drainage, it was about achieving household cleanliness and purchasing goods to help sanitise the home. Increasing pressure was extended to working-class households to demonstrate that their homes were clean. In working communities, this was often viewed as a realm of women's activity (Karskens, 1998: 158). At the turn of the century, working-class wives in urban areas were often criticised for the perceived sloppiness of their households. In addition to their income-generating work, they were judged (by middle-class reformers) in their ability to keep a clean and tidy home (Stearns, 1972: 103). Thus, for working homes, pride was believed to lie within 'the scrubbed doorstep, the polished window sill and the blazing hearth' (Briggs, 1988: 236). Just as the hearth evolved as an iconic symbol of the 'home' for Victorian England, cleanliness offered a similar (if blatantly gendered) metaphor of domesticity.

Artefacts and hygiene

At the Hagg Cottages, archaeological evidence demonstrated that numerous steps were taken to improve sanitation across the properties. Artefacts concerned with general sanitation were found in the southern Area A subdivided cottage. A galvanised steel-wire rat trap cage, dated to around 1900, was recovered in the demolition layer. By its very presence, it indicates that residents coped with pest control. Rat infestation was an international problem for industrial workers (see for example Beaudry, 1993: 100; Karskens, 1998: 192–194; Mayne, 1993). Since maintaining a pest-ridden, insanitary home was deemed to reflect directly upon female householders, the excavated rat trap may have caused particular social anxieties for the women living in the Hagg Cottages at the turn of the century.

As part of a cultural discourse on cleanliness (Briggs, 1988: 236), manufacturers prescribed methods for cleaning the home, thereby tapping into consumers' anxieties over sanitary living conditions. Cleanliness increasingly became a multi-sensory experience, with laundry detergents, for example, marketed as products for making clothes fresher and whiter (Pink, 2005: 279). Sensory evaluations of cleanliness came to be informed not only by what looked clean, but also by what smelled clean (Pink, 2005: 188). At the Hagg, excavations recovered a flat metal tin inscribed with the words 'pine scented', dated to the first half of the twentieth century. While the contents were unknown, it likely held a cleaning-related product. Such an artefact demonstrated how aspects of hygiene had become linked not only with the look and smell of a clean house, but also with the consumer choices necessary to achieve that cleanliness. The woman who purchased and used this product bought into an ideal of how the respectable home should appear (Mullins, 1999: 31). The fact that the product was pine-scented incorporated simultaneous metaphors of outdoor space. While nature was something to be kept outside of the cottages, if deployed properly it could be seen to enhance the domestic sphere.

Other archaeologically recovered cleaning products sanitised the home in a less pleasant manner. Two green hexagonal bottles, embossed 'Not to be taken', were included within the Area A assemblage. These may have held poison (to aid in the elimination of rats and other pests) or additional cleaning products. Containing generic preparations rather than scented commercial brands, these bottles may have represented the majority of late nineteenth- and early twentieth-century home cleaning products.

Sanitising the individual

As well as the sanitation of the domestic interior, archaeological evidence existed for the hygiene practices associated with the individual occupants

Plate I   Whiteware transfer-printed plate, Alderley Sandhills Project, 2003

Plate II   Glass pepperpot, Alderley Sandhills Project, 2003

Plate III Earthenware teapot fragments, including strainer and spout, Alderley Sandhills Project, 2003

Plate IV Detail of linoleum floorcovering, with reconstruction of
original encaustic tile pattern, Area A, Alderley Sandhills Project, 2003.
Upper left Excavated sample. *Upper right* Reconstructed pattern (detail).
Bottom Reconstructed pattern

Plate V   Floral painted vase, Alderley Sandhills Project, 2003

Plate VI   Hand figurine, Alderley Sandhills Project, 2003

Plate VII   Blackpool souvenir whiteware plate, Alderley Sandhills Project, 2003

Plate VIII   Whiteware Queen Victoria jubilee commemorative vessel, Alderley
Sandhills Project, 2003

of the Hagg Cottages. In Area A, artefacts included plastic toothbrushes (Figure 4.11) and the tops from three toothpaste tubes, one of which was stamped 'Gibb's'. A range of shaving equipment was also recovered. From the early twentieth century, one single handle for a safety razor and two safety razors for double-edged blades were recovered. A further safety razor for a single-edged blade was dated to the 1930s. Alongside these were two ceramic items, significant in terms of generating questions of personal hygiene (Larsen, 1994: 76). These consisted of a matching large bowl and jug, made of whiteware and decorated internally with a red rose transfer printed design. Externally, these items were relief-moulded with pink bands and gold overglaze flowers (Figure 4.12). Representing a matched set of washing implements, both were dated to the late nineteenth century through the early twentieth. Two Bakelite plastic combs provided further evidence of personal grooming by cottage residents over the early twentieth century. Invented in 1907 by Leo Baekeland, a Belgian-American chemist (Meikle, 1997: 5), 'Bakelite' quickly became a ubiquitous plastic, used for a multitude of domestic items and household furnishings until the post-war decade.

Paul Shackel (1993) interpreted grooming implements as an element of personal discipline developed as a consequence of industrialisation. Drawing on Pierre Bourdieu's (1977) notion of *habitus*, he observed that personal appearance, hygiene and care for the body became inculcated in the way in which modern workers came to understand their sense of individuality. Furthermore, hygiene and manners were more than just formality or display; they served as an integral part of the general regime of personal discipline (Shackel, 1994: 157). Toothbrushes, in particular, were related to having clean and inoffensive-smelling breath – increasingly a requirement for membership in polite society of late eighteenth-century Anglo-America. In addition, toothbrushes helped cerate a sense of personhood, as they were 'related to grooming and hygiene, and, therefore, to personal discipline, which required its regular and systematic use to create the individual' (Shackel, 1994: 21). Significantly, this argument demonstrated how toothbrushes and other personal hygiene objects such as wash basins and combs (Shackel, 1994: 8) were conceptually linked with wider techniques for disciplining workers in capitalist society.

Drawing from archival and oral history sources, the Hagg assemblage suggested alternative interpretations. Early twentieth-century residents, as we have already discussed, were increasingly part of a modern consumer society. Razors, toothbrushes, toothpaste and combs formed part of the repertoire of available commodities. George Barber, as a pharmacist's assistant, may have had a greater access to some of these personal hygiene products. But his role in the service economy of Alderley Edge village would also have necessitated a rigorous standard of personal grooming. Indeed, a shopworker would have been expected to habitually utilise a comb and razor in

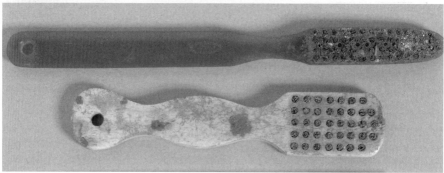

Figure 4.11   Artefacts of personal hygiene, Alderley Sandhills Project, 2003.
Upper Metal safety razor. *Lower* Bone and plastic brushes

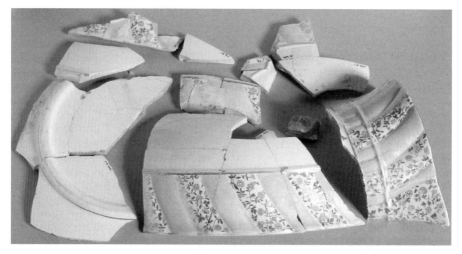

Figure 4.12   Whiteware washbowl set, Alderley Sandhills Project, 2003

an effort to maintain a certain personal appearance. It could be argued that the toothbrushes, toothpaste tubes, comb, razors and ceramic washing set all related to the daily practices of a specific worker at the Hagg site. These items may have therefore represented the etiquette and equipage required of turn-of-the-century service workers employed in the commuter town of Alderley Edge.

Following their invention in the early twentieth century, plastic hair combs came into widespread use, and have been found in other archaeological contexts, including the boarding houses of Lowell, Massachusetts (Mrozowski *et al.*, 1996: 78). The invention of disposable combs was stimulated by a desire to find a substitute for expensive ivory and tortoiseshell – imported materials essential for combs and brushes until the late nineteenth century. Plastic manufacturers in early twentieth-century America sought to associate their imitation goods with the comforts 'only available in a Sultan's harem.' (Meikle, 1997: 17). As well as simply engaging in disciplining behaviours of personal grooming, the purchase and use of plastic combs may have represented a perceived acquisition of luxury goods. Such items might have communicated an ability to purchase a personal 'luxury', even as their mass production simultaneously marked them as mundane implements.

Similarly, the bowl-and-jug washing set – when combined with the razors, combs, toothbrushes and toothpaste – spoke to a complex web of personal taste and social norms. These objects materially associated an interior space with personal hygiene, particularly as the cottages provided no indoor plumbing or separate bathrooms. Through these artefacts, Hagg Cottage residents were, in a sense, consuming hygiene. Such consumption patterns were widely shared. Even within the cellar dwellings of New Islington Wharf in Manchester, personal grooming items such as razors and toothbrushes were found (Oxford Archaeology North, 2005: 44). Thus, from the late nineteenth century, personal hygiene-related practices had permeated across the social classes.

Medicines and health

The final strand of evidence relating to health and hygiene involved the consumption of medicines. All artefacts related to this category were glass. A total of thirty-six bottles, jars and phials were firmly attributed to medicinal use either by form, or by embossed brand details on the bottle. Area B contained few vessels – two pill bottles and a single cylindrical phial. All of these artefacts were clear glass, and dated to the early twentieth century. None was branded. Area D contained medicinal containers in more significant quantities, with a total of eight vessels. One was an unbranded pill bottle. Three were late nineteenth-century medicine bottles: one was brown, embossed 'James Wolley, Manchester', and two were blue-green and embossed with

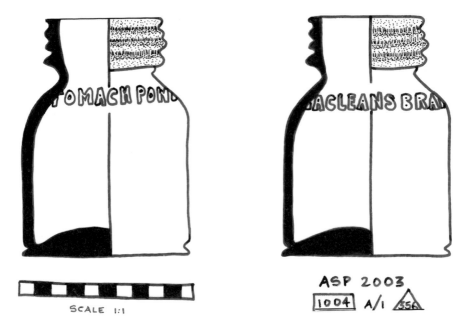

Figure 4.13   Medicinal glassware, Alderley Sandhills Project, 2003

tablespoon gradations. Two hexagonal brown medicine bottles were recovered. Embossed 'Milton' for milk of magnesia, both were dated from the late nineteenth through early twentieth centuries. Two unembossed early twentieth-century medicine bottles were also collected.

Area A contained the greatest proportion of medicine-related artefacts. A remarkable twenty-five glass vessels were collected from this trench. Temporal changes could be interpreted from this assemblage. Four vessels were recorded with a nineteenth-century date range. All phials, they consisted of one clear, one blue-green and two green – the latter two complete with droppers. Two further phials were found. One was blue-green, dated to the turn of the century, and the other clear, dating to the early twentieth century. Twelve medicine bottles were recovered from Area A, all dated to the early twentieth century. These appeared in a range of colours, including brown, green and clear. Two were ribbed (Figure 4.13). Four had embossed wording. Two of these were brown hexagonal bottles embossed 'Milton'. Matching those found in Area D, they would have contained milk of magnesia. A further seven vessels were pill bottles or medicine jars. Although one clear oval pill jar was nineteenth-century, the majority dated to the twentieth. One pill jar was embossed 'Yeast-vite' and three were embossed 'MacLeans Brand Stomach Powder'.

From the early twentieth century, residents of the Area A cottage seem to have maintained particular access to a wide variety of medicinal products. Although initially unsurprising, given George Barber's employment as a pharmacist's assistant, upon further reflection these medicines presented an ambiguous image of daily household practices. Did George Barber bring so many products home because someone in his family was afflicted with particular ailments? Or would other motivations have encouraged the consumption of medicinal products?

Historical archaeologists have viewed medicinal practices and the purchase of medicines as a part of creating and understanding social identities through practice (Larsen, 1994: 73). Health was of great importance to industrial era workers. Different types of medicine were available – those which might be prescribed by a doctor or apothecary of some sort, and patent (or 'proprietary') medicines, which could be home-dosed and were more widely marketed (Bonasera and Raymer, 2001: 50). One main motivation for purchasing medicines was the prevalence of diseases created by poor sanitary conditions and financial limitations. Bad health could result from dangerous materials, poor working environments, difficult work postures, communicable diseases, or workplace injuries. Chemicals and hazardous materials also commonly poisoned workers.

What then, were the motivations of the Area A residents in consuming medicines in such relatively large quantities? None of the oral histories suggested a chronically ill or invalid member of the Barber household. However, these narratives did reveal some common applications of different patent medicines. On being shown the Yeast-vite bottle, one of the Parkinson sisters commented that she continued to use the product: 'It's sort of a pick-you-up thing . . . It's supposed to make you untired . . . It sort of "puts a tiger in your tank," you know?' (Miss Pamela Parkinson, ASP Interviews, August 2003). Such a statement demonstrated the value ascribed to over-the-counter medicines as supplements to general health and well-being, rather than treatments for any specific illness.

Indeed, none of the medicinal containers at the Hagg Cottages site pointed to any particular affliction. 'Milk of Magnesia' was patented in the late 1870s, and was mostly used for constipation, although it also treated indigestion and heartburn (Bonasera and Raymer, 2001: 51). MacLean's brand stomach powder might be assumed to have similar soothing properties for the digestive system, suggesting that at least one member of the Barber–Perrin extended family suffered a recurrent mild stomach complaint. The other branded medicinal product, Yeast-vite, as discussed above, provided a general cure-all and pick-me-up.

As the nineteenth century progressed into the twentieth, medicinal containers at the Hagg site became increasingly branded. The health claims of these products would presumably have come from more distant, but increasingly marketed, sources. Certainly from the late nineteenth century health had become an important concern for the middle classes of Alderley Edge village. According to *Kelly's Trade Directory of Cheshire*, two pharmacies served the local community by 1896 (Hall, 2004: 33). For the Area A cottage occupants, George Barber brought home medicines, although these appeared to treat only very minor ailments, if ailments at all. The use of these products may have represented George Barber's ability to care for his family with a wide array of patent medicines. While these were obviously more available to this working man because of his pharmacy work, perhaps his daily exposure to commercial medicines helped cultivated his reliance on these products. Either way, excavation trenches within the Area B cottage recovered almost no comparable medicinal vessels. Perhaps this assemblage linked both George Barber and wider material practices of health from workplace to home.

Consuming domesticity

The evidence for medicinal products, as with so much else at the Hagg Cottages, demonstrated the polysemic meanings of household goods and spaces. Residents created their domestic interiors in accordance with the dominant model of Victorian homes. They drew on material aspects of gentility in their fireplaces, pianos, spatial demarcations, ornamentation and interior decor. Widespread social debates about cleanliness, sanitation, health and hygiene influenced their efforts to keep their homes and bodies clean.

Yet a single pattern did not characterise these practices within English working households. Particularly in later occupation phases, individual characters shaped the material signature of life at the Hagg. Mrs Lena Perrin, with her ornaments and figurines, created one unique sense of home – displaying a spectacular aesthetic which may well have seemed eccentric to friends, relatives and neighbours. Similarly, Mr George Barber created his own archaeological signature by providing commercial medicines for his family. The material world of this domestic site thus represented a delicate mix of both collective patterns, slowly accumulated over time, and unique practices of specific individuals.

Keeping home at the Hagg site was a complicated business. Over time the archaeological evidence suggested a lowering of status for the Hagg residents as the relatively comfortable farmhouses transformed into workers' cottages. But regardless of their socio-economic status, residents of the Hagg Cottages continued to actively modify their dwellings and their immediate environment, thereby changing their houses into homes. In addition to making living arrangements as comfortable as possible, Hagg residents would have enjoyed periods of leisure and relaxation, and it is to these moments that we now turn.

5

Recreation and relaxation

[Workers] have time to see more, do more, and incidentally buy more. This stimulates business and increases prosperity, and in the general economic circle the money passes through industry again and back into the workman's pocket.

(Ford, 1929: 17).

As observed above by the arch-industrialist Henry Ford, modern industry required the twin forces of labour and leisure. This chapter deals with the recreational and leisure activities of the Hagg residents, from the seventeenth-century farmers to the early twentieth-century service workers. Several categories of material evidence are drawn on in order to discuss these: glass bottles and ceramics relating to alcohol consumption, children's toys, smoking-related artefacts and souvenirs from fairs, festivals and holidays. In addition to these material categories, oral historical reminiscences of the daily play activities, holidays and special events richly supplement our understanding of the recreational practices of the later Hagg cottage residents. These categories of material evidence and oral historical strands are further integrated with comparable case studies of turn-of-the-century through inter-war period recreational pursuits. Thus this chapter offers a detailed discussion of the way in which the patterns we see at the Hagg site represent broader changes in recreational practices from the seventeenth through twentieth centuries.

Before presenting the relevant data and interpretations, it is important to discuss the historicity of the concepts that form the basis of this chapter. That the particular concept of 'leisure' could be separated from foodways and domestic care is a unique feature of a post-medieval period site. Leisure time, as a concept clearly delineated from work time, is itself a product of modernity (Burke, 1997: 195). This chapter also includes evidence relating to childhood play activities. These are again particular to recent periods, as it has been argued that the concept of 'childhood' as we understand it today, a period in which children should play and be given space to develop into adults, is an ideology developed only since the eighteenth century (Ariès, 1962). In this chapter we are therefore charting the way in which recreational practices have become a separate sphere of leisure and play.

The rapid growth of leisure industries, particularly at the end of the nineteenth and in the early twentieth centuries (Fischer, 1994; Rosenzweig, 1983) went hand in hand with the rise of industrial capitalism. The differentiation of time into periods for work versus leisure was part of the overall process of temporal regimentation which characterised the industrial era (Barton, 2005: 74). Of course, people engaged in recreational activities prior to industrialisation, but these activities were fundamentally different from those which followed the social changes of industrialisation, with festivals and informal and formal breaks from work all integrated *within* the patterns of working life (Barton, 2005: 9, emphasis added). Although many of the recreational activities discussed here – including county fairs, alcohol consumption and childhood play – were practised *prior* to English industrialisation, they were viewed as part of a wider continuum of practices that constituted daily life (Burke, 1997: 192; cf. Marfany, 1997).

As well as understanding leisure practices at the Hagg site in terms of overall historical changes, it is also imperative to try and understand how these were integrated within shifting identities for the site's residents over time. Historical archaeologists have argued that within working communities, leisure, or 'non-work' activities, provided the greatest opportunities for self-definition and self-expression (Beaudry *et al.*, 1991: 155; Casella, 2005: 167). Concomitant with the rise of work discipline in the industrial era was an attempt to regulate workers' lives by paternalistic industrialists and civic elites. As their efforts extended towards the domestic and recreational spheres, the hours outside of work became the focus of political debate and union activity (Rosenzweig, 1983). For archaeological purposes, leisure activities came to represent a set of contested practices central to the construction of working-class identities. Since the 1960s the history of leisure in the nineteenth and early twentieth centuries, particularly public sports and alcohol consumption, has provided an object of research in both England and North America (Burke, 1995: 136; Fischer, 1994; Rosenzwieg, 1983). As well as self-identified group identities, leisure practices also help us chart the way in which colonial relations were embedded in identities at the Hagg site. As was the case with tea, previously discussed in Chapter 3, tobacco and smoking pipes served as commodities of British colonial relations, for without the empire there would have been no tobacco, tea, pipes or teapots. From the eighteenth century, objects used to commemorate British rulers also reflected how British colonial identities became expressed within the home environment and reinforced through national public holidays. This chapter explores daily recreational practices at the Hagg site to interpret the complex ways these objects articulated with broader dynamics of industry and empire.

A world outside of work

Spaces of leisure and non-work activities, such as public houses, cinemas, parks and other specific recreational areas, provide a useful starting point for understanding leisure practices over the industrial era. Interestingly, the area immediately adjoining the Hagg site was itself a popular leisure space. In the second half of the twentieth century the land of Alderley Edge, once part of the Stanley estate, was gifted to the National Trust, an English non-governmental conservation trust, for public recreational use (Mrs Edna Younger, ASP interviews, July 2003). From the late nineteenth century, Alderley offered a favoured destination, with day visitors from Manchester riding by train to the Edge in order to enjoy the open woodlands and spectacular views across both Cheshire and Lancashire. The National Trust continue to advertise their property as one in which visitors can enjoy 'lovely walks through oak and beech woodlands' (National Trust, 2007) while visiting the Edge itself, a 'dramatic red sandstone escarpment, with impressive views'.

Although the Hagg site lies just immediately adjacent to the National Trust land, this conceptual boundary was less significant in the recent past. Following their closure, the abandoned mining shafts and metal ore-processing areas became a popular spot for recreational tours. Mrs Edna Younger (ASP interviews, July 2003) recalled that people would come from as far as Manchester on the bus or train to picnic on the sandhills themselves, frequently stating that they offered a 'playground' for visitors. In the early 1920s Mr Perrin (one of the Area A cottage residents) developed the entrepreneurial practice of selling half-candles to visitors to light their way in the mines, or taking them on tours of the mine workings himself (Whitehead and Casella, forthcoming).

The Hagg Cottage residents of the early twentieth century lived within an area that was, for outsiders, simply a recreational space, but most of the working classes in England enjoyed a range of their own local amenities for socialising. In the Staffordshire town of Stoke on Trent, for instance, leisure activities of the early twentieth century were 'expressed daily, weekly and annually in local and familiar spaces' which included pubs, clubs, dance halls, cinemas, church halls, oatcake shops, sports arenas, theatres, pageants, wakes and carnivals (Edensor, 2000: 7). While this range of recreational sites does not appear to be atypical, historical archaeologists working in the United Kingdom have also identified institutional sites as recreational venues. Multi-functional places such as churches, chapels and schools may have been established by workers themselves, by paternalistic employers, or may even have pre-dated industrialisation (see Hughes, 200, 2005, for a discussion of such buildings in Welsh industrial towns). One particularly well studied type of recreational venue consisted of places where alcohol was consumed. In England, research has focused on both inns (e.g. Boothroyd and Higgins, 2005) and public houses (e.g. Hutchinson, 1996), while in North America similar work has explored the archaeology of bars and saloons (e.g. Holder Spude, 2006; Seifert, 1991).

Thus Hagg Cottage residents would frequently have left their homes in order to participate in non-work activities. Some of their favoured establishments were located in the village of Alderley Edge and some in Nether Alderley. Oral histories indicated that the Trafford Arms Hotel of Alderley Edge village served as the local pub for male Hagg residents. In contrast, church and school-related activities were all closely tied to the traditional institutions of Nether Alderley (Mrs Edna Younger, ASP interviews, July and August 2003). This spatial differentiation may have partly reflected the short period of alcohol prohibition on the Stanley estate during the early years of the twentieth century (Mrs Edna Younger, ASP interviews, July 2003) – an atypical arrangement that appeared to reflect the paternalistic idiosyncrasies of one particular Stanley landlord. Close to the Hagg site was the Wizard of the Edge public house, possibly the traditional drinking establishment of the nineteenth-century Alderley miners, but by the 1920s the venue had been converted into a tearoom.

As detailed in the next chapter, community ties linked the Hagg residents with the parish of Nether Alderley. As a result, non-work activities related to longer-term hierarchical institutions – such as the church and school – were located in this traditional medieval village. The choice of the Trafford Arms as the favoured public house may have been motivated more by informal work ties than by formalised tenant and parishioner relations. By the early twentieth century the burgeoning rail commuter village of Alderley Edge was increasingly the location of work activities for the male residents of the Hagg. Thus the public house they would choose to drink in after work would be in that village.

Hagg residents would also have travelled farther than their local village for some recreational pastimes. Macclesfield, as the regional market town, may have been the destination for local fairs. From the early twentieth century cinemas were also becoming established in towns around Britain (Cook, 2000: 157). Both Mr Roy Barber (ASP interviews, August 2003) and Mrs Edna Younger (ASP interviews, August 2003) remembered being taken to the cinema in Manchester and Macclesfield by family members during the late 1920s. Although described as a special treat, cinema trips became increasingly affordable to working households over the inter-war decades. Hagg residents also increasingly participated in tourism from the late nineteenth century onwards. The word 'tourism' itself is only one which became embedded in the English language from the nineteenth century onwards (Burkart and Medlick, 1981: 3). Both the excavated assemblages and oral histories reflected the growing accessibility of holiday trips for working families over the industrial era.

Although certain spaces outside of the home were clearly linked with recreational activities, it was possible for *any* space to be constructed as a leisure space, including the home itself (Edensor, 2000; Lefebvre, 1991). While certain evidence supported the interpretation of leisure activities outside the immediate environment of the Hagg, most of this chapter examines recreational practices that occurred within and around this settlement site. In the following discussions, we chart the way in which recreational activities form a constituent part of daily domestic life (Beaudry *et al.*, 1991: 163). This focus on the domestic context of everyday leisure allows us to understand how recreational activities occurring away from the home became materially represented within the domestic sphere.

In order to approach the archaeology of recreation at the Hagg site, it has been necessary to attempt to segment artefacts relating to recreational activities from those discussed in Chapters 3 and 4. In the past artefacts did not easily fall within segregated realms of foodways, the creation of domestic space or recreational activities. They were instead entwined with the lived experiences and subjectivities of their users, causing them to cross-cut simple typological boundaries (Cochran and Beaudry, 2006). Previously introduced themes and classes of evidence are also interwoven within the material discussed below. The way in which leisure has become a consumer practice is considered and ceramic data previously introduced within the themes of foodways and of ornamenting the home are also included. To begin to discuss leisure practices we shall start with the artefacts relating to alcohol consumption at the site. Alcohol consumption in the industrial era has often been considered as a practice carried out predominantly in the public, male spaces of inns and public houses (Smith, 1983) such as the Trafford Arms of Alderley Edge village. The archaeological data from the Hagg site allow us to track the way in which alcohol was consumed in the home, and the importance of this as a recreational social practice within the domestic sphere.

Alcohol consumption at the Hagg

Drinking alcohol formed a common aspect of life at the Hagg site through all phases of occupation. One major change that does occur is the introduction of alcohol brewed on a mass industrial scale, with these new commodities marketed to consumers outside of the immediate region of manufacture. The types of alcohol consumed are also charted and the relative quantities of evidence for beer, spirit and wine consumption discussed in the context of wider practice in contemporaneous British society and overseas sites. The final point of interest within this section is the way in which oral history evidence documents one of the main ways of consuming alcohol at the site – that of home-brewed fruit wines. The limited archaeological visibility of this important practice is discussed, alongside the general significance of non-commercial informal alcohol for recreational life at the Hagg.

The history of alcohol consumption in England

In order to interpret the specific material evidence for alcohol consumption at the site, it is important to first consider the wider history of beer and alcohol production in England. Prior to the industrial era, it has been argued, domestic home brewing had been, alongside the baking of bread, one of the most economically important rural skills (Burnett, 1989: 49). Rather than being drunk for recreational purposes, in pre-industrial England beer formed part of the regular food intake of households. A significant shift in this pattern was caused by the introduction of tea as Britain became increasingly reliant on overseas colonial trade (Jamieson, 2001) and tea rapidly supplanted beer as the 'national drink' (Burnett, 1989: 175).

Alongside the increased availability of non-alcoholic beverages, wider social and mechanical changes also accounted for changing consumption patterns as beer transformed from the main household drink to a beverage tied only to recreational practices. Urbanisation, along with the introduction of long regular working hours for most adults, meant that it ceased to be practical for the majority of working families to brew at home. In terms of wider food and beverage production, beer brewing benefited from early mechanisation. By 1815 steam engines were in use by eleven breweries. These eleven were also England's foremost beer producers, brewing over 2 million barrels of beer a year (Burnett, 1989: 119).

The development of a modern transport infrastructure allowed the rapid distribution of bulk goods. It also impacted the availability of some beers to industrial-era consumers. Several English towns became centres of brewing over the early nineteenth century. By the mid-nineteenth century, half of England's total beer production was centred in Burton on Trent, Norwich, Liverpool and London (Burnett, 1989: 120). With the exception of London, railways played a crucial role in the growth of these centres, permitting large volumes of beer to be easily transported around the country from the 1830s onwards (Sigsworth, 1965: 544).

Continued mechanisation and industrialisation occurred in the British brewing industry throughout the late nineteenth century. Until the 1870s, beer brewing remained a seasonal activity – even at the largest commercial breweries: London-brewed porter, for example, between September and early June. And in Burton on Trent ale was brewed only between October and late April (Sigsworth, 1965: 563). This traditional pattern changed with the introduction of beer pasteurisation, perfected during the mid-1870s (Hull-Walski and Walski, 1994: 106; Sigsworth, 1965). Such rapid changes have been argued to make the brewing industry a precocious entry into the working-class consumer market – which expanded rapidly towards the end of the nineteenth century with increasing mechanisation of consumer goods such as boots, shoes and clothing (Dingle, 1972: 618). Turn-of-the-century improvements in glassware technology, such as bottling and capping, also had a significant impact on English beer production. This included the use of the Owens machine in 1898, which fully automated bottle manufacture, the decline of traditional opaque pewter or glazed ceramic beer mugs and the use of the crown cork to seal bottles (Sigsworth, 1965: 564; Jones *et al.*, 1989). Even by 1870, brewing had developed as an *industry*. Strengthened by the railway as a means of delivery, it formed the largest commercial food trade in Britain. Between 1880 and 1914, only forty-seven British firms accounted for approximately 45 per cent of all beer brewed in the country (Brunett, 1989: 120).

Set against this increasing dominance of brewing by large companies was the continued proliferation of smaller regional brewers. While they did not take such a large share in the market during the nineteenth century, they also remained significant producers. The taste of beer depended on the local water to a great extent, which was another factor in the location of certain towns as major brewing centres (Sigsworth, 1965: 543). Local producers brewed a range of types and strengths of beers aimed specifically at their surrounding market (Burnett, 1989: 120). Thus, despite a general trend towards industrial-scale production, regional specialisation continued into the twentieth century.

Trade directories can be used to gain a sense of the regional brewers in operation from the nineteenth century. The trade directories for Manchester and Salford in 1843 listed a total of eighty-seven breweries. The number of brewers in Manchester and Salford increased in the middle years of the nineteenth century, with 119 breweries listed in the 1854 directories (Hall, 2004: 55). The importance of local brewers was also highlighted by the collection of oral histories on commercial brands collected by Alice Hall (2004). All informants from north-west England recalled the full range of beer manufacturers represented by embossed bottles excavated from the Hagg Cottages. With the exception of Boddington's – originally a Manchester-based company but now an internationally marketed British beer brand – none of the Manchester, Stockport and Salford brewers was known by Hall's oral history participants from the south of England. Thus, even in the early decades of the twentieth century, local brewers remained an important component of beer consumption.

Although beer was the primary alcoholic beverage consumed in Britain during the late nineteenth century and early twentieth centuries, accounting for around 60 per cent of all alcohol sales (Dingle, 1972: 608), other types of alcoholic beverages were also consumed as part of recreational practices. Following beer, spirits (liquor) were the next most common type of alcohol drunk, forming around 30 per cent of alcohol consumption. As with beer, regional variations existed in patterns of spirit consumption. Gin and rum were the main types of spirits consumed in England, with locally distilled whiskies providing the preferred spirit in Scotland and Ireland (Dingle, 1972: 610).

The remainder of alcohol consumed consisted largely of wines and champagne. In the nineteenth century this was largely the preserve of the upper classes (Burnett, 1989: 80). In 1885 an estimate of the varying purchasing rates of alcohol by different social classes in Britain judged that the working classes purchased 75 per cent of all beers and spirits but only 10 per cent of all wine sold nationally. As wine bottles form a part of the Hagg Cottage assemblage, it is important to try and understand these within their broader context. In the global metropolis of nineteenth-century London, archaeological evidence suggests, wine may have been present in the recreational drinking patterns of the working classes. In the backfill of a brick-lined well used by the Crown public house, Lambeth Road, dating to the 1840s, several wine and liquor glasses, wine bottles and stemmed port and sherry glasses were recovered (Jeffries, 2006: 280). A nearby fill from a cesspit related to a tenement building occupation in the early 1850s also contained comparable evidence. Here both wine glasses and bottles were found, as was some pottery (in the form of spittoons), which may have been related to a nearby public house. Although these glasses and bottles all appear to have been related to wine consumption within the space of a public house, they are still suggestive that those living in poorer-quality housing in the capital city may have been drinking wine during the nineteenth century.

The assemblages from public houses in London also draw attention to the fact that during the nineteenth century there were major changes in the places that alcohol was consumed. The Beerhouse Act of 1830 had made licensing easier for public houses in Britain and increased the availability of beer generally (Burnett, 1989: 49). This was a continuation of the development of separate spaces for alcohol consumption during the period of urban expansion of the industrial era, also mirrored in North America (Rosenzweig, 1983). By the later nineteenth century, in urban areas of Britain, public drinking houses were regularly the foci of community life, criminal subculture, recreation, entertainment and sexual licence (Smith, 1983: 370). Victorian reformers in the nineteenth century viewed a clear connection between the 'excess of the drinking house evil' and criminal offences (Clay, 1857: 30).

In these public drinking houses gender divisions were clearly marked. In the understandings of working-class culture itself and in paternalistic discourses of 'respectability' in nineteenth-century Britain it was men only who populated public houses (Rose, 1993: 383). This was true in other nations also during this period. In mid-nineteenth-century Sydney the only women who frequented public bars were assumed to be prostitutes (Karskens, 1999: 164) and urban working-class bars in the United States were similarly gendered (Kingsdale, 1973: 473; Rosenzweig, 1983). In the rhetoric of Victorian reform in all of these countries, families and domesticity were seen as key to living a respectable life (Rose, 1993: 385). Such reformers urged the workers to eschew alcohol consumption as a leisure activity and instead participate in 'recreational relaxation', such as visiting parks, which could be shared by all family members. Reformers thought that this would produce a sober and respectable element into working-class society (Rosenzweig, 1983; Smith, 1983: 376).

Despite attempts at encouraging temperance, British industrial cities increasingly developed a male working-class drinking culture centred around popular public houses. Beer was called the 'quickest road out of Manchester' for Victorian working men in that city (Dingle, 1965: 543). Economic histories which track commercial alcohol sales have shown that it was agricultural counties in Britain that had the lowest *per capita* alcohol consumption over the period. Residents of these rural counties appear to have drunk far less alcohol when contrasted with industrial cities, ports and resort towns (Dingle, 1972: 622).

Excavated evidence from the Hagg site informed a range of archaeological questions. We can examine what kinds of alcohol were consumed in the homes of Hagg residents over time, and whether these beverages were home-brewed or commercially produced. The Hagg data also illuminated the domestic-based consumption of alcohol during the industrial era. Previous studies of urban communities have suggested that women may have purchased beer from public bars to bring home for consumption (Karskens, 1999: 162). Perhaps the Hagg Cottages provided a space for recreational drinking in which gendered practices were very different from those of public spaces. We can also examine the ways in which rural households participated in the purchase of national brands and test whether these rural working-class households materially appeared as low consumers of alcohol.

Drinking at the Hagg

Most of the evidence for alcohol consumption at the Hagg site comes from glass bottles that would have once held various kinds of alcoholic beverages. Through beer, wine and spirit bottles it is possible to begin to reconstruct some of the patterns of drinking at the site. Glass bottle remains are sometimes problematic, as they are often reused for other substances and may also have been returned to the bottler (Busch, 2000; Cook, 1989a; Casella, 2002). Nevertheless, the glass bottle assemblage from the site provides an entry point into understanding the different kinds of alcohol that were consumed in the home over time.

From the analysed material in Area A, 16 per cent of the total glass bottle and container assemblage sampled for analysis were clearly identifiable as alcohol bottles. This proportion may have been artificially lowered by the unusually large number of sauce and condiment bottles recovered from this excavation area. This proportional figure represented in total thirteen beer bottles, three wine bottles and fifteen quart bottles. Almost all of these dated to the early twentieth century. The wine and quart bottles were largely undiagnostic with regard to their precise contents. The only exception to this was a single clear glass quart bottle bearing the remains of a paper label for Vamour Vermouth, a type of low-strength spirit.

Only a single example of the beer bottles from Area A appeared to pre-date the twentieth century. This was blue-green in colour and had no embossed writing or label indicating the beer manufacturer. The remaining beer bottles all dated to the twentieth century. They were made from brown and green glass and represented a variety of North West regional companies, all from Manchester or the neighbouring towns of Stockport and Salford. The majority of these beer bottles were also clustered within the southernmost Area A cottage, suggesting that beer consumption was higher in the Barber family household than in the Perrin household of the northern cottage. One beer manufacturer was represented with a much greater frequency than those of other brewers. Eight of the thirteen total beer bottles from Area A were embossed with the name of the brewery Groves & Whitnall, Salford (Figure 5.1). The other embossed beer bottles were each single examples of different breweries. The now well known brand Boddington's (Figure 5.2), discussed above in the context of oral historical evidence, was embossed on one bottle. The other bottles were embossed with the brewers F. Robinson, Stockport, John Grundy, Stockport, G. Ray & Sons and Bell & Co. Ltd, Stockport.

Approximately 31 per cent of the Area B glass bottle and container assemblage consisted of alcohol-related bottles. The higher proportion of alcohol bottles in this excavation area also represented lower quantities of condiment bottles and jars within these assemblages. While the general amount of alcohol consumed between the two households may have been similar, the type consumed by the Area B residents appeared to have differed from those of Area A. Wine bottles represented a surprisingly high number of the total Area B bottles (Figure 5.3), with nine represented in the assemblage in contrast to the three from Area A. None of the recovered wine bottles was embossed or labelled. Some of the evidence relating to them is suggestive

Figure 5.1   Beer bottle, 'Groves & Whitnall, Salford', Alderley Sandhills Project, 2003

that wine may have formed a part of the drinking habits of the Area B householders prior to the nineteenth century.

In contrast only two beer bottles and a single quart bottle were included within the Area B assemblage. Of these beer bottles, one was unembossed and dated to the late nineteenth century. The other dated to the early twentieth century and was embossed 'Wray & Ward, Manchester'. The quart bottle was unembossed and dated to the early twentieth century. A final bottle from Area B was also embossed 'Daniel Judson & Son Mixing Liquid' and dated from the mid to late nineteenth century.

As with proportions of sauce bottles, previously discussed in Chapter 3, Area D contained an alcohol-related assemblage that proportionally fell between those recovered from Areas A and B. This related to just four beer bottles and a single quart bottle. The four beer bottles were all embossed with the names of Stockport brewers, replicating some of the beer brand choices from the Area A assemblage. One of these bottles dated from the late nineteenth century and was embossed 'Frederick Robinson, Stockport'. The three other beer bottles all dated to the early twentieth century. Two of these were embossed 'Groves & Whitnall, Stockport' and one with the brewer 'Bell & Co. Ltd, Stockport'. The quart bottle appeared to relate to a product

Figure 5.2   Beer bottle, 'Boddingtons, Manchester', Alderley Sandhills Project, 2003

manufactured by one of the beer brewers. It was embossed 'Bell & Co. Ltd, Stockport' and dated to the early twentieth century, contemporaneous with the beer bottle from the same brewer.

   In addition to glass bottles that would have held alcoholic beverages, glass, ceramic and metal artefact data are available to evince the way in which alcohol may have been served and drunk at the Hagg. Some glass tablewares related to alcohol consumption. From the Area A assemblage a single clear-glass bell-shaped decanter, decorated with vertical ribs, was recovered. This dated to the mid-nineteenth century. From Area B two glass drinking vessels were also recovered. One was a mid to late nineteenth-century facet-cut wineglass, quite a fine piece of glass tableware. A second wineglass dated to the late nineteenth or early twentieth century. This was also made of clear glass, but was manufactured with the inexpensive press-moulding technique (Figure 5.4). Area D yielded a single drinking glass, smaller than the wineglasses from Area B, suggesting that it may have been intended for port or sherry. Manufactured from clear glass, it was undecorated, and dated to the late nineteenth century. Two metal corkscrews were also included in the Area A assemblage. These were difficult to date, but

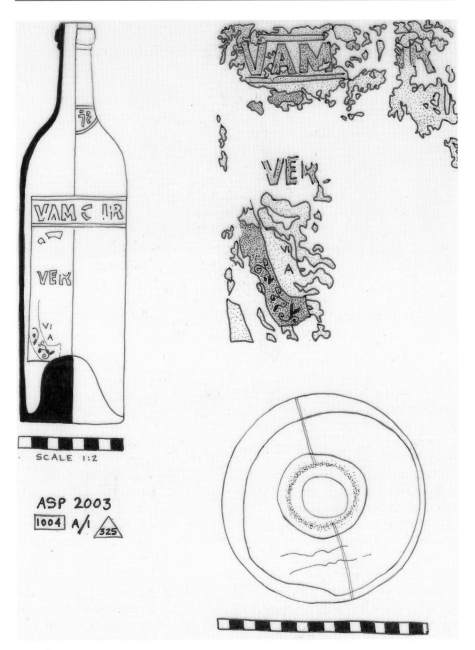

SCALE 1:2

ASP 2003
1004 A/1 325

Figure 5.3   Vermouth bottle, Alderley Sandhills Project, 2003

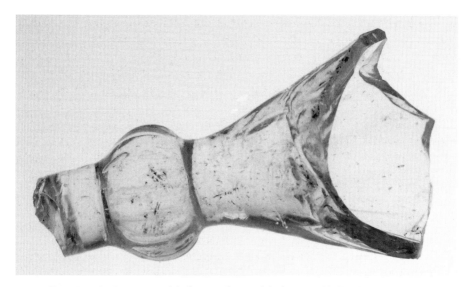

Figure 5.4   Press-moulded wineglass, Alderley Sandhills Project, 2003

despite the small numbers of wine bottles recovered from these trenches, twentieth-century cottage residents had access to wine, and thus needed to possess corkscrews.

The ceramic data presented in Chapter 3 can also be revisited in order to gain further insight on alcohol consumption at the Hagg Cottages. Of particular interest were mugs, as these commonly served for the consumption of beer prior to and throughout the Victorian era. Indeed, glass beer vessels superseded ceramic drinking mugs only when mechanisation reduced the cost of glass vessels over the early twentieth century (Sigsworth, 1965: 546). In total, mugs formed 6 per cent of the identified ceramic assemblage from the Hagg site, equalling that of teacups. While not all mugs were necessarily used for drinking beer, a significant number would have been, particularly given the importance of beer as a daily drink within the English diet.

The different proportions of ceramic ware types illuminate temporal patterns of mug use at the Hagg site. Of the slipwares, which form some of the earlier domestic wares at the site, 19 per cent were mugs. In contrast only 1 per cent of the identified creamwares and only 2 per cent of the pearlwares were mugs, although these low proportions may be related to the fact that these were both fine tablewares. In the later whitewares and porcelain/ bone china vessels, mugs continued to comprise an important element of the vessels represented. Surprisingly mugs become proportionally higher in both of these ware types as compared to earlier wares. Of the identifiable whiteware vessels 7 per cent were mugs, with 14 per cent of the porcelain/ bone china ceramic assemblage identified as mugs. The growth in mug forms in these later wares may not necessarily relate to increases in beer consumption, but may also represent changes in hot beverage consumption. Mugs are the most common form of vessels for drinking tea and coffee in the majority of British households today. It may be that it was during the phase of whiteware and porcelain/bone china use that mugs began to be an acceptable vessel for tea and coffee drinking, alongside cups.

As well as the mug data, some of the other ceramic forms may also have been used for beer and alcohol consumption. Four per cent of the identified brown glazed coarsewares appeared in jug forms. These may have been used to store and serve beer. Only in the nineteenth century with the increased mechanisation of glass bottle manufacture and growth of commercial brewing do beer bottles appear in the Hagg Cottage assemblage. Prior to this time ceramic vessels may have played the main role for both storage and serving beers, whether home-brewed or bought from other producers.

Drawing together the historical background and material data, alcohol consumption practices at the Hagg site suggested some interesting patterns. In the earliest phases of the site the slipware mugs and brown-glazed coarseware jugs may have indicated daily practices of beer consumption within the rural farming households. Women in the seventeenth and eighteenth centuries would have been fully involved in the home brewing of beer, and the beverage would have been drunk by all household members as a regular part of their daily diet. If beer was not brewed at the Hagg site itself, then it would have been purchased direct from neighbouring farms rather than from commercial breweries. The lack of mugs manufactured from creamware and pearlware suggests perhaps that beer mugs may not have formed part of 'genteel' table settings, with pewter or leather vessels perhaps being used to serve beer at the table. In the eighteenth century, tea may also have been replacing beer as the main beverage at mealtimes, with higher proportions of teacups than mugs manufactured from both creamwares and pearlwares (see Chapter 3).

Later beer drinking practices seemed to differ from these early assemblages. The nineteenth- and early twentieth-century beer bottles demonstrated the impact of industrialisation upon the British market. From the Victorian era onwards, beer consumers made choices from a range of manufactured goods on which to spend their household income. The late nineteenth century has been argued to be the peak period of beer consumption in Britain (Burnett, 1989: 107). Historically we know that beer would have been a constituent part of the lives of later nineteenth-century Hagg Cottage residents, as the 1881 census includes George Leaman, a 'commercial agent' for a brewery. We do not know which brewery employed him, or the exact nature of his job. Nonetheless, the very fact that a brewery required an agent demonstrated the commercial character of the late Victorian brewing industry. Beer brewers prior to industrialisation had no need of sales persons for their products. It is interesting that so few of the beer bottles from the Hagg assemblage date to the late nineteenth century. Perhaps a brewer's commercial agent would have been particularly vigilant in returning valuable glass bottles to his employer.

In the mid and late nineteenth century the male mineworkers may also have been fitting within the trends for urban workers and mostly consumed beer in nearby public houses. The lack of beer bottles from the nineteenth century could also be evidence of the increasing segmentation and separation of beer drinking as a recreational practice from the domestic sphere. It is difficult to reconstruct spirit-drinking practices from this period. While we clearly have a range of bottles that date to this phase of the cottages occupation, their lack of labelling or embossed wording makes it impossible to suggest the types of spirits people were drinking.

The beer bottles dating to the early twentieth century allow a consideration of consumer choice in beer-drinking practice. The evidence from the Hagg Cottages clearly shows a preference for beers manufactured by Salford and Stockport breweries. Whilst from the historical data discussed earlier we know that there was a proliferation of smaller breweries in these urban centres, it is interesting that it is these smaller breweries which appear to have had networks of delivery outside of their immediate urban area, to rural sites such as the Hagg Cottages. Given the historical trends in the increase in large-scale breweries, with supporting transport allowing them to distribute their product nationally, it is interesting to note that not a single non-regionally local beer appears to have been bought by Hagg residents. From the sample of bottles available it appeared that the Area A householders who were drinking beer had a clear preference for Groves & Whitnall's beers, with secondary choices from a range of Stockport breweries. Further contemporary assemblages are required from British rural sites in order to assess whether this represents the personal preferences of a single household, or whether archaeological data in fact contradict historical arguments for the dominance of nationally branded beers. The choice in beers by the southernmost of the Area A cottage households, as with the choice in ornaments by the different households, was not simply random. The people making the choices had particular desires when they did so, in this case the desire to enjoy a beer with a specific *taste*. In choosing Salford and Stockport beers against national products the Hagg beer consumers may also have been specifically choosing locally known products.

The data for the Hagg Cottages also raise some interesting questions about the home as a context of alcohol consumption. We have already suggested that in the nineteenth century local public houses may have been the main venue for alcohol consumption by male household members. Oral historical evidence suggested that this was still a regular part of behaviour for the adult male cottage residents during the early twentieth century (Mrs Molly Pitcher, ASP interviews, July 2003). Why then is there such clear evidence for the home consumption of commercial beers in the early twentieth century? Multiple interpretations provide plausible explanations for this material patterning. It may have been that an elderly male household member in the early twentieth century could no longer easily walk to the local public house. Alternatively it may have been that female household members also liked to drink beer, despite their exclusion from public houses through the dictates of socially acceptable norms of behaviour. Archaeological evidence from sites such as the Hagg Cottages has the opportunity to provide an interesting foil to working-class histories of nineteenth- and early twentieth-century Britain which focus on beer consumption as an almost exclusively male and non-domestic recreational practice. In doing so it may be possible in future to further explore the social importance of consumer choices of beer drinking in a range of social contexts of industrial-era Britain.

Detailed studies of workers' turn-of-the-century drinking patterns in the United States have discussed the importance of non-licensed commercial drinking places within domestic houses (Rosenszweig, 1983). In nineteenth-century Sydney, Australia, although respectable working-class women were socially prohibited from drinking in bars, this did not mean that they did not consume alcohol. Women went to hotels, or sent their children to fill jugs and decanters with beer and spirits that they could then drink at home. Although drinking was similarly gendered in nineteenth-century Sydney as it was in cities such as Manchester and London, this was gendered differentially between bars and domestic locales (Karskens, 1999: 164). But the practices of drinking may have related to localised social norms and we cannot simply apply the practices of nineteenth-century North American and Australian urban residents to their contemporaries of rural England. The patterns of socialisation that took place at the Hagg Cottages, in relation to recreational drinking, were clearly not limited only to drinking in public houses. Beer consumption in the home may have allowed Hagg residents to maintain an air of social respectability. A degree of sobriety may have been actively cultivated by the site occupants through minimising visitations to the public house in favour of home drinking.

The oral historical evidence of fruit wine production also intersects with our arguments here in an interesting manner. The wine bottle evidence from Area B does show a trend towards these households drinking wines rather than beers. Home-made fruit wines may also have been consumed. Mrs Edna Younger had vivid recollections of the neighbouring Ellam sisters brewing a range of fruit and vegetable wines in their half of the subdivided Area A cottage:

> You'll find a lot of bottles where it was Miss Ellams'. I mean, they brewed everything that grew – rhubarb wine! And of course, none of it was alcoholic, it was 'medicinal'. And then you came out and saw things twice!
> (Mrs Edna Younger, ASP interviews, July 2003)

Home-brewing wines appeared to have been a common practice among the working of the Alderley region. Mrs Younger also spoke of her great grand-mother and great grandfather, who had lived in a nearby cottage at Welsh Row (discussed in greater detail in Chapter 6), similarly brewing wines from different fruits. Mrs Younger remembered as a child seeing a 'whole lot of bottles' containing these wines in her great grandmother's pantry (Mrs Edna Younger, ASP interviews, July 2003).

Thus home brewing and the home consumption of these non-commercial beverages provided an important part of recreational practice for these rural cottagers. The imbibing of fruit wines is a practice ignored by the main-stream of histories of alcohol drinking among the working classes in the industrial era, as these tend to be centred on urban groups and on economic data which exclude home production (e.g. Dingle, 1972; Sigsworth, 1965). The archaeology of home brewing at rural working-class sites may be one way in which a more nuanced historical understanding of industrial-era alcohol consumption practices can be created. The assertion by historians that agricultural counties may have drunk less alcohol than their urban compatriots may be countered with evidence to suggest that rural drinking patterns differed significantly from those in industrial urban centres, even in the commercialised period of the early twentieth century.

Overall, the archaeological evidence for alcohol consumption at the Hagg Cottages presented a significant study of the consumer preferences and non-commercial brewing practices in a small-group households. Importantly, these disrupted the general historical narrative created for workers' drink-ing patterns over the industrial era. Although representative of a single community, the artefact assemblage clearly showed that rural communities were different from those of urban centres in their recreational practices. As further research is undertaken in historical archaeology of these later periods at British sites an exciting avenue of work may be the deepening of under-standings of drinking at a range of different sites. Archaeology clearly has a great deal to contribute to this particular aspect of British social history through the reconstruction of household consumption patterns.

Aerated waters and beverages

Fizzy drinks and mineral waters formed a second type of beverage con-sumption related to everyday recreational practices. Alongside techno-logical changes which altered the means of production and consumption of alcoholic beverages, rapid changes in glassmaking technology over the late nineteenth century made a new range of commercially produced non-alcoholic beverages available to Hagg Cottage residents (McNeil and Newman, 2006b: 189). Because of the sampling strategy developed for post-excavation analysis, very few of the non-alcoholic glass bottles recovered

Figure 5.5   Internal screw bottle stoppers, Alderley Sandhills Project, 2003

from Area A were subjected to specialist work. These materials included a single clear-glass elliptical mineral water bottle, embossed 'Salford', and several bottle stoppers that would have been used to seal non-alcoholic beverages (Figure 5.5).

In Area B a total of four mineral water bottle tops were recovered. One of these was moulded with a chequered pattern, and contained no company name. The second was marked 'Sumner Fulwood', and the remaining two were both marked 'Spardal Mineral Water Co. Ltd, Manchester'. Further evidence for non-alcoholic beverage consumption at the Hagg appeared in the form of four stoneware bottles dating from the late nineteenth century. Since all were unmarked, original contents could not be precisely determined, although bottles of this type were typically used for ginger beer. Two of these stoneware bottles were recovered from Area A; Areas B and D each contained a single example. The relative absence of glass mineral water bottles from the Hagg Cottage assemblages might have resulted from recycling activities, with residents returning empty containers to their local supplier. But when considered in combination with the bottle stoppers and ceramic bottles, archaeological evidence clearly demonstrated that occupants enjoyed non-alcoholic commercially prepared beverages.

The pattern of non-alcoholic drink consumption can be placed within a wider social context. Excavations at the contemporary English sites of Coalbrookdale (Belford and Ross, 2004: 223) and Kingsway (Oxford Archaeology North/John Samuels Consultants, 2006: 51) both recovered non-alcoholic drink bottles that were regionally rather than nationally sourced. The Hagg site data, whilst limited, seemed to follow this pattern of obtaining mineral waters via local supply routes – including Manchester-based companies like the Spardal Mineral Water Company. In contrast, excavations of contemporary sites in the United States suggested that American national companies began to dominate the non-alcoholic drinks market from the early twentieth century. The ever-ubiquitous 'Coke' bottle, for example, has been recovered from supposedly isolated sites, including cabins in the Blue Ridge mountains in Virginia (Horning, 2002: 139). Thus an emphasis on locally produced non-alcoholic beverages may potentially reflect a particularly English pattern of consumption.

As with most other categories of evidence, the late nineteenth through early twentieth centuries witnessed an growing shift to selection of mass-produced products, including beer and non-alcoholic beverages intended for recreational use within the home. A complex pattern, it appears that the choices made by Hagg Cottage occupants drew upon local tastes and supply networks. Since these items simultaneously reflected individual practices and tastes, greater regional and national comparative data are required before the commercial dynamics of this emerging regional market can be full understood.

Artefact evidence on beverage consumption also clearly indicated continued reliance on home-made alcohol, particularly in the form of fruit wines. This prevents us from simply glossing over changes in alcohol consumption at the site as a straightforward adoption of commercial products over those made within the community itself. It also adds a further layer of complexity to the changes and continuities of rural domestic recreation over the late nineteenth and early twentieth centuries. Interpreting the multiplicity of changing practices and social meanings within the realm of recreation is one we continue as we move forward to discuss evidence relating to tobacco smoking at the site.

Tobacco consumption at the Hagg

The data relating to tobacco consumption at the Hagg spans the entire known occupation of the site. In total, tobacco-related artefacts analysed totalled 185 clay tobacco pipe fragments, of which there were forty-nine bowls, 132 stems and four mouthpieces. In addition to this clay-pipe material, excavations recovered a single briar-pipe bowl, manufactured from a Mediterranean bush, and nine Vulcanite mouthpieces which would have attached to this organic pipe bowl. Since tobacco pipes are common throughout post-medieval sites, were short-lived in their use, and changed rapidly in both form and shape, they are ideal for the purposes of dating sites and soil deposits. Studies of clay tobacco pipes commonly focus on chronological sequences, with the diameter of pipe stem bores used to precisely date early post-medieval English and colonial North American sites

(Binford, 1962; Harrington, 1978). A reliance on these artefacts pervades even contemporary studies of tobacco pipes on archaeological sites (e.g. Mallios, 2005).

The importance of tobacco pipes

Interpretations of this important artefact category have also moved beyond simple chronological analysis. Scholarship has particularly emphasised the potential of clay tobacco pipes as indicators of past social roles. One early example of these studies (Cook, 1989c: 209) examined the clay-pipe data from the Boott Mills site of Lowell, Massachusetts. Cook argued that social class, gender and ethnicity were the primary factors in influencing past tobacco use, with minor choices such as whether to chew or smoke tobacco reflecting wider aspects of personal presentation and social identity (Cook, 1989b: 215). Recent studies have applied this social approach within Australia (Gojak and Stuart, 1999), North America (Brighton, 2004) and Europe (Hartnett, 2004). Through this literature, archaeological data relating to past use of tobacco offers a powerful tool for interpreting the common process of tobacco consumption as an essentially social practice.

Like tea consumption, the British history of clay tobacco pipes links directly to the history of colonial expansion into North America from the seventeenth century. Objects have complex genealogies of both form and use (Gosden, 2005) which can reveal the commonly 'hidden' colonial histories of regions such as the north-west of England (Poulter, 2006). The idea that everyday goods consumed within European households were enmeshed in complex world colonial relations is not a new one (see for instance Mintz, 1985, on sugar). A crop globally distributed as a result of European colonial activity in the Americas, tobacco production was enmeshed within the power relations of empire – particularly given its long history of production by enslaved Africans on British plantations. Thus smoking paraphernalia are in many ways analogous to the material culture of tea drinking, with both sets of objects providing an archaeology of colonial relations (Jamieson, 2001; Gosden, 2004).

Tobacco pipes and teapots took forms known from colonial contexts, which were then continually modified to suit changing tastes and technologies in Britain and other industrialised nations. The very fact that clay tobacco pipes became the common means of tobacco smoking in England represented a particular trajectory of colonial engagement. As a result of its close links with South American indigenous populations who smoked cigars, this particular form of tobacco consumption grew popular within Spain. Conversely, British colonists interacted with North American indigenous populations who traditionally smoked their tobacco from clay pipes (Baram, 1999; Orser, 1996: 127). What is important to consider with regard to the Hagg data is that clay tobacco pipes were not an apolitical object of recreational activity. The very existence, and specific material form, of these artefacts represented broader patterns of empire and acquisition.

Tobacco consumption evidence

The earliest tobacco pipe artefacts recovered from the Hagg Cottages were all found within Area B trenches. These artefacts were crucial to dating some of the earliest wall foundation cuts. Only a small proportion of the pipe data relates to this initial occupation phase. The earliest possible date of manufacture for any pipes found within Area B was *c.* 1610. Most of the pipe data from the area post-dated this. A distinct clustering of material dating between *c.* 1640 and *c.* 1710 appeared to entirely relate to contexts associated with the initial construction and occupation of the site in Area B. Of the seventeenth-century pipe material from Area B, the most complete early bowl fragment dated to between *c.* 1650 and 1670 (Figure 5.6A). This was a typical local product of the period, undecorated with a milled and bottered rim. While clay pipes in the North West region may have been imported from as far away as Brosley in south Shropshire, even in the seventeenth century (McNeil and Newman, 2006a: 162), it seems, the earliest residents at the Hagg site were sourcing their clay pipes from local manufacturers.

The majority of clay-pipe material from the site as a whole dated to between *c.* 1740 and 1950. This material appeared to be associated with the occupation phases of which we understand the most, including the final inhabitants of the early twentieth century. The forty-nine clay-pipe bowl fragments mostly dated to these later phases. Of these, six had decorated bowls or spurs of some kind, all of which dated to the nineteenth century. One fragmentary bowl, displaying a leaf-decorated seam, had a wide date range, spanning the nineteenth century. Two pipe bowls were decorated with Masonic motifs. The first of these was in five fragments, and dated to between *c.* 1810 and *c.* 1840. It contained several decorative elements; leaf-decorated seams, moulded milling, enclosed flutes and a panel (to the smoker's right) containing Masonic motifs. The second pipe bowl decorated with Masonic motifs was slightly later. It dated to between *c.* 1830 and *c.* 1860 and had a square and compass motif moulded on to the bowl (Figure 5.6B).

A more complete artefact was a long-stemmed pipe with a ring-and-dot motif on the spur, datable to the middle years of the nineteenth century, *c.* 1840 to *c.* 1870. A tall and elegant pipe bowl, dating between *c.* 1810 and *c.* 1850 was another visibly decorated example. This consisted of raised 'ribs' on the lower part of the bow, and the seams were decorated with panels of leaves. It also probably had a spur, although this had broken off. The final decorated bowl dated between *c.* 1840 and *c.* 1870, with narrow

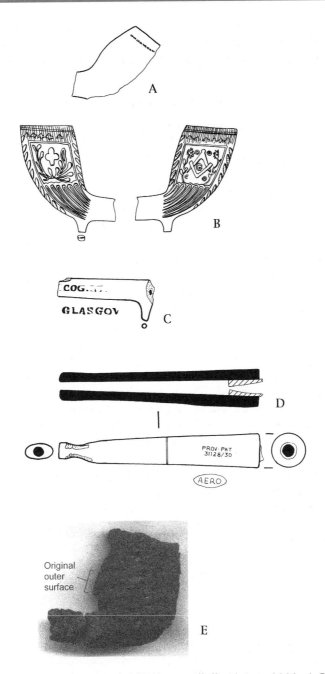

Figure 5.6 Tobacco artefacts, Alderley Sandhills Project, 2003. *A* Clay pipe heel bowl, *c.* 1650–70. *B* Clay pipe mould decorated bowl with Masonic motif, *c.* 1810–40. *C* Clay pipe stem marked COGHILL/GLASGOW, *c.* 1826–1904. *D* Vulcanite pipe mouthpiece, *c.* 1930+. *E* Briar pipe bowl, 'Billiard' type, *c.* 1880+

flutes on the lower bowl, broad panels above, leaf-decorated seams and a ring-and-dot motif either side of the spur. In addition to these bowls, nine plain bowls, with a date range of *c.* 1810 to *c.* 1860, were recovered and had leaf-decorated seams. Some of these also had dots on the spur and seams. The remaining pipe-bowl fragments were either from undecorated bowls, or were too fragmentary for any decoration to be discerned.

Over half of the clay-pipe artefacts (132 in total) were stem pieces only. The majority of these were fragmentary, and provided little information. Due to a general standardisation in manufacturing techniques, only clay-pipe stems made before about 1800 proved useful as date indicators (Gojak and Stuart, 1999; Mallios, 2005: 90). Most of the pipe stems from the Hagg assemblage postdated this, and were unmarked. Their fragmentary nature also made it difficult to reach firm conclusions as to the length of the pipe stems from which they had come, potentially an important tool in understanding the social meanings of clay pipes (Cook, 1989b). A single-faceted ground mouthpiece stem was most probably used for the secondary purpose of marking surfaces, akin to the way one might use a piece of chalk. Pipe stems used for such purposes have been found throughout Yorkshire and other parts of England as early as the seventeenth century.

Three pipe-stem fragments did, however, stand out from this assemblage. One example recovered from Area B held traces of green lead glaze. Although dated from *c.* 1750 to *c.* 1850, such a glaze on pipes was in fashion from around 1800 and had ceased to be used by around 1900. Two pipe stems were stamped with the names of their manufacturer, both of which were based in Glasgow. The first, unusually manufactured from red clay, was stamped 'W. White/Glasgow' on the side. This would have been made by William White & Son, a prolific company which manufactured pipes from 1846 through 1955. William White & Son were known to have made use of the distinctive red clay for pipe manufacture during the nineteenth century. The second marked pie was stamped 'Coghill/Glasgow' (Figure 5.6C). Coghill's were a successful pipe maker from Glasgow and operated between about 1826 and 1904.

Tobacco was one of the first commodities of colonialism to be mass-consumed in seventeenth-century European societies (Shammas, 1994: 179). Such consumption was particularly important in the North West region, which was intimately connected with Atlantic trade from the seventeenth century onwards through the port of Liverpool. Therefore alongside the growth of the port came the development of secondary industries related to these colonial products, particularly sugar refining and clay-pipe manufacture (McNeil and Newman, 2006a: 162). Similarly, the demand for tobacco in England drove its growth and production in Virginia plantations, affecting settlement patterns there (Deetz, 1993; Matthews, 2001; Noël Hume, 1982). The earliest clay-pipe evidence thus suggested that Hagg Cottage residents of the seventeenth century maintained access to tobacco, a luxury product only recently imported in bulk quantities.

While the particular milled and bottered rim-finishing technique located the early pipe fragments within the north-west of England, their overall form drew on forms adapted from Native Americans of the Virginia and Middle Atlantic coastline of the United States, with whom English colonists had the closest contact. Such artefacts begin to demonstrate the complexities of the way in which colonial goods entered the everyday world of English residents. Tobacco pipes, as with teapots, highlight the way in which seemingly mundane British artefacts were part of the wider material process of transatlantic colonialism (Gosden, 2004).

By the nineteenth century, when the clay-pipe assemblage from the Hagg Cottages became more abundant, tobacco importation to Britain was well established. Due to the fragmentary nature of the Hagg pipe data it is not possible to know whether Hagg Cottage residents were smoking long-stemmed 'churchwarden' pipes or shorter straight-stemmed variants. However, the collection did produce data related to the decorative motifs on the pipe bowls. While seventeenth-century pipe manufacturers were experimenting with a novel kind of recreational object, pipe manufacturing was a widespread British trade by the nineteenth century and was particularly extensive across the North West region. Pipe manufacturers existed in most towns, with factories operating from Carlisle in the north of the region to Northwich in the south, although often with just a single pipe maker in any one town (McNeil and Newman, 2006b: 186).

Such widespread manufacture means that we can reasonably speak of consumer choice in clay pipes by the Victorian era. Purchasers of pipes could likely choose from a range of designs and styles. Selections therefore may have indicated desired group affiliations and the social image the purchaser wished to present to others as they smoked (Cook, 1989a). The designs of the clay pipes from the Hagg site were therefore part of active processes of personal identification by cottage residents. Whilst much of this may simply have been related to general trends and prevailing tastes, such as the leaves, ribs, ring-and-dot motifs and fluting, some of these may have been related to quite specific aspects of personal identity. It would be interesting to speculate as to the kinds of identities that the smokers of the pipes with Masonic motifs wished to project within their community. Whist these motifs may simply have been a fashion of the time, they may also have been intended to communicate a particular aspect of the social identity of the smoker, as were patriotic motifs used by immigrants to New York's Five Points neighbourhood during the nineteenth century (Reckner, 2001).

The local identities of smokers may have been important in the choice of all elements of designs. While the available sample of clay tobacco pipe evidence from the Hagg was too small to be able to draw any firm comparative conclusions, it is worth noting some of the potential comparisons with other contemporaneous English sites. From a fill in the well of the Crown public house, in the Lambeth district of London, clay tobacco pipes were recovered with a date range spanning from 1820 to 1860 (Jeffries, 2006: 280). The majority of the decorated stems from this site had a wheat motif. Such a motif was entirely absent from the Hagg Cottages assemblage, thus raising the interesting possibility of regionally distinct pipe decorations within nineteenth-century Britain. As previously discussed in Chapter 2, miners from the south-west of England had relocated to the Hagg site for local industrial employment. Subtle difference in the decoration of clay pipes may have therefore provided a small material symbol of non-local regional identities.

The marked pipe stems also allow tracing of the routes of consumer practice. While clay pipes were being produced locally (McNeil and Newman, 2006b: 186), Hagg Cottage smokers appear to have purchased at least some from large-scale pipe manufacturers in Glasgow. Both makers' marks recovered from the Hagg pipes could be found in contemporary sites around the world. Pipes manufactured by Coghill's and William White & Son were found in nineteenth-century contexts in Old Sacramento, California (Humphrey, 1969), the Boott Mills boarding house and tenement site in Lowell, Massachusetss (Cook, 1989b), and numerous Australian sites (Gojak and Stuart, 1999: 43). The American Revolution also altered the purchasing patterns of tobacco pipes in the United States, with a wider range of European-manufactured pipes available to American smokers (Mallios, 2005: 101). By 1867 the Glasgow company of William White & Son alone was producing over 700 varieties of clay pipe (Humphrey, 1969: 18). Nineteenth-century tobacco smokers at the Hagg Cottages, in Australia and North America (Gojak and Stuart, 1999; Humphrey, 1969) shared similar consumption patterns in their selection of pipes. For archaeologists, clay pipes offer an opportunity to begin to understand international patterns of consumerism that shaped the global distribution of manufactured goods (Appadurai, 1996). As commodity production intensified, markets became flooded with products of particular manufacturers – in this case, Scottish pipe manufacturers – who came to dominate the international export market over the nineteenth century (Gojak and Stuart, 1999: 43). Thus local and regional preferences may have fed back to the pipe manufacturers, influencing pipe designs distributed through both the internal and export markets.

Briar pipes

The final period in which pipes were used at the site was the early twentieth century. By this point materials other than clay were being utilised for pipe manufacture in Britain. An unusual find from Area A was that of a single briar-pipe bowl, manufactured from the root burl of the white heather tree, a species commonly grown in North Africa. As an organic material, such pipe bowls rarely survive within archaeological contexts, and the surface of the Hagg briar pipe bowl had severely degraded (Figure 5.6D). Briar pipe bowls were first manufactured in England in 1879 (Linney, 1924: 106). By 1900 their manufacture had rapidly expanded and they were being produced by a range of factories in numerous styles. Pattern books from the period show these styles, named in words relating to the tastes and political sentiments of the date, including the 'Dublin', 'Apple', 'Bulldog' and 'Rhodesian'. The Hagg bowl was identified as a 'Billiard' style. As smoking fashions changed, briar pipes quickly supplanted clay pipes as the popular material for pipe manufacture. By the 1920s the increased popularity of cigarette smoking forced the majority of clay tobacco pipe manufacturers to cease production.

In the same context within Area A as the briar pipe bowl, nine Vulcanite pipe mouthpieces were recovered. Seven of these were within the northern half of the Area A cottage, with the remaining two from the southern half. As with the briar pipe, these were unusual among British archaeological assemblages. Vulcanite mouthpieces were intended for use with briar pipes, and their forms and styles were advertised alongside briar-pipe bowls in the trade catalogues of briar-pipe manufacturers of the late nineteenth and early twentieth centuries. Vulcanite was an innovative material for nineteenth-century manufacturers, created through the vulcanisation of natural rubber with sulphur, a process discovered only in 1839 which was then refined throughout the 1840s. Pipe mouthpieces of vulcanite first appeared in England from 1878 (Dunhill, 1977: 197) and their use has continued by pipe smokers to the present day.

The trade advertisements for these mouthpieces provide both their specific forms and link them with the types of briar-pipe bowls to which they could have been attached. Two of those from the southern half of Area A for instance were of a 'saddle' type. One was circular in section and could have been used with a range of briar-pipe bowls. The second of these 'saddle' mouthpieces was more unusual. It was square in section, and is therefore most likely to have been used with the Bulldog or Rhodesian pipe bowl forms. One of the vulcanite mouthpieces from the northern half of Area A, as with earlier clay mouthpieces, was marked. Unlike nineteenth-century pipe stems with simple manufacturers' names, these linked the vulcanite mouthpieces with specific registered designs. On this particular example (Figure 5.6C) the lettering 'Aero' in an oval was stamped to the smoker's left. On the smoker's right is the lettering 'Prov. pat.' above the number 31128/30. 'Prov. Pat.' was the abbreviation for 'provisional patent', suggesting that the patent for this particular mouthpiece had not been completely registered at the time of its manufacture. The number 31128 related to the patent number, with the suffix /30 denoting the year of the patent – in this case 1930 (P. Hammond, pers. comm.). As well as the shapes and marks affixed to Vulcanite mouthpieces by their manufacturers, seven of the nine examples from Area A also had evidence of tooth wear, suggesting continual use by their owners. When this briar pipe evidence is taken as a part of the larger tobacco pipe data, it showed the ways in which technology influenced prevailing fashions. As vulcanite became available for mouthpieces, pipes could be made from new durable materials. Advances in technology, such as the use of briar pipes with Vulcanite mouthpieces, were not limited to the materials and styles in which pipes were manufactured. They also aided a fundamental change in the way in which the majority of smokers in early twentieth-century Britain consumed tobacco, and it is this change that forms the final component of tobacco consumption at the Hagg site.

Cigarettes

The briar pipes and vulcanite mouthpieces were produced at a time when tobacco smoking in Britain had never been higher, with the *per capita* consumption of tobacco more than doubling between 1850 and 1914 (Hilton, 1995: 587). This rise was partly to do with the changing means of smoking tobacco. Growing numbers of younger men and boys began to smoke, attracted by the increased availability of cigarettes, the machine manufacture of which had been perfected in the 1880s. The relatively cheap price of mass-produced factory cigarettes and accompanying cigarette cards made them attractive to younger consumers (Hilton, 1995: 591), as did their portability and ease of smoking during short work breaks.

Cigarettes are, of course, difficult to recognise archaeologically. Nevertheless, one piece of evidence was collected to reflect this final change in the nature of tobacco smoking at the Hagg site. A tobacco or cigarette tin, 120 mm long, was found in Area A, contained within the same context as the briar pipe and vulcanite mouthpieces. This object dated to the early twentieth century and may either have been used to store tobacco for pipe smoking or to store cigarettes.

Whatever the exact contents of this tin, the lack of clay pipes dating to the twentieth century indicated a major shift in the ways in which tobacco was commonly consumed. Clay pipes had been the dominant means for smoking tobacco by British smokers for 300 years, but the emergence of technological innovation in the realm of consumer goods changed this pattern. As discussed above, Vulcanite was very much a product of the later industrial era. Cigarettes also became popular only because machinery was developed which could manufacture them extremely rapidly and very cheaply (Hilton, 1995: 589). Changing fashions in smoking were thus related to wider technological innovations.

As discussed in North American and Australian scholarship (Beaudry, 1993; Casella, 2000; Gojak and Stuart; 1999; Seifert, 1992), aspects of gender infused the everyday practice of smoking. Tobacco consumption in late nineteenth-century and early twentieth-century Britain was similarly an extremely gendered activity, with smoking by women symbolically associated with loose morals (Hilton, 1995). A variety of men and women at different stages of their lives occupied the Hagg Cottages during the late nineteenth and early twentieth centuries. If the cottage residents were all engaging in conservative social practices, then it is likely that all of the tobacco smoking-related artefacts discussed above were utilised by male household members. However, the position of these artefacts *inside* the home may suggest an alternative explanation. Perhaps the pipes and cigarette tin may represented the means through which one or more female member(s) of the Hagg Cottage households discreetly enjoyed the pastime of smoking without carrying this practice out within the observational range of non-household members. This would allow the maintenance of a polite feminine identity, whilst being able to partially disregard the social disproval extended to female smokers at this time.

Overall, the tobacco smoking evidence from the Hagg site shows a complex layering of meanings over time. In the seventeenth century tobacco smoking was interwoven with the development of colonial identities. By the nineteenth century, continuing into the twentieth century, tobacco-smoking artefacts were more engaged with the presentation of self and individual social identities. What is clear is that the tobacco-related evidence from the Hagg site offered far more than a dating tool. The styles of smoking artefacts may have represented particular local identities, international patterns of recreational consumption and technological influences on prevailing fashions. Providing a valuable insight into a recreational activity over time, the tobacco-related artefacts demonstrated that such everyday practices were far from static. That recreation practices changed through time with industrialisation and the increased participation in a consumer economy remains a theme as we turn to our next aspect of recreational life – the enjoyment of holidays and country fairs.

Holidays and fairs

Not all leisure time was spent within the household itself. Historical evidence of fairs, wakes and festivals, suggests that even the earliest Hagg residents would have spent some time engaged in seasonal festivals. With the increased segmentation of work time over the eighteenth and nineteenth centuries, the specific nature and content of these diversions evolved. Further, with the introduction of affordable rail travel by the mid-nineteenth century, seaside holidays began to form a wider part of recreational activities outside of the home. Although these leisure persuits were obviously not undertaken directly at the Hagg site, their existence was materially indicated through souvenirs of seasonal fairs and seaside resorts recovered during excavations. The overall category of ceramic souvenirs was small, forming less than 1 per cent of the total analysed ceramic assemblage. Nevertheless, these artefacts represented a significant component of the recreational patterns enjoyed by site residents. As with other types of household ornament, holiday souvenirs provide overt symbols of personal and social aspirations (Brighton, 2001: 18; Mullins, 1999). The assemblage is therefore vital for understanding the material dynamics of class, status and domesticity within the recent past.

Fairs, wakes and festivals

Holidays and festivities became redefined over the industrial era as leisure time and work hours became increasingly separated. From the medieval period, traditional local festivities were held within each English village and town. These were sometimes termed 'wakes', and were often tied to the church – commemorating the founding of the local church or celebrating its dedicated saint. Entertainments consisted of 'quasi-religious celebrations, followed by games, sports, drinking and dancing' (Barton, 2005: 74). Traditional festivities continued into the industrial era, and increasingly became associated with travelling carnivals. At the markets and fairs attached to these celebrations, stalls offered a range of exotic objects and curios from around the world (Barton, 2005: 75; Holliday and Jayne, 2000: 181). As part of the general regulation and supervision of society that accompanied late eighteenth-century industrialisation, wakes and carnivals were increasingly confined to official national and religious holidays, thereby limiting their compromise of productive work periods (Holliday and Jayne, 2000: 181).

Despite civic attempts at regulation, travelling fairs and circuses continued as important recreational diversions throughout the nineteenth century, often in opposition to industrial owners, whose employees would often absent themselves from work to enjoy the spectacular entertainment (Rosenzweig, 1983; Thompson, 1967). Travelling performers would journey between towns over the main wake season, which ran between Whitsun, or Pentecost, falling five weeks after Easter, and September (Barton, 2005: 80). The world of these travelling fairs showcased the bohemian and exotic, with imported wild animals (such as zebras) appearing on their stages from the early nineteenth century (Turner, 2003: 20). As events that encouraged folks to experience the 'exotic', these fairs helped English workers understand their own social identity in opposition to the increasingly familiar colonial 'other'. In addition to exotic animals, travelling fairs and carnivals were a place where local workers might come into contact with those of other races. Indeed, a circus owned by a black man, Pablo Fanque, toured English northern towns over the early through mid-nineteenth century, including Stockport and Altrincham, two market towns within the wider Alderley region (Turner, 2003: 30). Thus, as with tea and tobacco, concepts of exotic otherness were consumed by British working households through a variety of material objects and recreational encounters.

Prevailing ideologies of cleanliness and gentility, discussed within the previous chapter, were also mediated through the realm of leisure. In the town of Stoke on Trent, for example, the Board of Health – a civic body consisting largely of ceramic industrialists unhappy with their factory workers disappearing off to the fairs – shut down the local wakes in 1879 with the argument it was 'unsanitary' (Holliday and Jayne, 2000: 190). But at the same time as these traditional leisure pursuits were impinged upon by bourgeois classes, newly sanctioned leisure activities were becoming available for England's workers.

Seaside holidays

Enjoyment of the annual seaside holiday became a new practice across nineteenth-century Britain, forming 'part of the routine of respectable life' (Barton, 2005: 73). While this began with the middle classes, from the 1850s it became more widely available to workers as railway companies introduced dedicated service to regional coastal resorts and affordable accommodation was established within these seaside towns (Walton, 1981: 251). As wage rates and living standards in Britain began to improve after 1850, workers were able to emphasise their family lives and leisure expectations (Barton, 2005: 10). Additionally, paternalistic employers, Church leaders and temperance groups were particularly keen to promote seaside visits as a means of promoting physical health and personal improvement (Casella, 2005; Walton, 1981: 249).

For workers themselves, the annual seaside holiday became part of a newly realised consumerism. They could 'have a spree' away from the work environment and spend excess income on both 'rational recreations' and cheap consumer goods (Walton, 1981: 253). Rather than simply conforming to the ideals of the middle classes, workers shaped these seaside destinations in terms of their own desires, creating resorts in which the leisure pursuits available – of which drinking continued to play a key role – conformed to their own wants. In terms of wider landscapes of recreation, bourgeois anxieties over travelling fairs were also allayed by the growth of discrete coastal working-class resorts. The curious (and rather uncivilised) travelling fair became safely relocated away to summer seaside resorts (Barton, 2005: 80).

The Blackpool Tower, with its architecturally designed space for a circus, materially represented the growing regulation and commercialisation of these traditional country fairs. Blackpool's Pleasure Beach amusement grounds also contain examples of some of the oldest surviving English fair rides – including Maxim's Flying Machine, constructed in 1904 (McNeil and Newman, 2006b: 178; Walton 1998). Such pleasure rides provided dramatic new leisure experiences to working holiday makers over the turn of the century. By 1914, although still a luxury, the seaside holiday had evolved into a treasured part of British working culture (Barton, 2005: 11).

Souvenirs

The small percentage of ceramic souvenirs mentioned earlier consisted of three particular artefacts. The first was was a ceramic zebra figurine, recovered from Area A in several pieces. This was a whiteware artefact, moulded in the shape of a horse, its head actually adorned with reins (Figure 5.7). Black stripes had been painted under the clear glaze to make it appear as a zebra rather than a horse, thereby creating an exotic animal figurine for sale and display. Other ceramic figurines depicting exotic animals were commonly produced in the early to mid-nineteenth century in connection with fairs, circuses and touring beast shows (see Oliver, 1981, for an example). The whiteware zebra from Area A dated to the late nineteenth century.

Two further souvenir items were also found from the site. From Area A came a pair of souvenir plates from Douglas, in the Isle of Man, dated to between the late nineteenth century and the early twentieth century. They related to two small matching porcelain/bone china vessels with overglaze

Figure 5.7   Whiteware zebra figurine, Alderley Sandhills Project, 2003

transfer printed designs which depicted a seaside resort. Gold lustre paint had been applied to the rims and handles. The specific wording on one vessel was unclear, with remaining letters consisting of 'Do . . . glas/ . . . men . . .'. When interpreted in conjunction with the seaside resort picture, the object was sourced to Douglas, capital town of the Isle of Man, an island off the Lancashire coast of north-west England. From Area B one single fragmentary souvenir plate was recovered, although post-demolition recycling had spread its remains across four separate contexts. This second plate had been acquired from the popular North West holiday resort of Blackpool (Plate VII), its polychrome centre depicting the famous Blackpool Tower. Constructed specifically as a tourist attraction, the tower opened in 1894, incorporating an aquarium, circus and ballroom (Walton, 1998).

Oral histories of fairs and holidays

In addition to the artefactual data provided by souvenirs, a range of oral history referred to both fairs and seaside holidays. Mrs Edna Younger recalled a local fair: an organised event, it appeared to contrast with the pre-twentieth-century carnivalesque fairs described earlier in this chapter. By the 1920s the Wizard public house had changed into tearooms, providing the venue for this respectable family-oriented annual fair. Mrs Younger remembered a lady known as Donkey Warburton who used to bring donkeys for children's rides. Additionally, the fair offered swingboats, and Mrs Wright, who ran the tearooms, provided refreshments for 2s 6d (Mrs Edna Younger, ASP interviews, July 2003).

The fair at the Wizard tearooms in the 1920s was close to the Hagg Cottages, requiring only a short walk uphill for residents to enjoy the amusements. The Hagg families also travelled further for the purpose of holiday amusements. Both Mrs Edna Younger and Mrs Molly Pitcher, prompted by the seaside plate souvenir, had clear memories of seaside holidays taken from the Hagg over the 1920s. For the Barber family, holidays had consisted of an annual trip to the resort of New Brighton, located in Merseyside, opposite the port of Liverpool. When she saw the sherds of the Blackpool souvenir plate, Mrs Molly Pitcher commented that if any souvenirs were found from New Brighton they would have belonged to her family:

> We went to New Brighton every year. For as long as I can remember. And the waggon used to come up this road here and our trunk used to go sailing along Whitebarn Lane to the station. It went a month before we went away. So we'd have nothing to wear for a month before we went away, and then we'd have to wait another month for it to come back. But every year we went to New Brighton.
>
> (Mrs Molly Pitcher, ASP interviews, July 2003)

Even if the recollection that it took a month for the Barber family's possessions to travel between Alderley Edge station and New Brighton has stretched
this period a little, it demonstrated the degree of planning and careful preparation for a holiday if possessions were to be sent on in advance. Only forty-
five miles from the Hagg Cottages, the town of New Brighton was closer
than the other popular holiday resorts of the region, such as Blackpool, a
little over sixty miles away. A less prominent English seaside destination,
New Brighton did not feature in histories of holidays within Britain or the
North West region (Barton, 2005; Walton, 1981; 2000). It is one of the
closest coastal towns to Alderley, and as holidays were complex affairs to
plan and arrange, its proximity motivated the choice of resort.

Seaside holidays were also a regular experience of other families residing
at the Hagg Cottages in the early twentieth century. Mrs Edna Younger's
grandmother, grandfather and uncle had moved from the Hagg site to the
resort town of Colwyn Bay in Wales in the early 1920s. This move followed
a doctor's recommendation, as Mrs Younger's uncle suffered from chronic
chest infections, and the seaside air was appreciated for its restorative
qualities. Their move also meant that Mrs Younger, an only child, took an
annual seaside holiday without her parents. From around the age of six she
would travel by train all the way from Alderley Edge to Colwyn Bay (Mrs
Edna Younger, ASP interviews, July 2003). She specifically recalled how
her mother would hang a large label around her neck, and the train's guard
would be instructed to look after her, including seeing her safely through the
change of train at Crewe. She remembered that on such journeys she had a
'whale of a time!' because she was on her holidays. Her grandmother would
give her some pocket money, and encourage her grandfather to take her on
day trips to Llandudno so that they could go on the 'Dudno boat'. To her
gran's displeasure, these trips could involve a quick pint, with her grandfather
drinking in the bar while Mrs Younger sat on the deck of the boat 'watching all that was going on outside'. Mrs Younger's grandmother appeared to
find such diversions inappropriate, but the pleasure of an elderly man and
young girl cheerfully intersected on such trips, with Mrs Younger's memories
suggesting that they both had an excellent time on the 'Dudno boat'. These
memories also raise the point that even within the outwardly respectable
practice of taking a family holiday to the seaside, there was scope for a range
of recreational enjoyments, particularly that of alcohol consumption.

As well as these annual individual trips to Llandudno, Mrs Younger also
spoke of an additional family holiday to Torquay. Unlike the resorts of
Llandudno and New Brighton, both within an easy day of railway travel
to Alderley Edge, Torquay is 245 miles from the village, located in the
south-western county of Cornwall. Given the complexities of a family trip
to New Brighton, such a holiday would obviously have required similarly
careful planning, and shows a break from contemporaneous working-class

holiday patterns of visiting seaside resorts within one's region (Barton, 2005; Walton, 1981).

Interpreting holidays at the Hagg

The clarity of oral-historical reminiscences of childhood holidays by Mrs Pitcher and Mrs Younger highlights the importance of these in their lives. For the adult residents of the cottages as well, holidays would have been a break from the norm and a chance to relive the pressures of daily working life. The residents of the cottages were not wealthy, and such holidays would have required important investments by the cottage residents of precious excess income. In this context, the souvenirs on display in the cottages become particularly important. The root meaning of these artefacts comes from the French word *souvenir*, 'to remember' (Chaimov, 2001: 59). By bringing such objects home from holidays and fairs, Hagg residents had the chance to have within their daily living space a commemoration of these treasured events.

Souvenirs served as a material reminder of the leisure enjoyed during a summer trip. Although Blackpool and the Isle of Man did not feature in particular memories of Mrs Pitcher and Mrs Younger, this does not preclude the possibility that these families had visited the resorts. The Isle of Man is a short ferry ride from Liverpool, adjoining New Brighton. Blackpool may have been the destination of an excursion or holiday by members of the Perrin or Ellam households, or may simply have been forgotten as a holiday trip by Mrs Pitcher or Mrs Younger. Whatever the route through which these souvenir vessels entered the Hagg Cottages, the objects provided material devices for cottage residents to remember the leisure that would await them as they made their way through the monotony of everyday work.

The zebra figurine may have represented differing leisure practices. Exotic animals and peoples were made domestically familiar over the turn of the century through objects such as the zebra figurine. Given the nineteenth-century date of the artefact, it is possible that it may have been purchased at a travelling circus rather than the holiday world of a seaside resort. The purchase of curios and objects at these events may have been a way of reminding the purchaser of leisure activities, as with the souvenir plates. It may also have been a means of bringing an exotic and exciting experience into the home. Empire provided an explicit part of the British national identity over the turn of the century (see Lawrence, 2003). The type of fair with animals like zebras on show often also displayed people from other races, sometimes in dioramas of views from the empire (Armstrong, 1993; Qureshi, 2004; Russell, 1999).

As well as acting as prompts for aspects of identities and memories of leisure time away from the home, the souvenir plates and the zebra figurine were also all a part of the way in which cottage residents engaged with consumer culture, as discussed in previous chapters. Participating in seaside holidays and having the financial resources to be able to attend fairs and travelling shows provided a means through which Hagg Cottage residents did not simply take time off work, but actively participated in the cash economy of leisure consumerism. In buying objects to commemorate this they were able to exhibit their consumer status to visitors invited within their homes (Johnson, 1988: 40; Mullins, 2004; Praetzellis, 2004), at a time when a growing number of working households took such an annual holiday (Walton, 198: 258).

Buying and displaying souvenirs allowed the materialisation of holidaymaking. These leisure activities formed a part of turn-of-the-century consumer practices, in the same way as purchasing ornaments, vases and furnishings for the home. As with other categories of recreation, the changing practices and meanings of holiday activities were related to wider social changes of the same period. Thus, when juxtaposed with historical background and oral histories, they begin to reveal the complexities of meaning, lived through participation in holidays and fairs and the purchase of souvenirs at these. Before moving on from this topic, there is one further related set of souvenir artefacts to discuss, those related to royal jubilee celebrations.

Jubilee celebrations and imperial identities

During the nineteenth century new national festivals began to be celebrated, commemorating the crowning of the monarch, royal weddings and jubilee celebrations. Material culture produced in support of these national celebrations, including paintings, coins or souvenirs depicting the monarchy, can be contextualised within the particular socio-political milieu of the nineteenth century (Hackett, 2001: 823). Celebrations of the monarchy were an active part of presenting the royal family in order to cultivate a popular sentiment of 'Britishness' during a time of imperial expansion. Modern royal jubilee celebrations, promoting nationalist ideologies, have been argued to have begun only with the golden jubilee of George III in 1809 (Chase, 1990: 141). Prior to this most of the British population had little involvement with royal events. In 1809 events to commemorate the jubilee of George III began to involve even working communities. The wealthy social elite of the town of Brighton, for instance, treated 2,000 of the poorest local working classes to a celebratory feast. This simultaneously reified ties to a national identity and reinforced local social hierarchies (Chase, 1990: 142).

By the late nineteenth century British national identities had become further transformed, as reinforced through royal celebrations. The golden jubilee celebrations of Queen Victoria in 1887 were tied to spectacle, with events such as parades in London celebrating the institutions of late nineteenth-century

British society (Richards, 1987: 11). Although the celebrations had at their heart a very specific imperial British identity, these identities were also tied to the production of consumer goods. For the first time companies produced a massive range of material items, spawning a set of artefacts related to this single moment in history. This 'jubileeana' included embroidered samplers, rugs, plates, cups, spoons, toys, medals and scent bottles (Richards, 1987: 18). The ideology of imperialism and empire in Victorian Britain was therefore explicitly demonstrated through the production of items of jubileeana for British consumers. While these were sold only within the domestic market, some of them explicitly drew on ties with Britain's then flourishing Victorian empire (Lawrence, 2003: 11), with some including lines such as 'May be purchased throughout the Empire' alongside Victoria's image.

Such souvenirs were powerful and widely available. As a phenomenon it has been argued that they 'seemed to promise a familiar world wherever one went, a world created by English manufacturers, populated with English commodities, and depicted in the idiom of English advertising' (Richards, 1989: 19). Images of imperialism and empire within the British nationalist ideology and identity continued to be utilised and expanded upon through the end of the nineteenth century and into the twentieth. In 1897 Queen Victoria celebrated her diamond jubilee, by which point she had become, in the eyes of the British public, 'the charismatic centre of all the phantasmagoria of Empire' with popular newspapers such as the *Daily Mail* running headlines proclaiming the 'Greatness of the British race' (Richards, 1989: 32).

Royal celebrations of this latter period of the British Empire were explicit in the way in which they promoted a certain kind of national identity, and manifestations of this are visible in the material record of the Hagg cottages. From Area B part of a late nineteenth-century commemorative vessel, with a moulded plaque depicting the head of Queen Victoria and the letters 'VR' picked out in blue, was recovered (Plate VIII). It was a mass-produced piece, manufactured from low-cost whiteware. Aside from the moulded plaque it was also decorated by a moulded rilled line, emphasised with the use of blue paint, with hand-painted blue loops and possible sponged decoration on the body. Area B also yielded a second royal commemorative vessel, dating from the early twentieth century. This was the base of a whiteware mug, with an overglaze transfer print depicting a picture of King George V and his wife Mary. George was born in 1865, crowned in May 1910 and held his silver jubilee celebrations in 1935, a year before his death in 1936. Only a fragmentary base of this vessel was recovered, but it clearly showed the name 'Mary' printed and the name of the photographers 'W. & D. Downey'. This company of photographers regularly produced studio portraits of the royal family in the late nineteenth and early twentieth centuries that were used as the basis for transfer-printed items relating to the monarchy.

Historical accounts have indicated that by the late nineteenth century, celebrations for the royal family provided a holiday for British subjects across the empire. Although no direct material remains survived of specific locally hosted Alderley celebratory events, the purchase and display of jubileeana at Hagg Cottages may have publicly demonstrated their support for the royal family as well as feelings of national pride. Products tied to royal jubilees, coronations and weddings were actively promoted across the country in an attempt by manufacturers to expand their consumer markets (Lawrence, 2003). As with the seaside souvenir items, vessels depicting the royal family may have functioned as another bric-a-brac item to add to overall aesthetic presentation of home. Nonetheless, through their unique form, these particular vessels also made a clear statement of identity. While they may have commemorated the fun enjoyed during a particular royal celebration event, they simultaneously displayed patriotic feelings about the monarch and a sense of belonging to the British nation. In the final section of this chapter we turn to another aspect of recreational life at the Hagg – the childhood play activities that entered the archaeological record.

Childhood at the Hagg

While not simply a recreational activity at the Hagg, children's play activities appear to have offered adult residents a diversion from their everyday work patterns. The archaeology of childhood in post-medieval periods has been recognised in covering an important part of the development of our modern understanding of children. Concomitant with this is the growth of specific material culture relating to children. In addition to evidence from artefacts, the oral historical memories of childhood have allowed a rich interpretation of the way our project participants experienced Hagg life as children during the early twentieth century.

Childhood as an historical construct

The notion of a clear life stage of 'childhood' within the archetypal structure of a nuclear family is a social construct that has been articulated only within the very recent past of Western cultures (Buchli and Lucas, 2000: 135). Today childhood is viewed as a specifically designated period in the life course, with children as social dependants, obliged to be happy and with rights to protection and training, but with little personal autonomy (Sofaer Derevenski, 2000: 5). But it was not until the eighteenth century that the idea of an extended period of non-productive 'childhood' was first developed. Thus a clearly defined world of children engaged with toys and school – separate from the world of adults – is itself a very modern aspect of human life (Cunningham, 1998: 1196). Rather than simply assuming childhood roles at the Hagg conformed to present expectations, this chapter concludes by examining the material construction of pre-adult identities.

The material culture of childhood

A range of artefacts was recovered from the site that appear to be manufactured objects purchased for the purpose of childhood play. All of these dated to the nineteenth century or later, and most were manufactured of ceramic. Of these ceramic artefacts the majority were parts of dolls, totalling six dolls' heads and a small number of other ceramic dolls' parts. All of these artefacts were manufactured from unglazed porcelain/bone china, with hand-painted decoration. The earliest of these consisted of a child's head with a painted and moulded quiff of hair at the front of the head, dating to the nineteenth century. A further three dolls' heads, all simply decorated, dated to between the late nineteenth and early twentieth centuries. Two had only had painted eyelashes and the other (Figure 5.8) was decorated with both hand-painted eyebrows and eyelashes.

Two further dolls' heads, contextually dating from between the late nineteenth and early twentieth centuries, were painted with more detailed decoration. One had the appearance of a girl, with moulded wavy hair and painted cheeks, lips and eyes. The other represented the head of a baby, decorated with painted lips and eyes, the hair indicated by an incised line and quiff at the front. Two of these heads had been stamped with marks across the neck and shoulders. One of these was indecipherable. The other read 'Germany/275.19/0/**oppers**', indicating an import from Germany. Further decorated doll elements were in the form of a body and limbs. The shoes and socks were painted to depict black shoes and blue socks. Ceramic sherds were also recovered which formed the fragmentary remains of further doll elements. The final ceramic toy evidence was a single undecorated glazed whiteware doll's teaset plate.

In addition to these ceramic toys, a range of bone, metal, plastic and rubber artefacts were recovered from Areas A and B which appeared to relate to children's play around the Hagg site. The only bone item consisted of a doll's brush, potentially used with the ceramic toys detailed above. Metal artefacts from Area A included a mouth organ, table tennis net clamp, bike pedal and mechanical workings of a bike. Upper remnants of a bike bell were collected from Area B. Rubber toys came from Area A, and consisted of four small toy balls and a single larger tennis ball. From the early twentieth century, plastic began to appear in the manufacture of small children's toys. Several cream-coloured plastic tiddlywinks were recovered from Area A, while Area B contained a further single tiddlywink and a plastic male figure, stamped (in English) 'Made in Germany'.

The Hagg Cottage toy assemblage is broadly comparable to those from

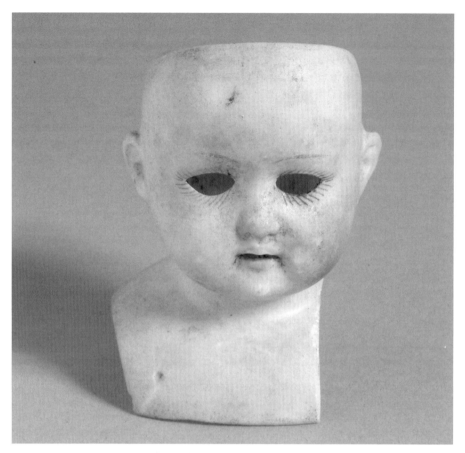

Figure 5.8   Bisque porcelain doll's head, Alderley Sandhills Project, 2003

British urban post-medieval archaeological sites. In Manchester, a range of toys were recorded from the New Islington Wharf site. These included a ceramic female painted earthenware figurine and painted porcelain pug dog, part of a writing slate and two slate pencils, glass and ceramic marbles and a plastic scuba diver and plastic tipper truck (Oxford Archaeology North, 2005: 44). From MOLAS excavations of a working-class district in urban London, a cesspit fill, dated to the 1860s, also contained a range of toys and childhood-related artefacts. These consisted of bone whistles and dice, glass marbles, ceramic toy cups, saucers and plates and a whiteware children's mug decorated with the 'Who killed Cock Robin?' nursery rhyme (Jeffries, 2006: 284). Hagg site data appears to be broadly comparable to that of these Manchester and London sites. Such similarities suggest that from the mid-nineteenth century the range of children's toys acquired by working households may have differed little between urban and rural contexts. This archaeological interpretation gains significance when we consider the role of these artefacts in the construction of modern childhood identities.

Creating childhood identities at the Hagg

The eighteenth-century emergence of modern childhood prompted the growth of a wide range of material culture related to this new stage of life. Such objects facilitated recreational activities for juveniles that, depending on socio-economic conditions, intermixed education and play. In addition to promoting a sense of childhood, these artefacts also communicated wider social values, particularly Victorian ideals of morality, gender and class. Previous scholarship has observed that such formal material culture was created by adults to instil particular values into their children, and did not reflect any statements made by the children themselves (Wilkie, 2000: 100). Therefore, the bourgeois classes quickly adopted porcelain dolls and teasets over the nineteenth century. This widespread popularity has been archaeologically interpreted as extending a particular ideology of domesticity across Victorian society. In other words, providing young girls with these toys may have reinforced an expected sense of feminine identity tied to the domestic sphere. Children's artefacts could also impart virtuous ideals through explicit textual messages. Particularly those ceramics marked with commendations for good children reinforced approved and expected behaviours (Praetzellis and Praetzellis, 1992: 90), in addition to subtle messages of private property, age and status distinctions within the family group (Brighton, 2001: 27).

The role of toys in helping to construct gendered identities for children is well recognised in studies from a range of disciplines (Messener, 2000). Toys function as crucial element in the development of personal identity, with the long-term cultural process of subjectification aided by the meanings adults attempt to convey through these childhood objects (Phillips, 2002: 124). The most obvious example of this gendering occurred in the provision of dolls and dolls teasets to the young girls of the Hagg. Helping to socialise girls into their presumed future role of mothering, these toys also provided idealised icons for the feminine appearance. Doll's teasets could function similarly, introducing girls to the essential ritual of the English 'tea party'. Dolls intended to reinforce a masculine gendered role were also provided, the plastic figure of a man perhaps representing a discarded toy soldier.

Alternative narratives of childhood at the Hagg

Supplementing the material evidence for childhood at the Hagg Cottages were detailed narratives of life at the cottages by Mrs Edna Younger, Mr Roy Barber and Mrs Molly Pitcher, all of whom were in early childhood when they resided at the site (Figure 5.9). Some of these tales involved

Figure 5.9   Hagg kids at play, 1920s

memories of specific toys. Mrs Edna Younger described a doll's house that her father had constructed for her and Mrs Molly Pitcher remembered a doll's tea set she had been given by her great-aunt, Mrs Lena Perrin (Mrs Edna Younger and Mrs Molly Pitcher, ASP interviews, July 2003). As well as simply reinforcing the values of society, the gifting of toys to children was a way of reinforcing kinship and community ties. Whether mass-produced or manufactured at home, the giving of a present represents the materiality of a kinship between the giver and receiver. The toy artefacts described above may thus represent ties between children and parents, grandparents, aunts, uncles and wider community members.

In these narratives toys formed only a small part of the memories of childhood at the site. The most vivid memories of all three oral history participants concerned the way in which the land around the Hagg had provided a playground for the cottage children. Favoured activities included winter tobogganing down the hill to the south-east of the cottages – identified as a 'belting' spot for this game. The sledges used by the children for this were all home-made by their fathers (Mrs Edna Younger, ASP interviews, July 2003). The Sandhills themselves also provided a favourite playground for children. Describing how during summer months they would slide down the Sandhills on a tray, Mrs Younger explained, 'And you'd go – whoosh! Right down to the bottom! It was very good.' Although the Sandhills had originated as waste material from the neighbouring mineworks, in the geography of children's play they were only associated with fun, games and family events.

These sledding teatrays formed part of a repertoire of domestic objects requisitioned by the children for their play activities. Mrs Edna Younger similarly recalled how all three of the children had played in tree houses formed in the base of hollowed-out trees in the neighbouring woods. Unsupervised by adults, they would take a frying pan, some lard and potatoes from their homes, and would make chips in their tree houses as part of their games. Even when prompted by specific artefacts such as the doll's tea plate and dolls' heads, it was the outdoor play, the fields, tree houses and Sandhills that figured most prominently in the recollections of childhood at the Hagg Cottages.

The oral historical evidence relating to the youth of Mrs Younger, Mr Barber and Mrs Pitcher permits an alternative narrative of childhood play at the Hagg site over the early twentieth century. Through the toys, it was possible to interpret distinct childhood identities, structured by gender and age. However, the stories narrated in participant oral histories did not reflect these interpretations. Instead, these were rooted in memories of being outside, playing in the woods, on the hills and in the snow. Rather than store-bought toys, it was home-made toboggans, dolls' houses and co-opted domestic items such as frying pans and teatrays which formed the core of their childhood material culture. Strict gender segregation of behaviour and play featured little in these accounts. Mr Roy Barber and Mrs Edna Younger both discussed regularly playing together during their first nine years of life. Mrs Edna Younger also specifically recalled her great-grandmother's general disapproval of her tomboy lifestyle at the Hagg (Mrs Edna Younger, ASP interviews, July 2003).

The importance of outdoor play for the Hagg children can be compared with the recognition of distinct geographies of childhood at other historical archaeological sites. Rather than oral histories, it is material evidence, such as the clustering of marbles in particular sheltered corners of domestic sites, which have allowed some archaeologists to associate particular spaces with children's play (Wilkie, 2000: 110). At the Hagg site, children's places were located far beyond the cottages themselves, with the gardens, woods, fields and Sandhills serving as playgrounds rather than spaces of routine adult activities. Childhood identities formed through play at this rural site, while not intentionally transgressing gendered roles, were not simply divided into masculine and feminine identities. While their memories of shared play may have also reflected a nostalgia for their perceived idyllic childhood, oral history participants recalled more communal than segregated play activities. Thus the small toy artefacts – such as rubber balls and tiddlywinks – may have been as important to their experience of childhood as the dolls and teasets. Childhood play at the Hagg cottages was involved in processes of consumer behaviour and the reinforcement of gendered roles, but children at this rural site also had the ability to ignore these messages and to create their own childhood community through shared play.

Conclusion: recreation and identity at the Hagg

Through the archaeology of the Hagg Cottages we can see the growth of clearly demarcated leisure time over the nineteenth and early twentieth centuries. Evidence for this modern phenomenon can be drawn from a number of different aspects of evidence. Souvenirs and oral histories of treasured holidays away from the Hagg Cottages, local fairs and royal commemorations all attested to the clear segregation of single days or groups of days away from work. Recreational activities also formed part of the routines of daily life, concentrated into evenings and weekends. While anecdotal evidence suggests that some of this may have happened away from the cottages, particularly male practices of drinking in public houses, the domestic space of the Hagg site was also the location for recreation. Drinking commercially brewed and home-brewed alcohol was a way for adult men and women to socialise and relax in their homes. Memories of the consumption of home-brewed fruit wines suggested that such home consumption of alcohol may have sustained a local Hagg community as households drank together. In Chapter 4 we discussed the creation of domestic space at the cottages, and in

Chapter 6 we discuss the spatiality of labour and work at the cottages. Thus the polyvalent site offered a location for leisure activities woven around the more mundane aspects of household life.

Archaeological evidence indicated that recreational and leisure practices at the Hagg site grew increasingly commodified throughout the nineteenth and early twentieth centuries. A specific manufactured and marketed leisure culture began to appear through the industrial era, with excavations recovering commercial beers, souvenirs, mass-produced pipes and manufactured toys. As leisure time became recognised as an essential part of workers' lives, a material consumerism of these practices powerfully emerged, but despite the glamour of these new objects, a non-commercial side of leisure activities continued to be treasured within this rural community. Drinking home-brewed fruit wines, and making toys such as toboggans and dolls' houses for children provided relaxation and recreation by and for the families themselves.

Recreation and leisure activities were also active in mediating many different aspects of identities and relationships. On a large scale, national identities were reinforced through the celebration of patriotic holidays. Colonial identities were also understood by the residents at the Hagg site through various aspects of recreational activities during different stages of the British Empire. Early colonial relations were bound up with the use of commodities like tobacco and the pipes in which it was smoked. Later, more explicit identities projected images of a proud British Empire. More subtle manifestations of imperial identities emerged through artefacts of exotic beasts, their curious appearance made fashionable through travelling circuses and fairs. Leisure activities also helped create a sense of belonging to community and extended family. Play activities helped create childhood identities, which were sometimes gendered. Drinking in public houses and smoking tobacco, while outwardly the domain of the working adult men of the Hagg, may have been simultaneously enjoyed by the ladies, who partook of their everyday indulgences in the comfort and respectability of their own homes. Community identities shared between the households of the Hagg Cottages may also have been reinforced through certain leisure practices, in particular home brewing and the sharing of alcohol between homes, and for children shared practices of play between households. This theme of community identities is the one we shall now turn to interpret through the following chapter.

6

Community life

Mrs Edna Younger. [Life at the Hagg] didn't worry Mother, because *her* mother lived up here . . . her brother was born here.

Mrs Molly Pitcher. But for anybody like, say, my mother, who came from, um, well, a *habited* place – I mean, she only came from Wilmslow, but to come here, well, it was a *little* village in those days.

(ASP Interviews, September 2003)

This chapter deals specifically with the ways in which rural community life can be interpreted from archaeological evidence. As observed in Chapter 1, no precise or singular definition can be adequately applied to the idea of a social community. For this study, community affiliations are understood as subjective feelings of 'belonging' to a social group not immediately defined by kinship. Such groupings frequently form as a 'node of social interaction' gathered around daily practices, with members self-identifying with one another (Kolb and Snead, 1997: 611). In attempting to interpret community identities through the archaeological record we seek to understand the ways in which Hagg residents formed coherent links through their work and recreational practices. We further explore how these bonds articulated with deeper ties of kinship, neighbourhood and patronage to create this unique social world.

Scales of community

What became immediately apparent through this analysis was the complex plurality of communities that simultaneously existed at the site. Hagg Cottage residents were closely bound into various overlapping social networks. Crucial relationships were sustained through a delicate interplay of work, kinship, tenancy and neighbourly ties. Multiple scales of community operated, with individuals simultaneously located within several networks. The internal hierarchies of these groups were both expressed and mediated through a range of power dynamics. While the emotive ties that bound people together created a desired degree of social cohesion, they did not preclude the presence of differential status within the community, nor tensions between community members of equal status.

On deference and duties

For the traditional English landscape, ties between landlords and tenants provided crucial element of community life. Before the Second World War most land in Cheshire was divided up among a series of large historic estates. Within this rural county, single landlords often owned large proportions of individual parishes (Barnwell and Giles, 1997: 122). While the specific regional history of land tenure was previously summarised in Chapter 2, it is worth noting that the Stanley family owned the majority of land for the parish of Nether Alderley. As a result, the Stanleys exercised a great deal of political and social control over this local area.

The Stanley family also maintained property on the island of Anglesey in Wales, a land holding that included industrial copper mines. As a result, they were not wholly reliant upon the rental income from their tenants, unlike the majority of nineteenth-century landlords (Thompson, 1980: 207). Rather than forcing their tenants on to shorter leases, or rationalising their land into new economically productive units – as was the case with most Cheshire landowners of the nineteenth and early twentieth centuries (Barnwell and Giles, 1997: 123) – the Stanley family expressed a notable degree of social largess towards their Nether Alderley parish tenants. This relationship cultivated an atmosphere of deference (Thompson, 1980: 8) towards the Stanleys, with the landlords remembered in benevolent, terms:

> *Edna Younger.* There were five [Stanley] daughters, and every Christmas they gave a party for local schoolchildren – Nether Alderley schoolchildren and schoolchildren of the parish. They were all invited to Alderley Park, anyone that belonged to the parish. And we had a wonderful tea. And then we'd go in the Tenants' Hall, and there was a gallery at the top. And those five girls would be sat in it. And Victoria, that's the one that's just been over from Canada, Lady Victoria. They were beautiful girls. And they made all these things to go on the tree. You know, they'd make cot covers and that sort of thing. Little things, but very pleasing to the people that received them. It was a different way of life.
> *Devin Hahn.* So the Stanleys . . .?
> *Edna Younger:* They were lords and ladies.
> *Devin Hahn.* And they were looked on favourably?
> *Edna Younger.* Very. It was the squire. And he was a very good squire. Very good to the people. I just met them, I think, possibly at two parties. They

were very good. Looked after everybody very well. And if they took somebody on to work there, they were there for life. There again, it all added to
a very nice way of life. You felt secure. You felt part of a big family.

(Mrs Edna Younger, ASP interviews, August 2003)

Thus traditional paternalistic bonds connected various social levels within
the parish community. In exchange for receiving annual rent, landlords were
expected to maintain a duty of care over long-established local families,
including the early twentieth-century residents of the Hagg Cottages. Over
the generations, this shared experience of tenancy cultivated a sense of local
community for rural working families.

Community as labour

In addition to the social bonds created through tenancy, working relations
across the Hagg site were also crucial in the formation of community identities. Over the industrial era, shared occupations were pivotal aspects of community life. The city of Sheffield, for instance, functioned as a 'community of
cutlers' (Symonds, 2002). Similarly, villages associated with particular occupations, such as pitmen, weavers and nailers, were typically associated with
distinct close-knit communities (Rule, 1986: 158). Work life was not simply
about the means of production and the generation of household income.
It also structured everyday social encounters, causing workers employed
by different professions to participate in different ways of life (Thompson,
1980: 256). In British industrial archaeology the social networks of labour
have been highlighted as a vital yet often overlooked aspect of past workers'
lives (Symonds, 2005: 49; see also Silliman, 2006). The concept of specific
communities formed through shared industrial occupations is therefore
highly relevant to the material world of the Hagg Cottages.

Workers who participated in the same occupation generally received
the same wages. Those working in labouring roles received less than those
in supervisory and managerial positions. This internal economic differentiation has often been crucial to the way in which historical archaeologists
have extrapolated community status from the economic scaling of artefacts
found within sites. Ceramics in particular have been the target of economic
scaling analyses, which compare the amount of money various households
were spending on goods (Miller, 1980, 1991; see also Brooks and Connah
2007). Such approaches have been frequently critiqued for producing simple
dichotomous or gradational constructions, which ignored the relational
aspects through which class identities were understood by those in the past
(Wurst, 1999, 2006; Wurst and Fitts, 1999). While class may have been an
important factor in understandings of labour communities, this would not
simply have equated to economic scales (Thompson, 1980: 230).

A sense of work-based community was often experienced differently by men and women. Traditional studies of shared labour identities tend to focus on the creation of male working identities (Palmer, 2005: 71). E.P. Thompson's seminal work, *The Making of the English Working Class*, for example, 'celebrated the making of a class with the women left out' (Vickery, 1998: 394), but the variable experiences of gendered workers offer a crucial dissonance within the creation of community. As with all other domestic and recreational practices at the Hagg site, the creation of community simultaneously bonded together and differentiated the men and women of these working households.

Shared labour

The social dynamics of informal domestic duties provided crucial insight on the maintenance of ties between the Hagg residents. Of particular importance were the inter-generational links between adults and children of the Hagg community as they shared basic tasks associated with life in these rural cottages. The immediate landscape surrounding the Hagg Cottages served as the major venue for this informal labour. Mr Roy Barber recalled that there was always a pile of wood in the gardens, gathered by the residents as a winter fuel supply (Mr Roy Barber, ASP interviews, September 2003). Mrs Edna Younger remembered the way in the different households participated together in the task of gathering this wood (Figure 6.1). She recalled, 'Gertie

Figure 6.1 The Misses Ellam in the western half of Area B cottage, *c.* 1920s

used to say – that was Miss Ellam – "We'll go sticking." And we used to go sticking up in the wood. Picking up sticks for the fire' (Mrs Edna Younger, ASP interviews, August 2003). As Hagg residents performed these daily tasks together, they sustained their neighbourly ties through the collection of materials for mutual benefit. Although the majority of work activities produced financial support for a single household, some labour clearly aided in the construction of a particular local community, with resources shared between the four households.

Children and the working community

Work activities offered a means for 'apprenticing' children into the adult working world. For example, Mrs Edna Younger discussed both the outside utilitarian space and the kitchen extension in Area B. When asked about a remnant stone-flagged surface and stoneware drain, her narratives described helping her mother with the laundry, some of which had been taken in from the nearby villas of Alderley Edge:

> *Devin Hahn.* Is it strange to be here, without the house?
> *Edna Younger.* It's very strange. Those stones were probably laid down by Father, as a path. And Mother had – well, they didn't have washing machines in those days. She had a mangle. And it had big rollers, and you could put the washing through, and it would take all the moisture out. And a washtub and a dolly tub. And the dolly you would push up and down and that got clothes clean. And then she would put them in another tub, out here, in the summer. We did it all outside, in this bit of spare land by the kitchen. We did it all together. I can remember turning the handle on the mangle to put things through. Oh, that was a job!
> (Mrs Edna Younger, ASP interviews, August 2003)

Through this domestic work Mrs Younger not only provided vital help for her mother, but was also socialised into a specific working role within the local community. In helping process laundry from the nearby villas she became familiarised with ideas of both gendered labour and socio-economic status.

When describing the kitchen of her Area B cottage, Mrs Younger similarly described the labour practices enacted within the excavated space. Rather than naming the room immediately, she explained, 'This was the area where we did all the washing up and that sort of thing – you know, the kitchen' (Mrs Edna Younger, ASP interviews, August 2003). She retained detailed memories for the layout of rooms that were clearly related to her childhood domestic chores. Mrs Younger knew 'we had a sink at this end' of the family kitchen. She also clearly traced the journey made out of the kitchen door of her home to the outside coalshed, remembering that it was possible to fetch only a single scuttle of coal at a time, when she gathered fuel for the copper boiler. Her detailed narrative contrasted with the memories of Mr Roy Barber. When faced with the excavated remains of his former childhood home in Area A, he simply observed, 'There was a kitchen here' (Mr Roy Barber, ASP interviews, September 2003). Although he did know further details of this space, including the location of a cooking range and boiler, the details were drawn out through interview prompts and did not represent his primary way for remembering the space.

Instead, Mr Roy Barber offered detailed stories of the birds and trees in the woods around the cottages and of working with his father and grandfather. The only interior household space that generated a narrative description was that of the mid-Victorian extension on the southern end of the Area A cottage. Although, as discussed in Chapter 4, the space had originally been constructed as a fancy parlour, by the early twentieth century it served a more utilitarian purpose. During a site visit, Mr Roy Barber remembered it as a space for storing coal and tools:

> *Roy Barber.* We had it like a coal cellar. That was the place where, after they were all gone, I came and found the gelignite. Over there, there was a big slab, a big slab of, call it granite, I don't know what it was.
> *Eleanor Casella.* A big stone slab?
> *Roy Barber.* A big stone slab. Well, six sticks of this gelignite was lying on there. Well, I didn't know what it was in those days. I picked them up and, weuurgh, it was sticky. It was what my granddad used for blowing up tree roots, for the farmers.
> (Mr Roy Barber, ASP interviews, September 2003).

Several aspects of group identity manifested in the different ways that the Hagg children experienced and remembered these working spaces. In contrast to play activities discussed in Chapter 5, work tasks appeared quite markedly segregated by gender. With the adult men and women of the Hagg differentially participating in domestic versus outdoor labour, perhaps the children were socialised into their expected gender roles through 'apprenticeship' in these activities. Kinship – a relationship partly negotiated through gender – also appeared significant to the process by which the children participated in daily working life. Close relatives invited children into their working tasks, with family ties reinforced through the shared completion of tasks around the Hagg Cottages.

Working life and the Alderley community

Oral histories illuminated how labour patterns sustained community life over the preceding generations. When describing her family history, Mrs

Figure 6.2   Edna Barrow with her great-grandparents, aunt and father, 1920s

Edna Younger mapped the working lives of her grandparents and great-grandparents across the local village. Although quite elderly, her great-grandparents were still alive in the 1920s when she was a small child (Figure 6.2).

Both were integrated within the parish community of Nether Alderley through a combination of formal and informal ties. Her great-grandfather had worked in the Alderley mines from the age of twelve:

> *Edna Younger.* My great-grandfather lived in Welsh Row, but as a child he lived in Chelford. It was on the road from Welsh Row. This lane at the back is Artist's Lane, and then Welsh Row is at the bottom, over the main road. And he apparently, as a child, came to work in the mines. And he used to walk up from Chelford. Well, it must be five miles, as the crow flies. And he'd start work at six o'clock in the mines, imagine that!
>
> *Devin Hahn.* Your grandfather?
>
> *Edna Younger.* Great-grandfather. And then he lived in Welsh Row, in one of Lord Stanley's cottages. There's two on the right. They're lovely old cottages. And he kept bees. There were about five hives in the garden. . . . And at twelve years old he started work. It's amazing, isn't it? A different way of life. But you see, he grew to be a wonderful gardener; he knew everything about gardens and how to grow them. And then he kept these bees, and they were quite a famous old pair really, he and Great-grandma.
>
> (Mrs Edna Younger, ASP interviews, July 2003).

While Mrs Younger's great-grandmother did not participate in the wage economy of the commuter village, she maintained an active, yet informal, role in the working life and structure of the wider community:

> *Edna Younger.* [S]he was a great worker. She went and cooked dinners at the school at one point, 'cause she'd heard they'd no cook. And I heard one story of her coming from Alderley village. And, of course, they always walked from Alderley village to the Welsh Row. Two miles. We walked two miles to school from here. And she met this gentleman who worked for the coal people in the village. Oh, what did they call it? – coal merchant. And she met this old chap coming up the hill, and he looked terribly ill. She said, he'd got flu. And she asked him where he was going, and he said, oh, So-and-so. So she pushed the barrow while he carried her shopping up.
>
> (Mrs Edna Younger, ASP interviews, July 2003)

Such stories demonstrated how friendly bonds of mutual assistance sustained a sense of belonging across the wider Alderley community.

By the end of the nineteenth century, the ancient Nether Alderley community, traditionally oriented towards the Stanley estate, was increasingly overshadowed as locals turned to the commuter village of Alderley Edge for their primary means of employment. In contrast to her great-grandparents, both Mrs Younger's parents and grandparents developed working lives more firmly entrenched in the service economy of Alderley Edge village. This was a crucial shift, reflecting the broad socio-economic transition into England's post-industrial era. Formed only along commercial lines, the new village did not articulate with traditional historic ties between landlord and parish. Despite the fact that the Hagg Cottages lay on Stanley family land, outside of the village boundary, the working lives of Hagg Cottage residents were increasingly focused on the Alderley Edge high street by the turn-of-century. Mrs Younger's paternal grandmother was the first in the family to be actively engaged in commercial trade. From 1908 through 1921 she ran a confectioner's shop in Orchard Green, at the centre of the village, and became rather well known for her home-made toffees (Mrs Edna Younger, ASP interviews, July 2003).

By the 1920s all adult Hagg residents were engaged with some aspect of the local service economy. Both Mr George Barber and Mr Frederick Barrow, fathers of our oral history participants, trained for their jobs in the village of Alderley Edge. As mentioned in Chapter 4 in relation to pharmaceutical products, Mr Barber worked as a pharmacy assistant in an Alderley Edge village chemist. Mr Barrow was a skilled tradesman, who serviced houses across the region. Starting a carpentry apprenticeship at age fourteen, he was fully qualified by the age of twenty-one. By 1932 he ran his own shop in the village and specialised in making furniture (Mrs Edna Younger, ASP interviews, July 2003).

Mr Barrow's carpentry shop and the chemists that employed Mr George Barber formed part of a wide range of village shops over the inter-war decades. Others included two general stores – Hibberby's and Broadbent's. Both were described as 'regular village shops' that 'provided for the ordinary people of Alderley'. Seymour Meats was a second-hand furniture shop owned by 'a great character, Amy Crossley' (Mrs Edna Younger, ASP interviews, July 2003). Like industrial labourers, the service economy workers of the Hagg Cottages shared a common material world based around their labour patterns. Such shared ties may have helped forge a particular sense of community through a combination of daily social interactions and familiar household goods – purchased from the same high-street shops they themselves worked in.

Other Hagg residents engaged with less commercial forms of the local service economy. Female householders maintained a range of private contracts with the neighbouring villas for domestic-service labour. For instance, as discussed above, Mrs Barrow took in laundry for processing at home. The Misses Ellam, residents of the western half of the Area B cottage, relied upon a resourceful mix of activities. While Miss Gertie Ellam undertook domestic service in the villas, her sister, Miss Mary Ellam, worked from home:

> *Edna Younger.* It was all beautifully laid out. The Miss Ellams' garden, I mean. Father kept ours tidy, but theirs was immaculate. And one did all the work outside, and the other did the inside work. And that was it, they were left two spinsters on their own, oh, until they were too old, really, to be living up here. And they were given a house, one of Lord Stanley's, at the school at Nether Alderley, so they could get a bus down to the village. Two wonderful old ladies.
>
> (Mrs Edna Younger, ASP interviews, September 2003)

Mr Jack Perrin, a member of the extended Area A household, appeared to hold casual local agricultural employment:

> *Roy Barber.* I've never known him to work, as such. I suppose he did at one time. But he was the one who used to go round the farms assisting in the pig killing.
>
> (Mr Roy Barber, ASP interviews, September 2003)

Mr Perrin also delivered the local newspaper by bicycle, with Mr Roy Barber describing how he enjoyed riding on the rear frame as company during delivery routes. When day trippers from Manchester began visiting Alderley Edge to explore the disused mine shafts, Mr Barber's great-uncle developed an ingenious source of supplementary income:

Roy Barber. They made him . . . custodian of the [disused] mines and he used
to sit on a rock just before the mine entrance . . . He used to sit there, selling
these candles.

Edna Younger. Ha'penny each.

Roy Barber. These candles he bought in Alderley Edge . . . He used to cut them
in half and sell them for about one half for about four times what he paid
for them. [*Laughter*.]

Roy Barber. And that was a little income for him . . .

(Mr Roy Barber and Mrs Edna Younger, ASP interviews, September 2003).

Thus Jack Perrin emerged from the oral history as a man of frugal means,
a well connected fellow who resourcefully drew from local agricultural,
service and emerging tourist industries to generate his livelihood.

By the 1920s adult residents of the Hagg Cottages drew almost exclusively
upon the post-industrial service economy. The railroad commuter village of
Alderley Edge had emerged as the prominent local settlement, eclipsing the
traditional medieval village of Nether Alderley. Working life at the Hagg not
only created social bonds and shared material assemblages, it cultivated a
sense of community and belonging across the local landscape.

Objects of community

Particular items of excavated material culture helped illuminate the dynamics of community identity at the Hagg site. As a material communication
with the outside world, clothing offered a ubiquitous marker of social
'belonging'. Similarly, the sharing of foodstuffs between Hagg households
materially demonstrated the neighbourly ties and celebrated events that
sustained their sense of 'mutuality'. Through these everyday artefacts Hagg
Cottage residents subtly affirmed the internal hierarchies of kinship, class,
affiliation, support, competition and obligation that structured life within
this rural English settlement.

Clothing: presenting self to the wider community

Dress could be separated into two distinct categories: mundane daily clothes,
and those reserved for special occasions. Artefacts related to both types were
recovered during excavations. A variety of fasteners were recovered from
Area A: three belt buckles – one with a remnant of leather belt, a buckle from
a pair of trouser braces, a white-painted metal shirt button and a blue-black
glass coat button. Decorative clothing accessories were also deposited across
the site. From Area A, these included three handbag frames (Figure 6.3) –
one with elements of original fabric still adhering – one black dress stud,
three pieces of metal jewellery, a metal brooch and a steel corset bone.

Figure 6.3 Metal alloy handbag frame, Alderley Sandhills Project, 2003

Figure 6.4 Umbrella frame, with black fabric adhering to metal, Alderley
Sandhills Project, 2003

Other dress-related metal and composite-material artefacts recovered
from Area A consisted of a set of wire-framed spectacles, two boot-heel
plates, a fine engraved silver metal clasp and wooden umbrella handle, and
frames of two undecorated umbrellas. Both of these last artefacts retained
fine, yet highly decayed, black fabric adhering to the metal struts and one
held the remains of a wooden handle (Figure 6.4).

Metal clothing elements were also recovered from Area B excavations.
These included a spiral metal corset bone, three shoe-heel plates, and one

shoe toe plate. The Area B assemblage also contained a metal coat button, a metal trouser button and a small metal shirt button. A final, and particularly treasured, find from Area B consisted of a nine-carat gold collar stud.

Non-metal clothing artefacts were also found throughout the Hagg site. From Area A, these mostly involved various components of jewellery. The assemblage included purple and red plastic beads, manufactured to appear as glass. A fake pearl earring, also manufactured of plastic, was recovered from Area A, in addition to a large quantity of glass beads in a variety of colours. Area B contained a single pink/red fragment of plastic hairslide and one leather shoe heel.

Working gear

Discussing a photograph of a tin dressing floor in Cornwall at the end of the nineteenth century, Palmer (2005: 63) observed the importance of clothing for signalling differential status within the workplace. In this example, different types of headgear and costume were argued to represent various forms of labour. Similar social relations could be interpreted from Hagg Cottage photographs, particularly one dated to the early 1920s (Figure 6.5). In this family snap, Mr Frederick Barrow, a skilled carpenter, was photographed

Figure 6.5   Mr George Barber and Mr Frederick Barrow, early 1920s

190   *The Alderley Sandhills Project*

wearing a flat cap, while Mr George Barber, a pharmacist's shop assistant, was pictured in his trilby. Thus the clothing represented within the image may have signalled an occupational difference through the medium of clothing. Although both ran high-street shops in Alderley Edge village, one provided customer service, while the other offered a skilled trade.

Clothing artefacts recovered from the Hagg site also communicated clearly defined social roles within the local community. Objects such as the umbrella frames, carefully decorated walking stick and smart metal shirt and coat buttons recovered from Area A may have formed part of Mr George Barber's work attire as a pharmacy assistant. In contrast, Mr Barrow would have been expected to appear as a skilled tradesman within the wider Alderley Edge community. The assemblage collected from Area B may have reflected this occupational difference, with the high concentration of solid metal boot and shoe plates ('segs') indicating the practical footgear required on a building site.

Dressing up

Other excavated items of clothing would have been worn only outside of work. Sunday church attendance, for example, would have required an alternative social appearance. Mrs Edna Younger told us that her family always attend Sunday services at the traditional parish church in Nether Alderley:

> *Edna Younger.* And we used to go to the church at Nether Alderley. My parents used to take me. And it was a long walk down to Nether Alderley church. But you enjoyed it! We used to go in winter and summer. Down through the snow, they were the things you had to do. The Stanleys – they had their own pew, and their own steps into it. And they'd all come in up these steps and sit in this special . . . it's still there.
> *Devin Hahn.* Did they own the church?
> *Edna Younger.* No, no. But they were the landowners. Old church, 1600s it was built. All my family were married there. And I was. And Jeffrey [her son] was christened there. You always felt a part of it. You felt you were part of it all. One big district, very well run.
> (Mrs Edna Younger, ASP interviews, August 2003)

With the Stanley family attending the Nether Alderley church, occupying the family pew, the Hagg residents collectively reaffirmed their roles within the estate community – their sense of social affiliation beyond that of the commercial village. Thus recovered items of clothing such as the gold collar stud and decorative umbrella may well have been purchased simply for use on special occasions – Sundays, holidays and formal 'dress-up' events.

Figure 6.6   Mrs Lena Perrin (*far right*), pictured in costume jewellery atop the
Sandhills, *c.* 1928

Social concepts of gender and class were also relayed through these
archaeological data. The metal corset bones, for example, have been associated with middle- and upper-class women of the Victorian era – ladies
'cramped by custom, corset and crinoline' (Vickery, 1998: 384). However,
corset bones were from both Area A and Area B, suggesting their use
across the social spectrum. The jewellery items could be similarly associated with female members of the Hagg community. Mrs Lena Perrin's
status as the great-aunt of the Barber family was materially reinforced
through her costume (Figure 6.6). Remembered by oral history participants
as a particularly formidable character within the Hagg community, Mrs
Perrin was inevitably associated with the unusual quantity of glass costume
jewellery recovered during excavations. Photographs from the inter-war
years depicted her 'spangly-danglies' in active use, worn to accompany her
somewhat outmoded Edwardian-era attire.

While the glass and plastic beads of Area A may well have affixed Mrs
Perrin a colourful role within the local community, other recovered items of
personal adornment conformed more closely to prevailing tastes in feminine
fashion. Bright plastic jewellery, in particular, was popular across North
America and Europe over the 1920s and 1930s (Meikle, 1997: 76) and

the simple linear design of the recovered metal brooch suggested inter-war period origins. Clothing-related artefacts thus provided a valuable insight into community life over time. Through their attire, Hagg Cottage residents could present themselves in relation to either their employment within the local service economy or their social position within the wider Stanley estate community.

Food and community

A final material correlate of community identities occurred through the sharing of food across the four Hagg Cottage households. Several of the oral history narratives referred to these friendly exchanges as habitual daily practices. Mrs Edna Younger recalled her childhood breakfasts with Mr Ellam, elderly father of the Misses Ellam, who occupied the adjoining half of the Area B cottage:

> *Edna Younger.* And their father, of course, was a very old Cheshire man. He used to say, 'Oo wants a strawberry, doesn't oo?' [*Laughs.*] You know, the old-fashioned way of talking . . . And I used to share his porridge in the morning. Father would bring the paper up from the night before, and the following morning I used to deliver it. Before I went to school, this was. When I was very young. I'd go round with the paper to Mr Ellam, and he'd be sat, having his porridge. And he'd say, 'Oo wants a bit of porridge, doesn't oo? Sit 'r' on me knee.' And I'd sit on his knee, and he'd give me another spoon, and we'd both have it out of the same dish. [*Laughs.*]
> (Mrs Edna Younger, ASP interviews, August 2003).

Recorded in family photographs shared by Mrs Molly Pitcher, Mrs Edna Younger's fifth birthday was a particularly festive event for the Hagg residents. The neighbouring Barber and Ellam families attended and a range of party foods accompanied the celebration. At other neighbourly gatherings, alcohol was shared between the households, with the Barber, Perrin and Barrow adults joining the Ellams in the consumption of home-made wine.

Kinship ties were also reinforced through the sharing of foods across the local community. Mrs Edna Younger recalled visiting her maternal grandparents for meals while they still lived at the Hagg. On one particularly memorable occasion, her grandmother fed her an egg because she was upset (Mrs Edna Younger, ASP interviews, July 2003). The preparation of food for extended kin was described as a key motivation in the relocation of family members between different households. Mrs Lena Perrin, for example, had originally moved to the Hagg Cottages to help look after her young nephew, George Barber. However, due to her lack of cooking skills, the youth was regularly sent to nearby Brynlow Farm to eat with other Barber cousins (Mrs

Molly Pitcher, ASP interviews, July 2003). Similarly, although archaeological evidence of two separate kitchens was recorded within the Area A subdivided cottage, Mrs Pitcher told of her mother cooking for both sides of the extended Perrin–Barber household. Following the departure of the Barber family from the Hagg site in 1928, Mrs Pitcher remembered her mother continuing to prepare meals for Mrs Lena Perrin. She would instruct Mrs Pitcher to bicycle over from Wilmslow to deliver these foods to her elderly great-aunt at the Hagg Cottages.

Material examples of such hospitality could be found within recovered assemblages. The cakestands in particular reflect the way in which certain social contexts required a polite presentation of food to visitors. Since informal food sharing also interconnected the Hagg community, formal ceramics were not required in all situations. Instead, dishes, plates, bottles and serving bowls from one household may have been transferred to another as foodstuffs were collectively consumed. In Chapter 3 the relative absence of matching plates or tewares was discussed. This ceramic pattern may have represented an interchangability of tablewares between excavated households. The careful maintenance of matched ceramic sets may have seemed superfluous if one knew that plates would be borrowed and returned, lost and recovered among the various cottage kitchens. Since food preparation within such a close community as the Hagg may have functioned separately from consumption, the distribution of ceramics could occur across all four households. Thus the scattering of domestic artefacts across the site itself reflected the everyday practice of neighbourly relations within this rural settlement.

Conclusion

This chapter has covered the range of experiences and material practices through which community identities were constituted. A sense of social 'belonging' was forged through workplace relations, the communal sharing of foods and annual events hosted by the Stanley landlords. Community life was a spatial experience, with the cottages connected to both the new railroad village and the traditional parish landscape. As people moved about for purposes of work and recreation, they reinforced certain experiences of belonging. Although a difficult concept to interpret directly through the material record, these 'bits and pieces' of everyday life forged a profound sense of community for residents of the Hagg Cottages.

7

The Hagg cottages: material life of a rural community

From food we are led to homes, from homes to health, from health to family life, and thence to leisure, work-discipline, education and play, intensity of labour and so on. From standard of life we pass to way-of-life. But the two are not the same.

(Thompson, 1980: 230).

How does archaeology link the 'bits and pieces' of everyday domestic life with the global transformations of the industrial era? Results of the Alderley Sandhills Project addressed the material world of the Hagg Cottages across a range of scales. Stratigraphic, artefactual and architectural phenomena were integrated to read the residue of site-specific events. These local features in turn revealed how underlying dynamics of household consumption, domestic labour and social identity shaped the nature of everyday domestic life. Finally, these broader socio-economic patterns reflected profound material changes in the basic fabric of English rural communities over the last three centuries.

As observed in the introduction to this volume, the Alderley Sandhills Project explored three roughly grouped categories of analysis: material, methodological and interpretive. Weaving together archival, material and narrative sources of evidence, the results of this work placed our excavated features and recovered assemblages within a living social landscape. These data explained how our Hagg residents lived and laboured within their rural hamlet. It demonstrated how specific research techniques could help reveal these unrecorded pasts and, most important, it illuminated what these ordinary domestic lives meant to the residents themselves.

Material

On the site-specific level, project results characterised the nature, distribution, deposition and demolition of archaeological resources from the Hagg

Cottages. Area A was the most archaeologically intact region of the site. Excavations revealed extensive preservation of the original structure, including interior and exterior walls and flooring of various fabrics. The layout conformed with the regionally characteristic 'double-pile' Georgian cottage, a common mid-eighteenth-century rural house form adopted by Lord Stanley for workers' dwellings across his Alderley estate. Excavated features also included a cellar, two kitchens, a mid-nineteenth-century lean-to extension to the south and a fireplace in the southern interior front room.

Fieldwork also revealed a significant transition from local to national sources of building materials. While local building materials, primarily sandstone and hand-made bricks, were exclusively used in the construction of the eighteenth-century double-pile cottage, the nineteenth-century lean-to extension on the southern side of the cottage was floored in ceramic quarry tiles. Mass-produced from the mid-nineteenth century in the Midlands, these architectural ceramics required rail transport for bulk distribution. As the village of Alderley Edge was established to service the rail link to central Manchester in the late 1840s, this rail link provided the facilities for transporting new and 'exotic' goods in to the area.

Results from analysis of the metal, glass and ceramic assemblages recovered from Area A suggested a primary deposition period spanning from the late nineteenth through mid-twentieth centuries. This date range linked artefact assemblages with oral histories on the Barber and Perrin households. Representing the final phase of site occupation, the collections reflected patterns of domestic consumption under deindustrialisation, as Hagg residents increasingly turned to the rail commuter town of Alderley Edge for work in the local service economy.

Located within Area B, the second cottage consisted of a two-storey lobby (or 'baffle') entrance house, of typical design for the mid- to late seventeenth century. Similar to the 'hall and parlour' vernacular houses of North America (Deetz, 1977), this multi-purpose structure functioned as a rural farmhouse for 'ordinary' tenants of the Stanley family. Significantly, excavations revealed the Area B cottage originally included a brick entrance porch – an unusual feature suggesting a degree of relative affluence for these early agricultural workers.

Evidence from clay-pipe and architectural analysis also suggested an earlier seventeenth-century origin for the Area B cottage, with complex modifications transforming its structural layout over the subsequent four centuries. The first major change occurred before 1808, when the orientation of this cottage was reversed and the seventeenth-century brick entrance porch was reused as a rear utility storeroom. The reorientation of the Area B house may have related to the construction of the Area A double-pile cottage in the 1740s, and consequent re-routeing of Hagg Lane to provide more direct access between the two dwellings.

By 1808, archival evidence indicates, both Hagg Cottages were subdi-vided to provide separate accommodation for a total of four households. While the heavy recycling of building materials from Area B obscured the interpretation of interior spaces within this dwelling, structural evidence was recovered Area A, where the pattern of interior walls, access routes and duplication of kitchens suggested a multiple-occupancy cottage. Historical evidence has indicated that the front wall and roof of the Area B cottage were reconstructed in 1828, with a new kitchen and boiler space added thereafter.

Post-excavation analysis of the recovered artefactual assemblages sug-gested two principal occupation periods: from the late eighteenth through early nineteenth century, and from the later nineteenth through the first half of the twentieth century. The absence of ceramic materials dating to the mid-nineteenth century was likely to represent changes in the nature and loca-tion of depositional activities rather than the absence of site occupation, as census and rental records demonstrate the Hagg Cottages were continuously occupied through the nineteenth century. Both archival and oral history sources indicated that the site was demolished during the 1950s.

Ultimately, these site-specific results transformed the various material residues of local events into a comprehensive stratigraphic sequence for the Hagg site. They allowed us to distinguish intact subsurface remains directly linked to cottage residents over various occupation phases. By helping target assemblages for deeper analysis and interpretation, these site-specific research results provided a detailed archaeological understanding of the site itself – an essential material framework, in other words, for interpreting the broader social meanings and patterns of this rural community.

Methodology

Methodological questions guided our adoption of two particular techniques for the data recovery. Over the course of the 2003 field season, all strati-fied deposits were subjected to coarse sieving through a combination of 4 mm and 2 mm mesh. By using such a fine-scale and systematic recovery method, the Alderley Sandhills Project experienced a dramatically high rate of recovery for small finds. While the bulk of recovered cultural material was non-diagnostic, highly fragmentary and subjected only to preliminary stages of post-excavation analysis before discard, the basic analysis of these small finds helped ensure a systematic calculation of weights and relative concen-trations for artefact classes – particularly ceramics, glass and metals – within the ASP Collection. Ultimately, subtle patterns in these relative concentra-tions of building materials or household-related objects helped refine our interpretation of the site narrative and stratigraphic sequence.

In addition, a significant minority of small finds recovered through coarse sieving included artefacts that held particular interpretive value in themselves. Since original research objectives related to changes in class identity and everyday lifeways over the industrial era, small finds related to domestic activities provided essential data. As described throughout this volume, artefacts recovered from the sieves included objects related to child rearing (ceramic, glass and plastic toys, slate pencils), home industry (nails, copper-alloy thimbles, copper-alloy pins, plastic, bone and glass buttons, fruit seeds), health and hygiene (bone and plastic comb tines, plastic toothbrush bristles, metal razor fragments, ceramic toothpaste jar fragments, glass medicine bottle fragments, etc.) and personal appearance (decorative glass beads, costume jewellery, plastic collar inserts, plastic cufflinks, plastic, bone and glass buttons).

A second focus of methodological research addressed the relationship between ethnographic and archaeological sources of evidence on the recent past. On a particularistic level, oral history interviews helped identify how specific objects and features were produced, distributed, consumed and discarded within the recent past of the Hagg Cottages. The tremendous value of such a 'living' record of an archaeological site could not be overstated. From the perspective of our archaeological fieldwork, the memories shared by previous residents helped determine the location of excavation trenches, establish working interpretations of site stratigraphy and architectural features and identify likely date ranges for recovered artefacts.

However, as demonstrated throughout this volume, the collected oral histories provided an even more profound form of knowledge about the study site. Memories of the former occupants helped illuminate relationships between the recovered artefacts and their broader social, economic and political contexts, thereby moving our study from descriptive into more analytical and interpretive realms. Post-excavation consideration of these audio-visual recordings indicated significant patterns of both harmony and divergence between the ethnographic and archaeological sources of data. By encouraging former residents and neighbours to tell their stories, this project collected a wide range of alternative (and sometimes conflicting) recollections on past objects, spaces and technologies. As scholars have noted, oral history is not the 'past', but rather what the present remembers about the past (Grele, 1985; Purser, 1992; Summerfield, 1998; Misztal, 2003). Due to the many different histories recorded, this project recorded the inevitable disagreements, ambiguities and contradictions with equal enthusiasm as the mutually agreed and materially validated narratives.

Dissonance sometimes resulted from the shifting nature of memory itself. During her numerous site visits, Mrs Edna Younger would interpret the visible architectural remains as they slowly emerged within Area B trenches. Her explanations of specific site features often changed between visits, particularly as elements pre-dating her occupation appeared from the lower stratigraphic layers. Certain features provided 'anchor points' for her recollections, allowing her to drape or overlay memories of her childhood home on the brick and sandstone foundations revealed by the trenches. The generally poor preservation of architectural features from Area B led to ambiguous interpretations of this cottage and frequent revisions to her memories of the interior spatial organisation, the relative size of rooms and the function of specific activity areas. Unsurprisingly, details of material fabric or spatial location tended to be recalled with greater certainty if related to a specific childhood experience – such as watching her mother use the mangle on the sandstone-flagged yard adjacent to their kitchen door, or learning to play the piano in a tiny alcove off the northern side of their parlour. Conversely, such details underwent greater revision and ambiguity when the architectural feature did not anchor a memory of place. For example, Mrs Younger sited the front door of the cottage in multiple locations along the northern wall foundation. In a later interview, she mentioned that as a child she had only ever used the kitchen entrance to the house – and her interpretation of its specific location varied little between site visits.

In contrast, Area A was characterised by a greater degree of archaeological preservation, with excavations revealing more fully intact architectural features. Oral histories provided by the two former residents, Mr Roy Barber and Mrs Molly Pitcher, tended to conform between their site visits. The correlation between versions of their narratives perhaps reflected a greater range of architectural 'anchor points' for securing their memories of place. What dissonance existed tended to reflect differences in social identity between the two participants. For example, during early stages of the project, both were asked about the existence of a basement or cellar feature. While Mrs Pitcher did not believe the house contained such a feature, Mr Barber was certain of its existence. Excavations subsequently revealed a cellar (see Figure 2.8). During their collective interview and site tour of 10 September 2003 the siblings teased each other about these discrepant memories. While Mr Barber, as young boy, had been warned away from the cellar with tales of rats, his younger sister had never been told of its existence. Archaeology provided a third alternative narrative for the same structural feature. Although both oral histories suggested the cellar was not in active use during their interwar occupation period, early twentieth-century glass artefacts (including an intact whisky bottle) were recovered from the damp soil fill of the lowest level. Somebody in their household obviously knew of its existence.

The types of stories collected as oral history also differed. Some participants told 'set piece' stories that could be repeated for interviewers, journalists and audiences with few variations. Others approached the recording process as an extemporaneous 'chat' and offered more conversational types of oral history. In some instances, this conversational approach generated stories that participants subsequently requested be removed from the public record. Indeed, these oral history interviews may have sometimes blurred the delicate boundary between 'private' stories, told in that specific context, and 'public' stories intended for a permanent research record (Summerfield, 1998: 16–17). While the privacy requests of oral history participants were always respected, such reintroduced 'silences' in some cases created an artificial dissonance between the oral history and material evidence – particularly when the censored story had originally validated or explained archaeological patterns in the use and discard of recovered artefacts.

Ultimately, ethnographic, oral history and archaeological sources of data must be approached as complementary, yet different, forms of evidence (Purser, 1992). As we juxtaposed and integrated various material and narrative elements, moments of both harmony and dissonance warranted further exploration. Ultimately, it was through the (non)correlation of these sources that new – and sometimes hidden – details emerged to illuminate the nature of daily life within the Hagg Cottages.

Interpretation

Finally, we turn to consider the transformative roles of industrialisation, and subsequent deindustrialisation, on the everyday material life of this rural English hamlet. To understand the archaeology of the Hagg site, four central themes were selected for interpretive analysis: feeding the family, keeping the home, recreation and relaxation, and community life. Representing the primary functions of a working settlement, these categories helped us characterise the materiality of domestic practice over three centuries of occupation.

Feeding the family

Ceramics appeared as the first mass-produced commodities, with examples of late eighteenth-century vessels recovered from early levels of the Area B structure. Thus, from the earliest years of the industrial era, the working residents of our Hagg Cottages adopted the new domestic commodities of the Midlands, with creamwares and pearlwares recovered from both household sites. In addition to this growing incorporation of factory-produced ceramics, local foodways continued to be reflected in the ceramic assemblage. Significant concentrations of utilitarian earthenwares were deposited through the eighteenth and nineteenth centuries. Primarily appearing as large open hollow vessels and pancheons (or 'milk pans') the continued importance of these locally produced ceramics may have reflected a tradition of home preparation for certain foods, particularly given Cheshire's history as a specialised dairying region. By the late nineteenth century, the importance of regional production and distribution was continued to be reflected in commercial beverages, with Manchester (Boddington's) and Stockport (Groves & Whitnall's) breweries particularly heavily represented in the embossed internal screw plastic closures of glass beer bottles.

Temporal changes in the nature and frequency of commercial market access were difficult to trace because of the relative lack of mid-nineteenth century deposits from excavated areas. Nonetheless, evidence from the demolition layers of the Area A cottage demonstrated the influence of national market access, with inhabitants collecting, discarding, and inheriting factory-produced ceramics through the first half of the twentieth century. Although whitewares had come to dominate the later assemblage, residents also enhanced their household collections with bone china and porcelain teawares. Indeed, by the late nineteenth century, tea had emerged as a standard beverage in British households, reflecting aspects of gender, class, kinship and even national affiliation in its daily consumption.

Intra-site comparative analysis suggested a difference in access to commodified goods between the two excavated cottages. Post-excavation analysis of the glass and ceramic assemblages demonstrated a more frequent purchase of cosmetics and pre-prepared foodstuffs within the eastern Area A cottage. Sauce bottles, beer bottles, marmalades, preserved fish and meats (such as Shippam's paste and tinned sardines), and cooking supplements (including Yeast-vite, Horlick's, Mason's OK Sauce and Bovril) were concentrated within the Area A trenches. These results could be interpreted as demonstrating a lower frequency of mass-produced household commodities in the twentieth-century Barrow household of the Area B, as opposed to the Perrin–Barber extended household of Area A. While issues of post-depositional recycling certainly impacted recovered assemblages, the Barber household appeared to favour the consumption of table sauces, with a number of local and regional brands represented within the glass assemblage from their Area A cottage.

Keeping the home

Changes to the built environment of the Hagg Cottages suggested deeper transformations in the nature of domestic practices over the post-medieval period. A seventeenth-century structure, the earlier Area B cottage would have been initially occupied by yeoman farming household – residents including both the tenant family and any domestic servants or field labourers. Its two downstairs rooms were likely used for a multitude of agricultural and residential activities and its upstairs rooms provided sleeping accommodation. In contrast, the layout of the eighteenth century Area A cottage suggested an increased concern with internal divisions of space, thereby allowing for more specialised activity areas within the household. A more 'modern' form of vernacular architecture, this symmetrical 'double pile' cottage reflected a paternalistic improvement of estate holdings by the local landlord.

Evidence from the glass, ceramic and metal assemblages suggested a general interest in the 'etiquette and equipage' (Paynter 2001: 138) of comfortable domestic life. From the late eighteenth century, site occupants acquired fashionable tablewares from the Potteries district of Staffordshire, discarding these off-white transfer-printed creamwares and pearlwares in favour of whitewares, as fashions changed over the nineteenth century.

In the Area A cottage, these practices of domesticity were augmented with the addition of decorative floorcoverings, sequentially laid over the original eighteenth-century sandstone floors. Consisting of various superposed layers of floorcloth, Congoleum and linoleum, and dated from 1860 through 1935, these gaudily patterned floorcoverings represented a degree of relative prosperity and domestic comfort for these working households. Although similar to the decor preferred by the genteel classes, these brash floorcoverings may well have expressed a distinctive domestic aesthetic.

Display items were recovered in particularly high concentration, with fragments of a Wedgwood Jasperware lidded bowl, highly decorated jugs, floral vases, and a number of nineteenth-century polychrome ceramic figurines found within Area A. Themes of personal adornment and hygiene intersected through the cosmetic containers recovered in relative concentration from the Area A cottage. These include ribbed perfume bottles, white cream jars and two facet-cut stopper tops from slightly more expensive scent bottles. While oral history linked these objects with the Victorian sensibilities of Mrs Lena Perrin, resident of the northern side of the 'double pile' cottage of Area A, decorative items were also recovered from the Area B cottage. These included fragments of two commemorative royal jubilee ceramic vessels, suggesting the commercial expression of monarchist sentiments and national identity by the twentieth-century residents of the Hagg. Glass assemblages from both excavation areas similarly contained decorative items, including a cut-glass decanter, various pressed glass vessels, colourful vases and fragments of a mirrored display case in the demolition deposits of Area A.

Sensitive issues of health, hygiene and sanitation were also interpreted from the recovered Hagg Cottage assemblages. Area A revealed a particularly high count and frequency of medicinal containers, particularly stomach remedies (Milk of Magnesia, McLean's stomach powder). These artefacts possibly reflected Mr Barber's employment as a chemist's assistant, although they also suggest that an inhabitant of the extended Barber–Perrin household suffered a chronic digestive ailment.

Another remarkable example of the increasingly specialist attention to health and hygiene issues over the early twentieth century included the recovery of a glass baby feeder bottle from the Area D trash dump. A clear double-ended, banana-shaped baby feeding bottle, embossed 'The Hygienic Feeder', this artefact suggested a growing material specialisation in domestic science and child-rearing practices over the early twentieth century. Evidence of increased attention to personal hygiene was also apparent in the number of artefacts related to bodily cleansing practices, particularly the plastic and bone toothbrushes discovered in both excavation areas and the various metal safety razors recovered from Area A. Finally, concepts of household sanitation were reflected in the appearance of household cleaners in Area A, including two green hexagonal bottles and a tin of 'pine-scented' product. A ferrous wire rat trap was recovered from interior demolition deposits of Area A, dated to *c.* 1900; this purchased, versus homemade, trap demonstrated increasing commercial attention to unpleasant, yet essential, domestic practices such as vermin control.

Recreation and relaxation

With a fluid overlap between work and residential activities characterising life at the Hagg Cottages, the materiality of this community was also shaped by recreational practices undertaken by site inhabitants. Although frequently an element of foodways, the consumption of alcohol provided an important leisure-time activity throughout occupation of the Hagg site. The relatively common presence of mugs in the slipware and whiteware assemblages may have represented the frequency of beer consumption throughout occupation of the cottages. The glass decanter and fifteen quart bottles recovered from Area A suggested that heavier spirits were also enjoyed by site residents.

While the twentieth-century glass assemblage of Area A contained a significant quantity of beer bottles, a greater concentration of dark-green olive glass wine bottles and two wine drinking glasses were recovered from the Area B trenches. These results might suggest a difference in consumption of alcoholic beverages. However, given that wine was an exotic and relatively expensive luxury item in Britain before the 1970s, the high frequency of wine bottles within the Area B cottage might also suggest that the Barrow household enjoyed a local exchange system with their adjoining neighbours. The 'Miss Ellams' were known for brewing fruit wine in their western half of the internally divided Area B cottage. With their removable cork closures, wine bottles may have been differentially used for distributing these home-made products. Perhaps the frequency of this artefact within Area B demonstrated a particular appreciation of the Ellam sisters' home vintages? Or, more significantly, perhaps a greater degree of integration with the local neighbourly exchange system than was sustained at the Perrin–Barber households of Area A? Ultimately, non-commercial home brews appeared to form an important component of domestic alcohol consumption for rural workers, perhaps indicating a difference from the 'pub' or 'saloon' traditions of their urban counterparts. Ultimately, the differential presence of commodified glass and ceramic goods between the Area A and B households, while possibly related to post-depositional removal and recycling activities, might also represent different adaptations to the burgeoning consumer economy of post-industrial-era Britain.

With smoking-related artefacts deposited across all three centuries of site occupation, tobacco consumption provided a popular recreational activity for various members of the Hagg community. Although seventeenth-century pipe fragments were recovered from the Area B cottage, the majority of clay-pipe artefacts dated after the mid-eighteenth century. As well as serving a functional purpose, the pipes may have communicated a social affiliation – particularly the two earlier nineteenth-century bowls decorated with Masonic motifs. In parallel with the embrace of tea as the 'national drink', tobacco consumption provided a mundane, yet profound, material link with the global processes of empire (Gosden, 2004). The turn-of-century organic briar pipe recovered from Area A illuminated these embedded colonial relations. Although surface decay prevented exact identification of the Hagg example, a number of English factories produced these fashionable carved tree-root pipes, naming their product ranges 'Dublin', 'Bulldog' and 'Rhodesian' in an echo of empire. By the twentieth century, tobacco consumption practices had also fallen under industrial mass-production, with tins of cigarettes appearing within the site deposits. While Vulcanite mouthpieces recovered from Area A suggested that at least one Hagg resident continued to enjoy a leisurely traditional smoke, others adopted the easy accessibility of the modern pre-rolled cigarette.

Not all leisure occurred at the Hagg. By the late nineteenth century, all site residents benefited from recreational travel. Seaside holidays provided a particularly favoured means of relaxation. Area A contained examples of souvenirs collected from two popular regional destinations – Blackpool, the quintessential destination for pre-war northern workers (Walton, 1998) – and Douglas, the capital of the Isle of Man, a fashionable holiday destination off the Lancashire coast (Walton, 2000). Both Mrs Molly Pitcher and Mrs Edna Younger recalled the excitement of the annual holiday trip, with the Barber family taking their vacation in New Brighton, Merseyside, while the Barrows sent their daughter to her grandparents, who by the 1920s had relocated from the Hagg to North Wales. Reflecting the enduring importance of seaside holidays to pre-1950s England, these stories and artefacts equally demonstrate a degree of participation in leisure consumerism. In other words, while firmly *working* households, Hagg residents of the early twentieth century were able to accumulate and mobilise enough disposable income to enjoy an annual vacation. In this sense, the post-industrial service economy of Alderley Edge village may have provided local workers with a valuable alternative to previous industrial and agricultural livelihoods.

Community life

As frequently observed both by social historians (Thompson, 1980; Rule, 1986; Summerfield, 1998) and by historical archaeologists (Silliman, 2006; Shackel, 2004; Symonds and Casella 2006; Groover, 2003; Horning, 2000) workers forge a sense of community through their shared experiences of labour. At the Hagg Cottages, residents maintained close-knit social and economic ties through their daily practices within both the household and the wider surrounding landscape. As children, the project's oral history participants were 'apprenticed' into the working world through a variety of 'helping' activities. The Misses Ellam took the children 'sticking' to fetch firewood from the surrounding woods. Mr Roy Barber rode pillion on his grandfather's bicycle during newpaper route deliveries. Mrs Edna Younger joined her mother in processing laundry collected from the local villas. After the Barbers left the Hagg, Mrs Molly Pitcher frequently cycled up to the cottages to deliver cooked meals to her elderly great-aunt, Mrs Lena Perrin.

Ultimately, these oral histories embedded the Hagg Cottages within the wider social landscape of Alderley Edge, with the 'intermingling of neighbourhood, friendship and kin links developed over time' produced through the reciprocal relationships that structured every life (Rule, 1986: 157).

Figure 7.1 Generations together. Roy Barber with his father and grandfather (*left*); Edna Younger with her mother, grandmother and great-grandmother (*right*)

Differences between the excavated domestic assemblages may have reflected alternative forms of waged non-industrial labour during the inter-war decades. The Barber household (Area A) were sustained through Mr George Barber's employment as a chemist's shop assistant in Alderley Edge. In contrast, the Barrows (Area B) relied upon local contracts, with Mr Frederick Barrow working as a skilled carpenter and Mrs Delphine Barrow (a member of the local Massey family clan) taking in laundry as a supplemental domestic income. Perhaps the higher presence of consumer goods within Area A was a result of closer economic ties with the village. Conversely, perhaps the lower presence of mass-produced commodities within Area B reflected a greater reliance on non-market forms of local exchange, with the Barrows drawing upon barter networks for home-prepared foods and fresh produce.

Despite these possible intra-site differences, the Hagg Cottages operated as a closely knit community, their shared sense of 'belonging' emerging through their material world. Internal hierarchies of class, age and gender were practised as residents ornamented their personal appearance with decorative pocket-books, costume jewellery and silver-handled umbrellas, or donned their flat cap, boots and house dress for a day of work. Their community life was sustained by the ability of inhabitants to 'know' each other both *socially* in the present and *temporally* through memories of previous generations.

Conclusion

In summary, the significant story of the Hagg Cottages is one of continuous socio-economic transformation, mapped from traditional post-medieval agrarian livelihoods, through nineteenth-century industrialisation, and into the earliest stages of twentieth-century deindustrialisation. When combined, the oral histories, archival accounts, family photographs and artefact assemblages demonstrated a growing participation in modern English consumer society. Structural evidence suggested a continuous process of adaptive economic flexibility, as represented through sequential modifications to the vernacular built environment. Material life within the Hagg cottages involved household-based commercial activities, food preparation and consumption patterns, health and hygiene practices, enhancement of living spaces, leisure pursuits, playtime, hierarchical status, inter-household relations and community networks. Ultimately, by engaging with these explicitly social themes, the Alderley Sandhills Project has offered a fresh archaeological perspective on the rapidly changing nature of rural community life over England's recent past.

Bibliography

Alderley Park Estate. 1939. *Illustrated Particulars with Plans and Conditions of Sale of the Alderley Park Estates*. Alderley: Estate Office, Alderley Park, Chelford, Cheshire.

Alexander, D. 1970. *Retailing in England during the Industrial Revolution*. London: Athlone Press.

Allen, Robert C. 1999. Tracking the Agrarian Revolution in England. *Economic History Review* 52(2): 209–235.

Andrews, M. 2006. Too Late to Save our Sauce? *Express and Star* www.expressandstar.com/cgi-bin/artman/exec/view.cgi?archive=35&num=90104 (accessed 10 December 2006).

Appadurai, A. 1986. Introduction: Commodities and the Politics of Value. In A. Appadurai (ed.), *The Social Life of Things: Commodities in Cultural Perspective*, 3–63. Cambridge: Cambridge University Press.

Appadurai, Arjun. 1996. *Modernity at Large: Cultural Dimensions of Globalization*. Minneapolis MN: University of Minnesota Press.

Ariès, Philippe (trans. Robert Baldick) 1962. *Centuries of Childhood*. London: Penguin.

Armstrong, Meg. 1993. 'A jumble of foreignness': The Sublime Musayums of Nineteenth Century Fairs and Expositions. *Cultural Critique* 23: 199–250.

Baram, U. 1999. Clay Tobacco Pipes and Coffee Cup Sherds in the Archaeology of the Middle East: Artifacts of Social Tensions from the Ottoman Past. *International Journal of Historical Archaeology* 3(3): 137–151.

Barker, D. and Majewski, T. 2006. Ceramic Studies in Historical Archaeology. In Hicks, D. and Beaudry, M.C. (eds) *The Cambridge Companion to Historical Archaeology*, 205–231. Cambridge: Cambridge University Press.

Barnwell, P.S. and Giles, C. 1997. *English Farmsteads, 1750–1914*. Swindon: Royal Commission on the Historical Monuments of England.

Barton, Susan 2005. *Working-class Organisations and Popular Tourism, 1840–1970*. Manchester: Manchester University Press.

Beaudry, M.C. 1993. Public Aesthetics versus Personal Experience: Worker Health and Well-being in Nineteenth-Century Lowell, Massachusetts. *Historical Archaeology* 27(2): 90–105.

Beaudry, M.C. and Mrozowski, S. 2001. Cultural Space and Worker Identity in the Company City: Nineteenth-Century Lowell, Massachusetts. In Mayne, A. and Murray T. (eds), *The Archaeology of Urban Landscapes*, 118–31. Cambridge: Cambridge University Press.

Beaudry, Mary C., Cook, Lauren J. and Mrozowski, Stephen A. 1991. Artifacts and Active Voices: Material Culture as Social Discourse. In McGuire, R.H. and Paynter, R. (eds) *The Archaeology of Inequality*, 150–191. Oxford: Blackwell.

Beaudry, M.C., Long, J., Miller, H.M., Neiman, F.D. and Stone, G.W. 1988. A Vessel Typology for Early Chesapeake Ceramics: The Potomac Typological System. In Beaudry, M.C. (ed.), *Documentary Archaeology in the New World*, 44–67. Cambridge: Cambridge University Press.

Beck, W. and Somerville, M. 2005. Conversations between Disciplines: Historical Archaeology and Oral History in Yarrawarra. *World Archaeology* 37(3): 468–483.

Belford, P. 2003. Forging Ahead in Coalbrookdale: Historical Archaeology at the Upper Forge. *Industrial Archaeology Review* 25(1): 59–62.

Belford, P. and Ross, R.A. 2004. Industry and Domesticity: Exploring Historical Archaeology in the Ironbridge Gorge. *Post-Medieval Archaeology* 38(2): 215–225.

Binford, L. R. 1962. A New Method of Calculating Dates from Kaolin Pipe Stem Fragments. *Southeastern Archaeological Conference Newsletter* 9(1): 19–21.

Bonasera, M.C. and Raymer, L. 2001. 'Good for what ails you': Medicinal Use at Five Points. *Historical Archaeology* 35(3): 49–64.

Boothroyd, N. no date (a). *Lawn Farm, Interim Report*. Unpublished report.

Boothroyd, N. no date (b). *Cotehouse Farm, Interim Report*. Unpublished report.

Boothroyd, Noel and Higgins, David. 2005. An Inn Clearance Group, *c.* 1800, from the Royal Oak, Eccleshall, Staffordshire. *Post-Medieval Archaeology* 39(1): 197–203.

Bourdieu, Pierre. 1977. *Outline of a Theory of Practice*. Cambridge Studies in Social and Cultural Anthropology. Cambridge: Cambridge University Press.

Brennand, M. (ed.) 2006. *The Archaeology of North West England: An Archaeological Research Framework for the North West Region*. Vol. I, *Resource Assessment*. Archaeology North West 8(18). Alford: Association of Local Government Archaeological Officers.

Brennand, M. 2007. *Research and Archaeology in North West England*. Vol. II, *Research Agenda and Strategy*. Manchester: Council for British Archaeology North West.

Briggs, A. 1988. *Victorian Things*. London: Penguin.

Brighton, S.A. 2001. Prices that Suit the Times: Shopping for Ceramics at the Five Points. *Historical Archaeology* 35(3): 16–30.

Brighton, S.A. 2004. Symbols, Myth-Making and Identity: The Red Hand of Ulster in Late Nineteenth-Century Paterson, New Jersey. *International Journal of Historical Archaeology* 8(2): 149–164.

Brooks, A. 1997. Beyond the Fringe: Transfer Printed Ceramics and the Internalisation of Celtic Myth. *International Journal of Historical Archaeology* 1(1): 39–55.

Brooks, A. 2003. 'Crossing Offa's Dyke: British Ideologies, Welsh Society and Late Eighteenth- and Nineteenth-Century Ceramics in Wales'. In S. Lawrence (ed.), *Archaeologies of the British*, 119–137. London: Routledge.

Brooks, A. and Connah, G. 2007. A Hierarchy of Servitude: Ceramics at Lake Innes Estate, New South Wales. *Antiquity* 81: 133–147.

Brunskill, R.W. 1982. *Houses*. London: Collins.

Buchli, V. and Lucas, G. 2000. Children, Gender and the Material Culture of Abandonment in the Late Twentieth Century. In Sofaer Derevenski, Joanna (ed.), *Children and Material Culture*, 131–138. London: Routledge.

Burkart, A.J. and Medlik, S. 1981. *Tourism: Past, Present and Future*. London: Heinemann.

Burke, P. 1995. The Invention of Leisure in Early Modern Europe. *Past and Present* 146: 136–150.

Burke, P. 1997. The Invention of Leisure in Early Modern Europe: Reply. *Past and Present* 156: 192–197.

Burnett, J. (1989) *Plenty and Want: A Social History of Food in England from 1815 to the Present Day* (3rd edn). London: Routledge.

Busch, J. 1981. An Introduction to the Tin Can. *Historical Archaeology* 15(1): 95–104.

Busch, J. 2000. Second Time Around: A Look at Bottle Reuse. In Brauner, D.R. (ed.), *Approaches to Material Culture: Research for Historical Archaeologists*, 175–188. Rockville MD: Society for Historical Archaeology.

Caffyn. L. 1983. *Workers' Housing in West Yorkshire*. London: HMSO.

Cantwell, A. and Wall, D. 2001. *Unearthing Gotham: The Archaeology of New York City*. New Haven CT: Yale University Press.

Casella, E. 2000 Bulldaggers and Gentle Ladies: Archaeological Approaches to Female Homosexuality in Convict-Era Australia. In Schmidt, R. and Voss, B. (eds), *Archaeologies of Sexuality*, 143–159. London: Routledge.

Casella, E. 2002. *Archaeology of the Ross Female Factory: Female Incarceration in Van Diemen's Land, Australia*. Records of the Queen Victoria Museum and Art Gallery 108. Launceston, Tasmania: QVMAG Publications.

Casella, E.C. 2005. The Excavation of Industrial Era Settlements in North West England. *Industrial Archaeology Review* 27(1): 77–86.

Casella, E. C., Griffin, D. and Prag, A.J.N.W. 2004. The Alderley Sandhills Project: Final Report. Unpublished report prepared for English Heritage and the National Trust, London.

Casey, M. 1999. Local Pottery and Dairying at the DMR Site, Brickfields, Sydney, New South Wales. *Australasian Historical Archaeology* 17: 3–37.

Cassell's *The Book of the Household, or, Family dictionary of everything connected with housekeeping and domestic medicine: with the treatment of children, management of the sick room, the sanitary improvements of the dwelling, the duties of servants, and full information on all other subjects relating to personal and domestic comfort / compiled by competent persons, under the superintendence of an association of heads of families and men of science*. London and New York: London Printing & Publishing Co. [1862–1864].

Castle, C. 2003. The Representation of Africa in mid-Victorian Children's Magazines.

In Gerzina, G.H. (ed.), Black Victorians, Black Victoriana, 145–158. Piscataway NJ: Rutgers University Press.

Cattell, M.G. and Climo, J.J. 2002. Introduction. Meaning in Social Memory and History: Anthropological Perspectives. In Climo, J.J. and Cattell, M.G. (eds), *Social Memory and History: Anthropological Perspectives*, 1–36. Walnut Creek CA: AltaMira Press.

Chaimov, John. 2001. Hummel Figurines: Moulding a Collectible Germany. *Journal of Material Culture* 6(1): 49–66.

Chase, Malcom 1990. From Millennium to Anniversary: The Concept of Jubilee in Late Eighteenth and Nineteenth-Century England. *Past and Present* 129: 132–147.

Clark, B. 2005 Lived Ethnicity: Archaeology and Identity in 'Mexicano' America. *World Archaeology* 37(3): 440–452.

Clarke, D. 1977. *Spatial Archaeology*. London: Academic Press.

Clay, John. 1857. On the Relation between Crime, Popular Instruction, Attendance on Religious Worship, and Beer-Houses. *Journal of the Statistical Society of London* 20(1): 22–32.

Cochran, M.D. and Beaudry, M.C. 2006. Material Culture Studies and Historical Archaeology. In Hicks, D. and Beaudry, M.C. (eds), *The Cambridge Companion to Historical Archaeology*, 191–204. Cambridge: Cambridge University Press.

Cook, Lauren J. 1989a. Tobacco-related Material and the Construction of Working-class Culture. In Beaudry, Mary C., and Mrozowski, Stephen A. (eds), *Interdisciplinary Investigations of the Boott Mills, Lowell, Massachusetts*. Vol. III, *The Boardinghouses System as a Way of Life*, 209–230. Cultural Resources Management Study No. 21. Boston MA: Division of Cultural Resources, North Atlantic Regional Office, National Park Service, United States Department of the Interior.

Cook, Lauren, J. 1989b. Descriptive Analysis of Tobacco-related Material from the Boot Mills Boardinghouses. In Beaudry, Mary C., and Mrozowski, Stephen A. (eds), *Interdisciplinary Investigations of the Boott Mills, Lowell, Massachusetts*. Vol. III, *The Boardinghouses System as a Way of Life*, 187–208. Cultural Resources Management Study 21. Boston MA: Division of Cultural Resources, North Atlantic Regional Office, National Park Service, US Department of the Interior.

Cook, Lauren J. 1989c. Tobacco-related Material and the Construction of Working-Class Culture. In Beaudry, Mary C., and Mrozowski, Stephen A. (eds), *Interdisciplinary Investigations of the Boott Mills, Lowell, Massachusetts*. Vol. III, *The Boardinghouses System as a Way of Life*, 209–230. Cultural Resources Management Study 21. Boston MA: North Atlantic Regional Office, National Park Service, US Department of the Interior.

Cook, L. 2000. Cinemagoing in Stoke-on-Trent and Newcastle-under-Lyme. In Edensor, Tim (ed.), *Reclaiming Stoke-on-Trent: Leisure, Space and Identity in the Potteries*, Stoke-on-Trent: Staffordshire University Press

Cunningham, Hugh. 1998. Histories of Childhood. *American Historical Review* 103(4): 1195–1208.

Dawson, G. 1994. *Soldier Heroes: British Adventure, Empire and the Imagining of Masculinities*. London: Routledge.

Deetz, J. 1977. *In Small Things Forgotten: An Archaeology of Early American Life*. New York: Anchor Books.

Deetz, J. 1993. *Flowerdew Hundred: The Archaeology of a Virginia Plantation, 1619–1864*. Charlottesville VA: University Press of Virginia.

Derbyshire Caving Club. 2007. The Alderley Edge Mines, Cheshire. www.derbyscc. org.uk/alderley/index.html (accessed 14 May 2007).

Dingle, A.E. 1972. Drink and Working-Class Living Standards in Britain, 1870–1914. *Economic History Review* new series 25(4): 608–622.

Dunhill, A, 1977 *The Pipe Book*, London: Alfred Dunhill.

Edensor, T. (ed.). 2000. *Reclaiming Stoke-on-Trent: Leisure, Space and Identity in the Potteries*, Stoke-on-Trent: Staffordshire University Press

Edis, R.W. 1881. *Decoration of Furniture and Town Houses*. London: Kegan Paul.

Ferguson, L.G. 1992. *Uncommon Ground: Archaeology and Early African America*. Washington DC: Smithsonian Institution Press.

Fine, B. and Leopold, E. 1993. *The World of Consumption*. London: Routledge.

Fischer, Claude S. 1994 Changes in Leisure Activities, 1890–1940. *Journal of Social History* 27(3): 453–475.

Flannery, K.V. 1976. *The Early Mesoamerican Village*. New York: Academic Press.

Ford, B. 1994. The Health and Sanitation of Postbellum Harper's Ferry. *Historical Archaeology* 28(4): 49–61.

Ford, H. 1929. *My Philosophy of Industry*. New York: Coward-McCann.

Friends of Berryhill Fields. 2007. Friends of Berryhill Fields, www.friendsofberryhill-fields.org/dig2006_4.htm (accessed 14 March 2007).

Gaimster, D.R.M. 1997. *German Stoneware, 1200–1900*. London: British Museum Press.

Gaimster, D.R.M. 1999. The post-Medieval Ceramic Revolution in Southern Britain, c. 1450–1650. In Egan G. and Michael, R.L. (eds), *Old and New Worlds*, 214–225. Oxford: Oxbow Books.

Gauldie, Enid. 1974. *Cruel Habitations: A History of Working-Class Housing, 1780–1918*. London: Unwin.

Gibbs, Patricia E. 2005. Eighteenth-Century Redware Folk Terms and Vessel Forms: A Survey of Utilitarian Wares from Southeastern Pennsylvania. *Historical Archaeology* 39(2): 33–62.

Giddens, A. 1984 *The Constitution of Society*. Berkeley CA: University of California Press.

Glassie, Henry H. 1975. *Folk Housing in Middle Virginia: A Structural Analysis of Historic Artifacts*. Knoxville TN: University of Tennessee Press.

Gojak, Denis and Stuart, Iain. 1999. The Potential for the Archaeological Study of Clay Tobacco Pipes from Australian Sites. *Australasian Historical Archaeology* 17: 38–49.

Gooderson, P.J. 1996. *Lord Linoleum: Lord Ashton, Lancaster and the Rise of the British Oilcloth and Linoleum Industry*, Keele: Keele University Press.

Gosden, C. 2004. *Archaeology and Colonialism: Cultural Contact from 5000 BC to the Present*. Cambridge: Cambridge University Press.

Gosden, C. 2005. What do objects want? *Journal of Archaeological Method and Theory* 12(3): 193–211.

Grele, R.J. 1985 *Envelopes of Sound: The Art of Oral History*. Chicago: Precedent Publishing.

Groover, Mark D. 2003. *An Archaeological Study of Rural Capitalism and Material Life: The Gibbs Farmstead in Appalachia, 1790–1920*. New York: Kluwer/Plenum.

Guillery, P. 2006. Housing the Early Modern Industrial City: London's Workshop Tenements. In Green A. and R. Leech (eds) *Cities in the World, 1500–2000*, 117–132. Leeds: Society for Post-Medieval Archaeology/Maney.

Gwyn, D. 2006. *Gwynedd: Inheriting a Revolution: The Archaeology of Industrialisation in North West Wales*. Chichester: Phillimore.

Hackett, Helen. 2001. Dreams or Designs, Cults or Constructions? The Study of Images of Monarchs. *Historical Journal* 44(3): 811–823.

Halbwachs, M. 1992 [1950] *On Collective Memory*. Coser, L.A. (ed. and trans.). Chicago: University of Chicago Press.

Hall, A.M. 2004. What can Bottle Evidence from Alderley Edge Reveal about Domestic Life during the Industrial Revolution? Unpublished B.A. dissertation. Manchester: Archaeology, School of Arts, Histories and Cultures, University of Manchester.

Hall, M. 2000. *Archaeology and the Modern World*. London: Routledge.

Hamilakis, Y. 1999. Food Technologies/Technologies of the Body: The Social Context of Wine and Oil Production and Consumption in Bronze Age Crete. *World Archaeology* 31(1): 38–54.

Harrington, J.C. 1978. Dating Stem Fragments of Seventeenth and Eighteenth Century Clay Tobacco Pipes. In Schuyler, R.L. (ed.), *Historical Archaeology: A Guide to Substantive and Theoretical Contributions*, 63–65. New York: Baywood.

Hartnett, A. 2004. The Politics of the Pipe: Clay Pipes and Tobacco Consumption in Galway, Ireland. *International Journal of Historical Archaeology* 8(2): 133–147.

Heawood, R., Howard-Davis, C., Drury, D., and Krupa, M. 2004. *Old Abbey Farm, Risley: Building Survey and Excavation at a Medieval Moated Site*. Lancaster: Oxford Archaeology North.

Hebbert, M. 2000. Transpennine: Imaginative Geographies of an Interregional Corridor. *Transactions of the Institute of British Geographers* 25(3): 379–392.

Hicks, D. and Horning, A. 2006. Historical Archaeology and Buildings. In Hicks, D. and Beaudry, M.C. (eds), *The Cambridge Companion to Historical Archaeology*, 273–292. Cambridge: Cambridge University Press.

Hilton, Matthew. 1995. 'Tabs', 'Fags' and the 'Boy Labour Problem' in Late Victorian and Edwardian Britain. *Journal of Social History* 28(3): 587–607.

Holder Spude, C. 2006. *The Mascot Saloon: Archaeological Investigations in Skagway, Alaska*, Vol. X. Anchorage, AK: National Park Service, US Department of the Interior.

Holliday, Ruth and Jayne, Mark. 2000. The Potters' Holiday. In Edensor, T. (ed.), *Reclaiming Stoke-on-Trent*. Stoke-on-Trent: Staffordshire University Press.

Horning, A. 2000. Archaeological Considerations of 'Appalachian' Identity: Community-based Archaeology in the Blue Ridge Mountains. In M. Canuto and J. Yaeger (eds), *The Archaeology of Communities*, 210–230. London: Routledge.

Horning, Audrey J. 2002. Myth, Migration, and Material Culture: Archaeology and the Ulster Influence on Appalachia. *Historical Archaeology* 36(4): 129–149.

Hoskins, W.G. 1955. *The Making of the English Landscape*. London: Hodder & Stoughton.

Howard-Davis, C. 2004. The Finds. In Heawood, R., Howard-Davis, C., Drury, D. and Krupa, M. (eds), *Old Abbey Farm, Risley: Building Survey and Excavation at a Medieval Moated Site*, 109–144. Lancaster: Oxford Archaeology North.

Hughes, S.R. 2000. *Copperopolis: Landscapes of the Early Industrial Period in Swansea*. Aberystwyth: Royal Commission on the Ancient and Historical Monuments of Wales.

Hughes, Stephen. 2004. Social Archaeology: A Possible Methodology of the Study of Workers' Settlements based on the Eighteenth- and Nineteenth-Century Copper Industry of Swansea. In David Barker and David Cranstone (eds), *The Archaeology of Industrialization*, 137–153. Leeds: Maney Publishing.

Hughes, Stephen. 2005. Institutional Buildings in Worker Settlements. *Industrial Archaeological Review* 27(1): 153–161.

Hull-Walski, D.A. and Walski, F.L. 1994. 'There's trouble a-brewin'': The Brewing and Bottling Industries at Harper's Ferry, West Virginia. *Historical Archaeology* 28(4): 106–121.

Humphrey, Richard V. 1969. Clay Pipes from Old Sacramento. *Historical Archaeology* 3: 12–33.

Hurst, G. 2006 [1987]. Appendix B. Mascot Saloon Group Container Glass Identification and Dating. In Holder Spude, C. (ed.), *The Mascot Saloon: Archaeological Investigations in Skagway, Alaska*, Vol. X, 257–286. Anchorage, AK: National Park Service, US Department of the Interior.

Hurst, J.G., Neal, D.S. and Van Beuningen, H.J.E. 1986. *Pottery Produced and Traded in North West Europe, 135 –1650*. Rotterdam Papers VI. Rotterdam: Museum Boymans-van Beuningen.

Hutchinson, Joanne. 1996. The Post-Medieval Pottery and Glass from the Bowling Green Public House, 44 Oxford Street, Leicester. Unpublished M.A. thesis, School of Archaeological Studies, University of Leicester.

Hyde, Matthew. 1999. *The Villas of Alderley Edge*. Altrincham: Silk Press.

Jamieson, Ross W. 2001. The Essence of Commodification: Caffeine Dependencies in the Early Modern World. *Journal of Social History* 35(2): 269–294.

Janowitz, M.F. 1993. Indian Corn and Dutch Pots; Seventeenth-Century Foodways in New Amsterdam/New York. *Historical Archaeology* 27(2): 6–24.

Jeffries, Nigel. 2006. The Metropolis Local Management Act and the Archaeology of Sanitary Reform in the London Borough of Lambeth, 1856–1886. *Post-Medieval Archaeology* 40(2): 272–290.

Johnson, M. 1993. *Housing Culture: Traditional Architecture in an English Landscape*. London: UCL Press.

Johnson, M. 1999. Rethinking Historical Archaeology. In Funari, P.P.A., Hall, M. and Jones, S. (eds), *Historical Archaeology: Back from the Edge*, 23–36. London: Routledge.

Johnson, Paul. 1988. Conspicuous Consumption and Working-Class Culture in Late Victorian and Edwardian Britain. *Transactions of the Royal Historical Society* fifth series 38: 27–42.

Jones, Olive R. 1993. Commercial Foods, 1740–1820. *Historical Archaeology* 27(2): 25–41.

Jones, O., Sullivan, C., Miller, G., Smith, E.A. and Harris, J. 1989. *The Parks Canada Glass Glossary for the Description of Containers, Tableware, Flat Glass, and Closures*. Studies in Archaeology, Architecture and History. Ottawa: Parks Canada.

Jordan, S.C. 2000. Coarse Earthenware at the Dutch Colonial Cape of Good Hope, South Africa: A History of Local Production and Typology of Products. *International Journal of African Historical Archaeology* 4(2): 113–143.

Karskens, G. 1998. *The Rocks: Life in Early Sydney*. Melbourne, Vic.: Melbourne University Press.

Karskens, G. 1999. *Inside the Rocks: The Archaeology of a Neighbourhood*. Sydney: Hale & Iremonger.

Karskens, G. 2003. Exporting Culture: Archaeology and the Nineteenth-Century British Empire. *Historical Archaeology* 37 (1): 20–33.

King, J.A. 2006. Household Archaeology: Identity and Biographies. In Hicks, D. and Beaudry, M.C. (eds), *The Cambridge Companion to Historical Archaeology*, 293–313. Cambridge: Cambridge University Press.

King, J.A. 2007. Still Life with Tobacco: The Archaeological Uses of Dutch Art. *Historical Archaeology* 41(1): 6–22.

Kingsdale, Jon M. 1973. The 'Poor Man's Club': Social Functions of the Urban Working-Class Saloon. *American Quarterly* 25(4): 472–489.

Koehn, Nancy F. 1999. Henry Heinz and Brand Creation in the Late Nineteenth Century: Making Markets for Processed Food. *Business History Review* 73(3): 349–393.

Kolb, M.J. and Snead, J. 1997. 'It's a small world after all': Comparative Analyses of Community Organization in Archaeology. *American Antiquity* 62(4): 609–28.

Larsen, E.L. 1994. A Boardinghouse Madonna: Beyond the Aesthetics of a Portrait Created through Medicine Bottles. *Historical Archaeology* 28(4): 68–79.

Lawrence, S. 2000. *Dolly's Creek*. Carleton, Vic.: Melbourne University Press.

Lawrence, Susan. 2003. Introduction: Archaeological Perspectives on the British and their Empire. In Lawrence, Susan (ed.), *Archaeologies of the British: Explorations of Identity in Great Britain and its Colonies, 1600–1945*, 1–13. London: Routledge.

Lawton, R. and Pooley, C.G. 1992. *Britain, 1740–1950: An Historical Geography*. London: Edward Arnold.

Lefebvre, H. 1991. *The Production of Space*. Oxford: Blackwell.

Leone, Mark P. and Potter, Parker B. (eds). 1999. *Historical Archaeologies of Capitalism*, 219–32. New York: Kluwer/Plenum.

Leone, M. and Shackel, P. 1987. Forks, Clocks and Power. In Ingersoll, D. and Bronitski, G. (eds), *Mirror and Metaphor: Material and Social Construction of Reality*, 45–61. Latham MD: American University Press.

Leone, M. with Creveling, M. and Nagle, C. 1999. Ceramics from Annapolis, Maryland: A Measure of Time Routines and Work Discipline. In Leone, M.P. and Potter, P.B., Jr (eds), *Historical Archaeologies of Capitalism*, 195–216. New York: Kluwer/Plenum.

Levenstein, H. 1983. 'Best for Babies' or 'Preventable Infanticide'? The Controversy over Artificial Feeding of Infants in America, 1880–1920. *Journal of American History* 70(1): 75–94.

Lillehammer, Grete. 2000. The World of Children. In Sofaer Derevenski, Joanna (ed.), *Children and Material Culture*, 17–26. London: Routledge.

Linney, A. 1924. Hats off to King Cole, *White Star Magazine*, November 1924, 106–110.

Lummis, T. 1987. *Listening to History: The Authenticity of Oral Evidence*. London: Hutchinson.

Lyons, D. 2008. Integrating African Cuisines: a Rural Example of Local Cuisine and Identity in Tigray Region, Highland Ethiopia. *Journal of Social Archaeology*.

Macclesfield Canal Society. 2007. History of the Macclesfield Canal. http://adkins-family.org.uk/macclesfieldcanal/history/index.htm (accessed 14 May 2007).

MacLean, R. and Insoll, T. 1999. The Social Context of Food Technology in Iron Age Gao, Mali. *World Archaeology* 31(1): 78–92.

McClure, H.R. 1939 An Historical and Regional Survey of the Village of Styal, Cheshire. *Geographical Journal* 93(6): 512–520.

McGuire, Randall H. and Reckner, Paul. 2002. The Unromantic West: Labor, Capital, and Struggle. *Historical Archaeology* 36(3): 44–58.

McNeil, R. and Newman, C. 2006a. The Post-Medieval Period Resource Assessment. In Brennand, M. (ed.), *The Archaeology of North West England: An Archaeological Research Framework for the North West Region*. Vol. I, *Resource Assessment*. Archaeology North West 8(18): 145–164. Alford: Association of Local Government Archaeological Officers.

McNeil, Robina and Newman, Richard. 2006b The Industrial and Modern Period Resource Assessment. In Brennand, M. (ed.), *The Archaeology of North West England: An Archaeological Research Framework for the North West Region*. Vol. I, *Resource Assessment*. Archaeology North West 8(18): 165–194. Alford: Association of Local Government Archaeological Officers.

Mallios, Seth. 2005. Back to the Bowl: Using English Tobacco Pipebowls to Calculate Mean Site Occupation Dates. *Historical Archaeology* 39(2): 89–104.

Marfany, Joan-Luís. 1997. The Invention of Leisure in Early Modern Europe. *Past and Present* 156: 174–191.

Marriott Watson, R. 1897. *The Art of the House*. London: George Bell.

Matthews, C. 2001. Political Economy and Race: Comparative Archaeologies of Annapolis and New Orleans in the Eighteenth Century. In Orser, C.E. (ed.), *Race and the Archaeology of Identity*, 71–87. Salt Lake City UT: University of Utah Press.

Matthews, K. 1999. Familiarity and Contempt: The Archaeology of the 'Modern'. In Tarlow, S. and West, S. (eds), *The Familiar Past? Archaeologies of Later Historical* Britain, 155–179. London: Routledge.

Mayne, A. 1993. *The Imagined Slum*. Leicester: Leicester University Press.

Meikle, J.L. 1997. *American Plastic: A Cultural History*. New Brunswick NJ: Rutgers University Press.

Messer, E. 1984. Anthropological Perspectives on Diet. *Annual Review of Anthropology* 13: 205–249.

Messener, Michael A. 2000. Barbie Girls versus Sea Monsters: Children Constructing Gender. *Gender and Society* 14(6): 765–784.

Miller, G.L. 1980. Classification and Economic Scaling of Ninteenth Century Ceramics. *Historical Archaeology* 14: 1–40.

Miller, G.L. 1991. A Revised Set of CC Index Values for Classification and Economic Scaling of English Ceramics from 1787 to 1880. *Historical Archaeology* 25(1): 1–25.

Mintz, S.W. 1985. *Sweetness and Power: The Place of Sugar in Modern History*. New York: Penguin.

Misztal, B. 2003. *Theories of Social Remembering*. Maidenhead: Open University Press.

Mitford, N. (ed.). 1939. *The Stanleys of Alderley: Their Letters between the Years 1851–1865*. London: Chapman & Hall.

Mrozowski, Stephen A. 2000. The Growth of Managerial Capitalism and the Subtleties of Class Analysis in Historical Archaeology. In Delle, James A., Mrozowski, Stephen A. and Paynter, Robert (eds), *Lines that Divide: Historical Archaeologies of Race, Class, and Gender*, 276–305. Knoxville TN: University of Tennessee Press.

Mrozowski, S. 2005. Cultural Identity and the Consumption of Industry. In Casella, E.C. and Symonds, J. (eds), *Industrial Archaeology: Future Directions*, 243–260. New York: Springer.

Mrozowski, S.A. 2006. Environments of History: Biological Dimensions of Historical Archaeology. In Hall, M. and Silliman, S.W. (eds), *Historical Archaeology*, 23–41. Oxford: Blackwell.

Mrozowski, S.A., Ziesing, G.H. and M.C. Beaudry. 1996. *Living on the Boott: Historical Archaeology at the Boott Mills Boardinghouses, Lowell Massachusetts*. Amherst MA, University of Massachusetts Press.

Mullins, P.R. 1999. *Race and Affluence: An Archaeology of African America and Consumer Culture*. New York: Kluwer/Plenum.

Mullins, Paul R. 2004. Consumerism, Living Conditions and Well-being. In Praetzellis, M. and Praetzellis, A. (eds), *Putting the 'There' There: Historical Archaeologies of West Oakland*, 85–116. Rohnert Park CA: Anthropological Studies Center, Sonoma State University Academic Foundation.

National Trust. 2007. *Alderley Edge*. www.nationaltrust.org.uk/main/w-vh/w-visits/w-findaplace/w-alderleyedge/ (accessed March 2007).

Nevell, M. and Walker, J. 1999. *Tameside in Transition: The Archaeology of the Industrial Revolution in two North West Lordships, 1642–1870*. Ashton under Lyne: Tameside Metropolitan Borough Council/Carnegie.

Newman, L.F. 1946. Some Notes on Foods and Dietetics in the Sixteenth and

Seventeenth Centuries. *Journal of the Royal Anthropological Institute of Great Britain and Ireland* 1: 39–49.

Noël Hume, Ivor. 1982. *Martin's Hundred*. New York: Knopf.

Nuttall, S. and Coetzee, C. 1998. *Negotiating the Past*. Cape Town: Oxford University Press.

Oliver, A. 1981. *Staffordshire Pottery: The Tribal Art of England*. London: Heinemann.

Orser, C.E. 1996. *The Historical Archaeology of the Modern World*. New York: Kluwer Academic/Plenum.

Orser, C. 1999. Negotiating our 'Familiar Pasts'. In Tarlow, S. and West, S. (eds), *The Familiar Past? Archaeologies of Later Historical Britain*, 273–285. London: Routledge.

Orser, C.E., Jr. 2005. Symbolic Violence, Resistance and the Vectors of Improvement in Early Nineteenth-Century Ireland. *World Archaeology* 37(3): 392–407.

Oxford Archaeology North. 2005. *New Islington Wharf, Ancoats, Manchester: Archaeological Investigation*. Unpublished report, December.

Oxford Archaeology North. 2006. *Piccadilly Place, Piccadilly, Manchester: Archaeological Excavation*. Unpublished report, April.

Oxford Archaeology North and John Samuels Archaeological Consultants. 2006. *Kingsway Business Park, Rochdale, Greater Manchester: Archaeological Survey and Excavation*. Unpublished report, May.

Palmer, M. 2005. Understanding the Workplace: A Research Framework for Industrial Archaeology in Britain. *Industrial Archaeology Review* 27(1): 9–17.

Palmer, M. and Neaverson, P. 2003. Handloom Weaving in Wiltshire and Gloucestershire in the Nineteenth Century: the Building Evidence. *Post-Medieval Archaeology* 37(1): 126–158.

Palmer, M. and Neaverson, P. 2004. Home as Workplace in Nineteenth-Century Wiltshire and Gloucestershire. *Textile History* 35: 27–57.

Palmer, Marilyn and Neaverson, Peter. 2005. *The Textile Industry of South West England: A Social Archaeology*. Stroud: Tempus.

Paynter, R. 2001. The Cult of Whiteness in Western New England. In Orser, C.E. (ed.), *Race and the Archaeology of Identity*, 125–142. Salt Lake City UT: University of Utah Press.

Pennell, S. 1999. Consumption and Consumerism in Early Modern England. *Historical Journal* 42(2): 449–564.

Pelto, G.H. and Pelto, P.J. 1983. Diet and Delocalization: Diet and Dietary Changes since 1750. *Journal of Interdisciplinary History* 14(2): 507–528.

Pevsner, N. and Hubbard, E. 1971. *The Buildings of England: Cheshire*. Harmondsworth: Penguin.

Phillips, Kendall R. 2002. Textual Strategies, Plastic Tactics: Reading Batman and Barbie. *Journal of Material Culture* 7(2): 123–136.

Pink, Sarah. 2005. Dirty Laundry: Everyday Practice, Sensory Engagement and the Constitution of Identity. *Social Anthropology* 13: 275–290.

Poulter, E. 2006. Revealing Histories: The Impact of Slavery in Greater Manchester. Unpublished report, Manchester: Revealing Histories Museums Consortium.

Prag, A.J.N.W. 2005. Introduction. The Alderley Edge Landscape Project. In Timberlake, S. and Prag, A.J.N.W. (eds), *The Archaeology of Alderley Edge: Survey, Excavation and Experiment in an Ancient Mining Landscape*, 1–5. Oxford: John and Erica Hedges/BAR.

Praetzellis, Adrian. 2004. Consumerism, Living Conditions and Well-being. In Praetzellis, M. and Praetzellis, A. (eds), *Putting the 'There' There: Historical Archaeologies of West Oakland*, 47–83.

Praetzellis, M. and Praetzellis, A. 1990 *'For a good boy': Victorians on Sacramento's J Street*. Rohnert Park CA: Anthropological Studies Center, Sonoma State University.

Praetzellis, A. and Praetzellis, M. 1992. Faces and Facades: Victorian Ideology in Early Sacramento. In Yentsch, A.E. and Beaudry, M.C. (eds), *The Art and Mystery of Historical Archaeology: Essays in Honor of James Deetz*. Boca Raton FL: CRC Press.

Praetzellis, M., Praetzellis, A. and Brown, M.R. 1988. What Happened to the Silent Majority? Research Strategies for Studying Dominant Group Material Culture in late Nineteenth-Century California. In Beaudry, M.C. (ed.), *Documentary Archaeology in the New World*, 192–202. Cambridge: Cambridge University Press.

Purser, M. 1992. Oral History and Historical Archaeology. In Little, B. (ed.), *Text-aided Archaeology*, 25–38. Boca Raton FL: CRC Press.

Purser, M. 1999. *Ex occidente lux?* An Archaeology of Later Capitalism in the Nineteenth-Century West. In Leone, M.P. and Potter, P.B., Jr (eds), *Historical Archaeologies of Capitalism*, 115–41. New York: Kluwer /Plenum.

Qureshi, Sadiah. 2004. Displaying Sara Baartman, the 'Hottentot Venus'. *History of Science* 42: 233–257.

Reckner, Paul E. 2001. Negotiating Patriotism at the Five Points: Clay Tobacco Pipes and Patriotic Imagery among Trade Unionists and Nativists in a Nineteenth-Century New York Neighborhood. *Historical Archaeology* 35(3): 103–114.

Reitz, E.J. 1994. Zooarchaeological Analysis of a Free African Community: Gracia Real de Santa Theresa de Mose. *Historical Archaeology* 26(1): 23–40.

Reitz, E.J., Ruff, B.L. and Zierden, M.A. 2006. Pigs in Charleston, South Carolina: Using Specimen Counts to Consider Status. *Historical Archaeology* 40(4): 104–124.

Richards, T. 1987. The Image of Victoria in the Year of Jubilee. *Victorian Studies* 31(1): 7–32.

Richards, Thomas. 1990. *The Commodity Culture of Victorian England: Advertising and Spectacle, 1851–1914*. Stanford CA: Stanford University Press.

Richardson, C.J. 1870. *The Englishman's House: From a Cottage to a Mansion*. London: John Camden Hotton.

Rock, James T. 1984. Cans in the Countryside. *Historical* Archaeology 18(2): 97–111.

Rose, S.O. 1992. *Limited Livelihoods: Gender and Class in Nineteenth-Century England*. Berkeley CA: University of California Press.

Rose, Sonya O. 1993. Respectable Men, Disorderly Others: The Language of Gender and the Lancashire Weavers' Strike of 1878 in Britain. *Gender and History* 5(3): 382–397.

Rosenzweig, R. 1983. *Eight Hours for What we Will*. Cambridge: Cambridge University Press.

Rule, John. 1986. *The Labouring Classes in Early Industrial England, 1750–1850*. London: Longman.

Russel, Lynnette. 1999. 'Well nigh impossible to describe': Dioramas, Displays and Representations of Australian Aborigines. *Australian Aboriginal Studies* 2: 35–45.

Saitta, D. 1994. Agency, Class, and Archaeological Interpretation. *Journal of Anthropological Archaeology* 13: 201–27.

Sarin, S. 2004. Oilcloth, *Wachstuch* and *Toile cirée*: The Floorcloth, its Origins, Continental Connections and Place in the Eighteenth Century London Interior. M.Phil. dissertation. London: Royal College of Art/Victoria and Albert Museum.

Sayer, K. 2000. *Country Cottages: A Cultural History*. Manchester: Manchester University Press.

Schrager, S. 1983. What is Social in Oral History? *International Journal of Oral History* 4(2): 76–98.

Scholliers, Peter. 2004. Goods and Stores for the Workers: The Shaping of Mass Retailing in Late Nineteenth-Century Ghent. In Barker, David and Cranstone, David (eds), *The Archaeology of Industrialization*, 257–267. Leeds: Maney.

Seifert, D. 1991. 'Within sight of the White House': the Archaeology of Working Women. *Historical Archaeology* 25(4): 82–108.

Shackel, P.A. 1994. *Personal Discipline and Material Culture: An Archaeology of Annapolis, Maryland, 1695–1870*. Knoxville TN: University of Tennessee Press.

Shackel, P.A. 1996. *Culture Change and the New Technology: An Archaeology of the Early American Industrial Era*. London: Plenum Press.

Shackel, P.A. 2004. Labor's Heritage: Remembering the American Industrial Landscape. *Historical Archaeology* 38(4): 44–58.

Shammas, Carole. 1994. The Decline of Textile Prices in England and British America prior to Industrialization. *Economic History Review* 47(3): 483–507.

Sigsworth, E.M. 1965. Science and the Brewing Industry, 1850–1900. *Economic History Review* new series 17(3): 536–550.

Silliman, Stephen W. 2006. Struggling with Labor, Working with Identities. In Hall, M. and Silliman, S.W. (eds), *Historical Archaeology*, 147–166. Oxford: Blackwell.

Simmons, Jack. 1984. Railways, Hotels, and Tourism in Great Britain, 1839–1914. *Journal of Contemporary History* 19(2): 201–222.

Simpson, E.S. 1957. The Cheshire Grass-dairying Region. *Transactions and Papers, Institute of British Geographers* 23: 141–162.

Smith, Michael A. 1983. Social Usages of the Public Drinking House: Changing Aspects of Class and Leisure. *British Journal of Sociology* 34(3): 367–385.

Sofaer Derevenski, Joanna. 2000. Material Culture Shock: Confronting Expectations in the Material Culture of Children. In Sofaer Derevenski, Joanna (ed.), *Children and Material Culture*, 2–16. London: Routledge.

Stearns, P.N. 1972. Working-Class Women in Britain, 1890–1914. In Vicinus, M. (ed.), *Suffer and be Still: Women in the Victorian Age*, 100–120. Bloomington IN: Indiana University Press.

Stoller, P. and Olkes, C. 1986. Bad Sauce, Good Ethnography. *Cultural Anthropology* 1(3): 336–352.

Stratton, M. and Trinder, B. 2000. *Twentieth Century Industrial Archaeology*. London: E. & F.N. Spon.

Styles, J. 2000. Product Innovation in Early Modern London. *Past and Present* 168: 124–169.

Summerfield, P. 1998. *Reconstructing Women's Wartime Lives*. Manchester: Manchester University Press.

Symonds, J. 2002. *The Historical Archaeology of the Sheffield Tableware and Cutlery Industries, 1750–1900*. British Archaeological Reports, British Series 341, ARCUS Studies in Historical Archaeology I. Oxford: Archaeopress.

Symonds, James. 2005. Experiencing Industry: Beyond Machines and the History of Technology. In Casella, E.C. and Symonds, J. (eds), *Industrial Archaeology: Future Directions*, 33–58. New York: Springer.

Symonds, J. 2006 Tales from the City. Brownfield Archaeology: a Worthwhile Challenge? In Green, A. and Leech, R. (eds), *Cities in the World, 1500–2000*, 235–248. Leeds: Society for Post-Medieval Archaeology/Maney.

Symonds, J. and Casella, E.C. 2006 Historical Archaeology and Industrialisation. In Hicks, D. and Beaudry, M. (eds) *The Cambridge Companion to Historical Archaeology*, 143–167. Cambridge: Cambridge University Press.

Tarlow, S. 2005. Death and Commemoration. *Industrial Archaeology Review* 27(1): 163–169.

Thompson, E.P. 1967. Time, Work Discipline and Industrial Capitalism. *Past and Present* 38: 56–97.

Thompson, E.P. 1980. *The Making of the English Working Class*, 2nd edn. London: Penguin.

Tibbles, J. 2000. *An Archaeological Evaluation by Trial Trenching on Land at South Beckside, Beverley, East Riding of Yorkshire*. Humber Archaeology Reports 52. Hull: Humber Field Archaeology.

Tibbles, J. forthcoming. The Ceramic Building Materials. In Atkin *et al.*, *Excavations at St Peter's Church, Barton on Humber*.

Timberlake, S. 2005. The Archaeology of Alderley Edge and the North-east Cheshire Hinterland: a Review. In Timberlake, S. and Prag, A.J.N.W. (eds), *The Archaeology of Alderley Edge: Survey, Excavation and Experiment in an Ancient Mining Landscape*, 6–19. Oxford: John & Erica Hedges/BAR.

Timberlake, S. and King, C. 2005. Archaeological Excavations at Engine Vein, Alderley Edge, 1997. In Timberlake, S. and Prag, A.J.N.W. (eds), *The Archaeology of Alderley Edge: Survey, Excavation and Experiment in an Ancient Mining Landscape*, 33–57. Oxford: John & Erica Hedges/BAR.

Timberlake, S. and Prag, A.J.N.W. (eds). 2005. *The Archaeology of Alderley Edge: Survey, Excavation and Experiment in an Ancient Mining Landscape*. Oxford: John & Erica Hedges/BAR.

Timberlake, S., Burke, T., King, C. and Pye, C. 2005. A Topographical and Archaeological Landscape Survey of the AELP Core Area of Alderley Edge, Cheshire, with Additional References to its Hinterland. In Timberlake, S. and Prag, A.J.N.W. (eds), *The Archaeology of Alderley Edge: Survey, Excavation and*

Experiment in an Ancient Mining Landscape, 124–168. Oxford: John & Erica Hedges/BAR.

Timmins, G. 1998. *Made in Lancashire: A History of Regional Industrialisation*. Manchester: Manchester University Press.

Timmins, G. 2000. Housing Quality in Rural Textile Colonies, *c.* 1800–1850: the Ashworth Settlements Revisited. *Industrial Archaeology Review* 22(1): 21–37.

Timmins, G. 2005. Domestic Industry in Britain during the Eighteenth and Nineteenth Centuries: Field Evidence and the Research Agenda. *Industrial Archaeology Review* 27(1): 67–76.

Trinder, B. 1993. The Archaeology of the British Food Industry, 1660–1960: A Preliminary survey. *Industrial Archaeology Review* 15: 119–139.

Trinder, B. 2001. Coming to Terms with the Twentieth Century: Changing Perceptions of the British Industrial Past. *Journal of the Society for Industrial Archaeology* 26(2): 65–80.

Trinder B. 2002. Eighteenth and Nineteenth Century Market Town Industry: an Analytical Model. *Industrial Archaeological Review* 34(2): 75–89.

Tringham, R. 1973 *Territoriality and Proxemics: Archaeological and Ethnographic Evidence for the Use and Organisation of Space*. Andover MA: Warner.

Tringham, R.E. 1991. Households with Faces: the Challenge of Gender in Prehistoric Architectural Remains. In Gero, J. and Conkey, M. (eds), *Engendering Prehistory: Women and Production*, 93–131. Oxford: Blackwell.

Turner, J.M. 2003. Pablo Fanque, Black Circus Proprietor. In Gerzina, G.H. (ed.), *Black Victorians/Black Victoriana*, 20–38. New Brunswick NJ and London: Rutgers University Press.

Van Bueren, Thad M. 2002a. The Changing Face of Work in the West: Some Introductory Comments. *Historical Archaeology* 36(3): 1–7.

Van Bueren, Thad M. 2002b. Struggling with Class Relations at a Los Angeles Aqueduct Construction Camp. *Historical Archaeology* 36(3): 28–43.

Vickery, A. 1998. *The Gentleman's Daughter: Women's Lives in Georgian England*. New Haven CT: Yale University Press.

Wall, D. D. 1994. *The Archaeology of Gender: Separating the Spheres in Urban America*. New York: Plenum Press.

Wallis, B.C. 1917. Central England during the Nineteenth Century: the Breakdown of Isolation. *Geographical Review* 3(1): 28–52.

Walton, J.K. 1981. The Demand for Working-Class Seaside Holidays in Victorian England. *Economic History Review* new series 34(2): 249–265.

Walton, J.K. 1998. *Blackpool*. Edinburgh: Edinburgh University Press.

Walton, J.K. 2000. *The British Seaside: Holidays and Resorts in the Twentieth Century*. Manchester: Manchester University Press.

White, Susie. 2004. Tobacco Pipes. In Casella, E.C. (ed.), The Alderley Sandhills Project: The Archaeological Excavation of Two Rural Working-Class Cottages, Alderley Edge, Cheshire. Unpublished report.

Whitehead, S.E. 2005. Mrs Perrin's 'Tracklements': An Exploration of Class through an Interdisciplinary Approach. Unpublished essay, Manchester: University of Manchester.

Whitehead, S. and Casella, E.C. forthcoming. Mrs Perrin's 'Tracklements': Community Life and Class Distinction in (Post-)Industrial Era Cheshire. In Beaudry, M. and Symonds, J. (eds), *Interpreting the Early Modern World: Transatlantic Perspectives*. New York: Springer.

Wilkie, Laurie. 2000. 'Not merely child's play': Creating a Historical Archaeology of Children and Childhood. In Sofaer Derevenski, Joanna (ed.), *Children and Material Culture*, 100–113. London: Routledge.

Willmott, H. 2004. Glass. In Casella E., Griffin D., and Prag, A.J.N.W. (eds), The Alderley Sandhills Project: The Archaeological Excavation of Two Rural Working-Class Cottages, Alderley Edge, Cheshire. Unpublished report for English Heritage and the National Trust.

Winstanley, M. 1996. Industrialization and the Small Farm: Family and Household Economy in Nineteenth-Century Lancashire. *Past and Present* 152: 157–195.

Wurst, L. 1999. Internalising Class in Historical Archaeology. *Historical Archaeology* 33(1): 7–21.

Wurst, L. and Fitts, R.K. 1999. Introduction. Why Confront Class? *Historical Archaeology* 33(1): 1–6.

Yaeger, J. and Canuto, M. 2000. Introducing an Archaeology of Communities. In Canuto, M. and Yaeger, J., *The Archaeology of Communities*, 1–13. London: Routledge.

Yentsch, A. 1991. Engendering Visible and Invisible Ceramic Artifacts, Especially Dairy Vessels. *Historical Archaeology* 25(4): 132–155.

Index

Page references in **bold** refer to illustrations.

Barber, Ernest 21, 23–5
Barber, George (elder) 21, 23, 49, **204**
Barber, George (junior) 23, 49, 119,
    127, 131, 132, 185–6, **189**, 190,
    192, **204**, 205
Barber, Roy 5, 21, **22**, 23–5, 71, 119,
    120, 136, 173–6, 181, 183, 186–7,
    198, 204, **204**
Barker, D. 51
Barrow, Delphine 205
Barrow, Frederick 22, 185–6, **189**,
    189–90, 205
Barton, George 16
Beachtree Lodge 16
Beerhouse Act,1830 140
Berryhill, Stoke on Trent 77–8, 82
Blackpool 163–4, 165, 167, 203, **plate
    VII**
bone, animal 71
Bourdieu, Pierre 127
Brennand, M. 74
brewing 138–9, 147–8, 149–50, 202
Brighton, Steve 119, 124
Bronze Age 4, 12
Brooks, Alisdair 78, 79–80
Brunskill, R.W. 89, 92, 96
Brynlow Farm 13–14, 49
Burnett, J. 44
Burton on Trent 138–9

canals 17, 76
canned goods 70
capitalism 41, 45, 46–8, 134
carnivals 162–3
census returns
    1841 16–17
    1851 17–18
    1861 18–19
    1871 19
    1881 19, 21, 147
    1891 21
    1901 21
ceramics 45, 51, 199
    black-glazed coarseware 60
    black-glazed redware 74, 75
    brown-glazed coarseware **52**, 52–3

brown-glazed coarseware vessel
    forms 60
brown salt-glazed stoneware 53
change in styles 55
changing food consumption patterns
    72–3
chronology 50–5
creamware 51, 53, 72–3, 199
creamware vessel forms 58–9
cups, mugs and drinking vessels 56,
    57, 58, 59, 61, 73, 74, 79–80,
    80–1, 146–7
data 50
dating 53
decreasing cost of 45
earthenware 47–8
economic scaling analyses 180
figurines 112, 114, **114**, 164, **164**,
    plate VI
flatwares 56, 58, 59, 61, 72, 73
foodway-related totals 50
garden wares 113–14
holiday souvenirs 162, **164**, 164–5,
    167–8, **plate VII**
hollow wares 56, 58, 59, 60, 61
mass-produced wares 51, 53–4, 55
matched 193
miscellaneous **57**, 57–8
national comparisons 78–80
Old Abbey Farm 74–5
open vessels 60, 62, 199
ornamental 50, 111–13, 117,
    119–21, 201, **plate V**, **plate VI**
pancheons 48, 56, 60, 62, 72, 75,
    79–80, 199
pearlware 51–2, 53, 73, 77, 199
pearlware vessel forms 58–9
porcelain/bone china 52, 55, **62**, 73,
    112
porcelain/bone china vessel forms
    61–3
regional comparisons 74–8
rise of consumerism, the 49
royal commemorative vessels
    169–70, **plate VIII**
serving vessels 73